European
Food & Drink Guide

Berlitz Publishing/APA Publications GmbH & Co. Verlag KG,
Singapore Branch, Singapore

Contacting the Editors

Every effort has been made to provide accurate information in this publication, but changes are inevitable. The publisher cannot be responsible for any resulting loss, inconvenience or injury. We would appreciate it if readers would call our attention to any errors or outdated information by contacting Berlitz Publishing, 95 Progress Street, Union, NJ 07083, USA. Fax: 1-908-206-1103, email: comments@berlitzbooks.com

Cover photo: ©Brian Leatart/Photolibrary

ISBN: 981-246-618-5

Printed in Singapore by Insight Print Services (Pte) Ltd.

First printing November 2004

ABOUT THE EUROPEAN FOOD & DRINK GUIDE

This invaluable course-by-course food and drink guide includes more than just a listing of menu items you'll find in restaurants, bars, and cafés. Explanations of meal times, traditional food, and country specialties, along with details on restaurant types, help the savvy traveler know when to eat, what to eat, and where to eat. Also included are some of the most common expressions you'll need in a restaurant or bar, such as reserving a table, ordering, paying, and—should the need arise—making a complaint.

This book is organized into 11 languages: Czech, Dutch, French, German, Greek, Italian, Polish, Portuguese, Russian, Spanish, and Swedish. Each section on eating out includes simplified phonetic transcriptions for every expression. Read the transcription as if you're reading English text—there are no rules or symbols to memorize. Finally, consult the conversion tables in the back of the book for weights and measures, and the handy tipping guide for the appropriate gratuity in the country of your visit.

Enjoy!

TABLE OF CONTENTS

CZECH

ESSENTIALS	
Hello.	**Nazdar.** *nazdar*
Good evening.	**Dobrý večer.** *dob-ree vecher*
A table for ..., please.	**Stůl pro ... , prosím.** *stuhl pro' ... proseem*
1/2/3/4	**jednoho/dva/tři/čtyři** *yed-no-ho'/dva/trzhih/chti-rzhih*
Thank you.	**Děkuji.** *dye-koo-yih*
The check, please.	**Účet, prosím.** *uh-chet proseem*
Good-bye.	**Na shledanou.** *nas-khledanoh*

PLACES TO EAT

Rychlé občerstvení *rikh-leh opchers-tve-nyee*
Snack bars serving sandwiches, hot meals, and beverages; generally standing places only

Pivnice/Hospoda *piv-nyi-tseh/hospoda*
Bars serving draft beer and sometimes simple meals

Vinárna *vinahr-na*
Restaurants offering a wide selection of wine and Czech cuisine; often open for dinner only

Cukrárna *tsook-rahr-na*
Pastry shop offering pastries, cakes, and ice cream; some have seating and serve coffee, iced coffee, tea, and cold drinks, too

Kavárna *kavahr-na*
Coffeehouse; offers a good selection of coffees, and a limited selection of cakes or ice cream

Restaurace   *res-ta-oora-tseh*

Traditional restaurant ranging from the simple to the stylish

Pizzerie   *pi-tse-ri-yeh*

Pizzeria; some with traditional ovens and pizzas true to the Italian original

MEAL TIMES

Breakfast (**snídaně** *snyee-da-nyeh*): 6:00–9:30 a.m.

Lunch (**oběd** *ob-yed*): 11:30 a.m.–2:00 p.m. A two- or three-course meal, often offered as a set menu; generally the main meal for Czechs

Dinner (**večeře** *veche-rzheh*): 6:00–10:00 p.m.

CZECH CUISINE

Czech cuisine is traditionally meat based, with pork and poultry being the most popular. Dumplings are a frequent accompaniment to meat often prepared in a rich gravy or a cream sauce. Potatoes are also popular and are served in a variety of ways. Many local soups can be a meal in themselves. You will probably find the range of vegetarian dishes limited.

Most fish on offer will be fresh-water fish like the carp and trout. Seafood is still a bit of a rarity. When you do find it, it is usually frozen. If you find fresh seafood, it is likely to be very expensive. Czechs are very fond of desserts, cakes, and rich coffee.

FINDING A PLACE TO EAT

Can you recommend a good restaurant?	**Můžete mi doporučit dobrou restauraci?** *muh-zheteh mih doporoochit dobroh res-ta-oora-tsih*
Is there a(n) … restaurant near here?	**Je tu poblíž … restaurace?** *yeh tooh pob-leezh … res-ta-oora-tseh*
inexpensive	**levná** *lev-nah*

traditional Czech	**tradiční česká** *tra-dich-nyee cheskah*	
vegetarian	**vegetariánská** *vegetari-ahn-skah*	
Where can I find a(n) …? *(masc./fem.)*	**Kde bych našel/našla …?** *gdeh bikh nashel (nashla)*	
café/coffeehouse	**bufet/kavárnu** *boofet/kavahr-nooh*	
restaurant	**restauraci** *res-ta-oora-tsih*	
fast-food restaurant	**rychlé občerstvení** *rikh-leh op-chers-tve-nyee*	
ice-cream parlor	**cukrárnu se zmrzlinou** *tsook-rahr-nooh se-zmur-zli-noh*	
pizzeria	**pizzerii** *pi-tse-ri-yih*	

RESERVATIONS

I'd like to reserve a table …	**Chtěl(a) bych si zamluvit stůl …** *khuteyl(a) bikh sih zamloovit stuhl*
for two	**pro dva** *pro dva*
for this evening/ tomorrow at …	**na dnes večer/na zítra na …** *na-dnes vecher/na-zeet-ra na*
We'll come at 8:00.	**Přijdeme v osm hodin.** *purzhiye-demeh vo-sum ho-dyin*
A table for two, please.	**Stůl pro dva, prosím.** *stuhl pro-dva proseem*
We have a reservation.	**Máme to rezervaci.** *mah-meh to' rezerva-tsih*

YOU MAY HEAR

Na kolik hodin?	For what time?
Na jaké jméno?	What's the name, please?
Je mi líto. Máme obsazeno.	I'm sorry. We're very busy.

Could we sit …?	**Mohli bychom si sednout …?** _moh-lih bi-khom sih sed-noht_
over there	**tamhle** _tum-hleh_
outside	**venku** _ven-kooh_
in a non-smoking area	**v části pro nekuřáky** _fchahs-tyih pro' ne-koo-rzhah-kih_
by the window	**u okna** _oo-okna_

ORDERING

| Waiter!/Waitress! | **Pane vrchní!/Paní vrchní!** _paneh vur-khnyee/panyee vur-khnyee_ |
| May I see the wine list, please? | **Mohl(a) bych vidět nápojový lístek?** _mohl(a) bikh vi-dyet nah-po-yo-vee lees-tek_ |

YOU MAY HEAR

Chcete si objednat?	Are you ready to order?
Co byste si přáli?	What would you like?
A co si přejete k pití?	What would you like to drink?
Doporučil(a) bych …	I recommend …
Nemáme …	We don't have …
Nechte si chutnat.	Enjoy your meal.

Do you have a set menu?	**Máte hotové menu?** _mah-teh hotoveh menooh_
Can you recommend some typical local dishes?	**Můžete mi doporučit nějaké typické místní jídlo?** _muh-zheteh mih doporuchit nye-ya-keh meest-nyee yeed-lo'_
Could you tell me what … is?	**Můžete mi říci, co je …?** _muh-zheteh mih rzhee-tsih tso yeh_

What's in it?	**Co v tom je?** *tso' ftom yeh*
I'd like …/I'll have …	**Chtěl(a) bych …/Vezmu si …** *khutyel(a) bikh/vezmooh sih*
a bottle/glass/carafe of …	**láhev/sklenici/džbánek …** *lah-hef/skle-nyi-tsih/duzh-bah-nek*

SPECIAL REQUESTS

With a side order of …	**Jako přílohu …** *yako' przhee-lo-hooh*
Could I have salad instead of vegetables, please?	**Mohu dostat čerstvý salát místo zeleniny?** *mohooh dostat chers-tvee salaht meesto' zele-nyi-nih*
Does the meal come with vegetables/with potatoes?	**Je jídlo se zeleninou/s bramborem?** *yeh yeed-lo' sezele-nyi-noh/sbrum-bo-rem*
May I have some …?	**Mohu dostat …?** *mohooh dostat*
bread	**chleba** *khle-ba*
butter	**máslo** *mah-slo'*
lemon	**citrón** *tsi-tron*
mustard	**hořčici** *horzh-chi-tsih*
pepper	**pepř** *peprzh*
salt	**sůl** *suhl*
oil and vinegar	**olej a ocet** *oleye ah o-tset*
sugar	**cukr** *tsoo-kur*
artificial sweetener	**umělé sladidlo** *oomye-leh sla-dyi-dlo'*
vinaigrette	**francouzskou zálivku** *fran-tsohs-koh zah-lif-kooh*

| Could you bring a child's seat, please? | **Můžeme dostat dětskou sedačku?** *moo-zhemeh dostat dyets-koh se-duch-kooh* |
| Where can I change the baby? | **Kde mohu přebalit dítě?** *gdeh mo-hooh purzhe-balit dyee-tyeh* |

GENERAL QUESTIONS

Could I/we have (a/an) …, please?	**Mohu/Můžeme dostat …?** *mohooh/muh-zhemeh dostat*
(clean) ashtray	**(čistý) popelník** *chis-tee popel-nyeek*
(clean) cup/(clean) glass	**(čistý) šálek/(čistou) sklenici** *chis-tee shah-lek/chis-toh skle-nyi-tsih*
(clean) fork/(clean) knife	**(čistou) vidličku/(čistý) nůž** *chis-toh vid-lich-kooh/chis-tee nuhzh*
(clean) plate/(clean) spoon	**(čistý) talíř/(čistou) lžíci** *chis-tee ta-leerzh/chis-toh luzhee-tsih*
(clean) napkin	**(čistý) ubrousek** *chis-tee oob-roh-sek*
I'd like (a) …	**Chtěl(a) bych** *khutyel(a) bikh*
beer	**pivo** *pivo'*
tea	**čaj** *chuy*
… coffee	**… kávu** *kah-vooh*
black/with milk	**černou/bílou** *cher-noh/bee-loh*
I'd like a … of red/white wine.	**Chtěl(a) bych …** **červeného/bílého vína.** *khutyel(a) bikh … cher-ve-neh-ho'/bee-leh-ho' veena*

glass/carafe/bottle	**skleničku/džbánek/láhev** *skle-nyich-kooh/duzh-bah-nek/lah-hef*
I'd like a … beer.	**Chtěl(a) bych … pivo.** *khutye(a) bikh … pivo'*
bottled/draft	**láhvové/točené** *lah-voveh/to-cheneh*
That's all, thanks.	**To je všechno, děkuji.** *to' yeh vushekh-no' dye-koo-yih*
Where are the restrooms?	**Kde jsou záchody?** *gdeh yesoh zah-khodih*

SPECIAL REQUIREMENTS

I can't eat food …	**Nesmím jíst nic …** *nes-meem yeest nits*
containing salt/sugar	**se solí/s cukrem** *se-solee/s-tsook-rem*
Do you have any dishes/ drinks for diabetics?	**Máte jídla/nápoje pro diabetiky?** *mah-teh yeed-la/nah-po-yeh pro-di-abe-tikih*
Do you have vegetarian dishes?	**Máte vegetariánská jídla?** *mah-teh vegeta-ri-ahn-ska yeed-la*

COMPLAINTS

That's not what I ordered.	**To jsem si neobjednal(a).** *to' yesem sih ne-ob-yed-nal(a)*
I asked for …	**Objednal(a) jsem si …** *ob-yed-nal(a) yesem sih*
I can't eat this.	**Nemohu to jíst.** *ne-mo-hooh to' yeest*

7

The meat is …	**Maso je …** *maso' yeh*
overdone	**převařené** *przhe-va-rzhe-neh*
underdone	**nedovařené** *ne-do-va-rzhe-neh*
too tough	**moc tuhé** *mots too-heh*
The food is cold.	**Jídlo je studené.** *yeed-lo' yeh stoo-deneh*
This isn't fresh.	**Není to čerstvé.** *ne-nyee to' chers-tveh*
How much longer will our food be?	**Jak dlouho budeme ještě na jídlo čekat?** *yak dloh-ho' boo-demeh yesh-tyeh na-yeed-lo' chekat*
We can't wait any longer. We're leaving.	**Už nemůžeme déle čekat. Odcházíme.** *oozh ne-moo-zhemeh deh-leh chekat. ot-khah-zee-meh*

PAYING

Tipping: See page 332.

I'd like to pay.	**Zaplatím.** *zapla-tyeem*
The check, please.	**Účet, prosím.** *uh-chet proseem*
We'd like to pay separately.	**Budeme platit každý samostatně.** *boodemeh pla-tyit kazh-dee samos-tut-nyeh*
It's all together.	**Všechno dohromady.** *vushekh-no' do-hro-ma-dih*
I think there's a mistake in this bill.	**Myslím, že v účtu je chyba.** *mis-leem zheh vuh-chtooh yeh khiba*
What's this amount for?	**Za co je tato částka?** *za-tso' yeh tato' chahs-tka*

8

I didn't have that. I had …	**To jsem neměl(a). Měl(a) jsem …** *to' yesem ne-myel(a). myel(a) yesem*
Can I pay with this credit card?	**Mohu zaplatit touto kreditní kartou?** *mo-hooh zapla-tyit toh-to' kre-dit-nyee kar-toh*
Could I have a receipt, please?	**Mohu dostat stvrzenku, prosím?** *mo-hooh dostat st-vur-zen-kooh proseem*
That was a very good meal. *(for a man/woman)*	**Výborně jsem se najedl/najedla.** *vee-bor-nyeh yesem seh na-yedul/na-yed-la*

COURSE BY COURSE

Breakfast Snídaně

I'd like …	**Chtěl(a) bych …** *khutyel(a) bikh*
eggs	**vejce** *veye-tseh*
boiled/fried/scrambled	**vařená/smažená/míchaná** *va-rzhe-nah/sma-zhe-nah/mee-kha-nah*
fruit juice	**ovocný džus** *ovots-nee dzhoos*
grapefruit/orange	**grepový/pomerančový** *gre-po-vee/po-me-run-chovee*
honey	**med** *met*
jam	**džem** *dzhem*
marmalade	**pomerančovou marmeládu** *po-me-run-chovoh mar-me-lah-dooh*
milk	**mléko** *mleh-ko'*
rolls	**rohlíky** *ro-hlee-kih*
toast	**topinky** *topin-kih*

Appetizers Předkrmy

ham with pickles	**šunka s okurkou**	
	shoon-ka so-koor-koh	
salami with pickles	**salám s okurkou**	*sa-lahm so-koor-koh*
egg mayonnaise	**ruské vejce**	*roos-keh veye-tseh*
cod livers with onion	**tresčí játra s cibulkou**	
	tres-chee yah-tra s-tsi-bool-koh	
rolled pork with onion	**tlačenka s cibulí**	
	tla-chen-ka s-tsi-boo-lee	
smoked tongue	**uzený jazyk**	*oozenee ya-zik*
ham and horseradish roll	**křenová rolka**	
	kurzhe-novah rol-ka	
ham in aspic	**šunka v aspiku**	*shoon-ka vas-pi-kooh*
pickled herring	**zavináče**	*za-vi-nah-cheh*

Soups Polévky

potato soup	**bramborová polévka**	*brum-borovah po-lehf-ka*
garlic soup	**česneková polévka**	*ches-nekovah po-lehf-ka*
lentil soup	**čočková polévka**	*choch-kovah po-lehf-ka*
bean soup	**fazolová polévka**	*fazolovah po-lehf-ka*
consommé (with vermicelli)	**hovězí vývar (s nudlemi)**	*ho-vye-zee vee-var (snood-lemih)*
pea soup with smoked meat	**hrachová polévka s uzeným**	*hra-kho-vah po-lehf-ka sooze-neem*
cabbage soup	**kapustová polévka**	*ka-poos-tovah po-lehf-ka*
chicken soup (with vegetables)	**kuřecí vývar (se zeleninou)**	*koo-rzhe-tsee vee-var (se-ze-le-nyi-noh)*
tomato soup	**rajská polévka**	*rai-skah po-lehf-ka*
fish soup	**rybí polévka**	*ribee po-lehf-ka*
vegetable soup	**zeleninová polévka**	*zele-nyi-novah po-lehf-ka*

Bramboračka *brum-bo-ruch-ka*
A thick soup with cubed potatoes, vegetables, mushrooms, and a touch of garlic

Zelňačka *zel-nyach-ka*
A thick soup with cubed potatoes, chopped sauerkraut, and cream

Hovězí vyvar s játrovými knedlíčky
ho-vye-zee vee-var syah-tro-vee-mih kuned-leech-kih
Beef broth (sometimes with shredded vegetables) and little round dumplings of finely chopped liver seasoned with nutmeg

Fish and seafood Ryby

candát	*tsan-daht*	pike perch
garnát	*gar-naht*	shrimp
humr	*hoo-mur*	lobster
chobotnice	*kho-bot-nyi-tseh*	octopus
kapr	*ka-pur*	carp
kaviár	*ka-vi-ahr*	caviar
krab	*krub*	crab
losos	*losos*	salmon
platýz	*pla-tees*	flounder
pstruh	*pus-trooh*	trout
rybí filé	*ribee fi-leh*	fish filet
slaneček	*sla-ne-chek*	herring
štika	*shtyi-ka*	pike
treska	*tres-ka*	cod
tuňák	*too-nyahk*	tuna
ústřice	*uhs-turzhi-tseh*	oysters

Smažený kapr *sma-zhe-nee kapur*
Pieces of carp fried in bread crumbs

Kapr na černo *kapur na-cher-no*
Pieces of carp baked in a sauce of vegetables, beer, and prunes

Kapr na česneku *kapur na-ches-nekooh*
Pieces of carp grilled with butter and garlic

Pstruh na másle *pus-trooh na-mah-sleh*
Grilled trout with butter, garnished with lemon

Egg dishes Vaječná jídla

omelet	**omeleta** *omeleta*
omelet with ham/cheese	**omeleta se šunkou/se sýrem** *omeleta se-shoon-koh/se-see-rem*
scrambled eggs with bacon	**míchaná vejce na slanině** *mee-kha-nah veye-tseh na-sla-nyi-nyeh*
scrambled eggs with onion	**míchaná vejce na cibulce** *mee-kha-nah veye-tseh na-tsi-bool-tseh*

Dumplings Knedlíky

Dumplings, a traditional part of Czech cuisine, are usually served as a savory accompaniment to meat dishes. They are cooked in long rolls and then sliced and served with sauce. Sweet dumplings are usually filled with fruit, traditionally fresh plums, and sprinkled with sieved curd cheese and sugar, and covered with melted butter.

houskové knedlíky	*hoh-skoveh kned-leekih*	bread dumplings
bramborové knedlíky	*brumboroveh kned-leekih*	potato dumpling
švestkové knedlíky	*shvest-koveh kned-leekih*	plum dumplings

Meat and poultry Maso a drůbež

bažant	*ba-zhunt*	pheasant
biftek	*bif-tek*	steak
hovězí	*ho-vye-zee*	beef
husa	*hoosa*	goose
jehněčí	*yeh-nye-chee*	lamb
kachna	*kakh-na*	duck
klobásy	*klo-bah-sih*	sausages
králík	*krah-leek*	rabbit
krůta	*kruh-ta*	turkey
kuře	*ku-rzheh*	chicken
párky	*pahr-kih*	chunky sausages
slanina	*sla-nyi-na*	bacon
šunka	*shoon-ka*	ham
telecí	*tele-tsee*	veal
vepřové	*vep-rzho-veh*	pork
zajíc	*za-yeets*	hare
zvěřina	*zvye-rzhi-na*	venison

Smažený vepřový řízek *sma-zhe-nee vep-rzho-vee rzhe-zek*
Wiener schnitzel with potatoes (**s bramborem**) or potato salad
(**bramborovým salátem**)

Uzené se zelím a knedlíky *oozeneh sezeleem a kned-leekih*
Smoked pork with sauerkraut and dumplings

Svíčková na smetaně *sveech-kovah na-sme-ta-nyeh*
Roast tenderloin slices in a creamy root vegetable sauce, garnished
with cranberries and served with dumplings (**s knedlíkem**)

Pečená kachna *pechenah kakh-na*
Roast duck with cabbage or sauerkraut, accompanied by dumplings

Meat cuts Části masa

játra	*yah-tra*	liver
ledvinky	*led-vin-kih*	kidneys
kotlety	*kot-letih*	chops
kýta	*kee-ta*	leg
plec	*plets*	shoulder
řízek	*rzhee-zek*	cutlet

Vegetables Zelenina

brambory	*brum-borih*	potatoes
celer	*tse-ler*	celery root
cibule	*tsi-booleh*	onions
cukety	*tsoo-ketih*	zucchini
červená řepa	*cher-venah rzhe-pa*	beets
česnek	*ches-nek*	garlic
fazolové lusky	*fazoloveh loos-kih*	green beans
houby	*hoh-bih*	mushrooms
hrášek	*hrah-shek*	peas
jarní cibulka	*yar-nyee tsi-bool-ka*	spring onions
květák	*kvye-tahk*	cauliflower
lilek	*lilek*	eggplant
mrkev	*mur-kef*	carrots
okurka	*okoor-ka*	cucumber
paprika	*pap-rika*	peppers
pórek	*paw-rek*	leeks
rajčata	*rai-cha-ta*	tomatoes
rýže	*ree-zheh*	rice
salát	*sa-laht*	lettuce

šalotka	sha-lot-ka	shallots
zelí	zelee	cabbage
žampiony	zhum-pi-onih	mushrooms

Smažený květák s bramborem
sma-zhe-nee kvye-tahk s-brum-borem
Cauliflower fried in bread crumbs, with potatoes and tartar sauce

Salad Saláty

bramborový salát	brum-borovee sa-laht	potato salad
míchaný salát	mee-kha-nee sa-laht	mixed salad
okurkový salát	okoor-kovee sa-laht	cucumber salad
rajčatový salát s cibulkou	rai-cha-tovee sa-laht s-tsi-bool-koh	tomato and onion salad
zelený salát	zelenee sa-laht	green salad
zelný salát	zel-nee sa-laht	cabbage salad

Cheese Sýry

jemný sýr	yem-nee seer	mild cheese
kozí sýr	kozee seer	goat cheese
měkký tvaroh	mye-kee tva-rokh	cottage cheese
ostrý sýr	os-tree seer	sharp/tangy cheese
ovčí sýr	of-chee seer	ewe's milk cheese
plísňový sýr	plees-nyo-vee seer	blue cheese
smetanový sýr	sme-tanovee seer	cream cheese
tvrdý sýr	tuvur-dee seer	hard cheese

Niva® *nyi-va*
The most common brand of blue cheese often on menus as
… s Nivou (… with blue cheese)

Smažený sýr *sma-zhe-nee seer*
Slices of Edam or Gouda fried in bread crumbs

Syrečky *si-rech-kih*
A cheese with a strong smell and sharp taste made with beer

Dessert Moučníky/Zákusky

jablečný závin	apple strudel
koblihy	donuts
makový koláč	poppy seed cake
ovocný koláč	fruit cake
ovocný koláč s drobenkou	fruit crumble pie
palačinky	pancakes
sachr dort	Sacher torte [Black Forest gateau]
trubičky se šlehačkou	brandy snaps with cream
tvarohové taštičky	cottage cheese pastries
zmrzlinový pohár	ice-cream sundae

Lívance *lee-vun-tseh*
Small pancakes, spread with plum cheese and a layer of cottage cheese, and topped with yogurt or thick sour cream

Švestkové knedlíky *shvest-koveh kned-leekih*
Plum dumplings with curd cheese and sugar, covered with butter

Fruit Ovoce

banány	*banah-nih*	bananas
borůvky	*bo-roof-kih*	blueberries
broskve	*brosk-veh*	peaches
cukrový meloun	*tsook-rovee me-lown*	melon
grepy	*grepih*	grapefruit
hroznové víno	*hroz-noveh veeno'*	grapes
jablka	*ya-bul-ka*	apples
jahody	*yahodih*	strawberries
maliny	*malinih*	raspberries

meloun	*me-lown*	watermelon
meruňky	*me-roony'-kih*	apricots
pomeranče	*pome-run-cheh*	oranges
švestky	*shvest-kih*	plums
třešně	*trzhesh-nyeh*	cherries
višně	*vish-nyeh*	morello cherries

DRINKS
Aperitifs Aperitivy

| meruňkovice | apricot brandy |
| slivovice | plum brandy/slivovitz |

Karlovarská Becherovka® is a famous herb brandy from
Karlsbad. Generally served chilled as an aperitif or as a liqueur
with strong coffee.

Beer Pivo

Beers in the Czech Republic are lagers, not ales. They are
generally quite strong and bitter and always served chilled.

plzeňské	pilsner
Budvar	Budweiser
černé	black (slightly sweet)

| Do you have … beer? | **Máte … pivo?** *mah-teh … pivo'* |
| bottled/draft | **láhvové/točené** *lah-voveh/to-cheneh* |

Wine Víno

Bohemia and the warmer region of Moravia have a number of
local wines. Many **vinárna**—a type of restaurant with a wide
selection of wines—serve local wines; they are open late and offer
regional snacks and/or meals. Look for the mature "archive" wine
(**archívní víno**).

Popular Czech wines to look for:

white:	**Vlašský ryzlink, Rulandské bílé, Müller-Thurgau, Veltlínské zelené**
red:	**Frankovka, Vavřinec**

Can you recommend a … wine?	**Můžete mi doporučit … víno?** *moo-zheteh mih doporuchit … vee-no'*
red/white/blush [rosé]	**červené/bílé/růžové** *cher-veneh/bee-leh/ruh-zhoveh*
dry/sweet/sparkling	**suché/sladké/šumivé** *soo-kheh/slut-keh/shoo-miveh*
I'd like a corkscrew.	**Chtěl(a) bych vývrtku.** *khutyel(a) bikh vee-vrut-kooh*

Spirits and liqueurs Destiláty a likéry

Apart from slivovitz and apricot brandy, another Czech drink worth trying is **borovička**, which is made with juniper berries.

straight [neat]	**čistý** *chis-tee*
on the rocks [with ice]	**s ledem** *sledem*
with water/with tonic water/ with lemon	**s vodou/s tonikem/s citrónem** *zvo-doh/sto-ni-kem/s-tsi-tro-nem*
I'd like a single/double …	**Chtěl(a) bych malou/dvojitou …** *khutyel(a) bikh maloh/dvo-yei-toh*
brandy/whisky/vodka	**brandy/whisky/vodku** *bren-dih/vis-kih/vot-kooh*
Cheers!	**Na zdraví!** *nahs-drahvee*

Non-alcoholic drinks

Mineral water (**minerálka**) comes in many different varieties. The brand "Dobra Voda" is sold in large bottles in most supermarkets. Look for "Mattoni," the well-known and highly regarded mineral water from Karlsbad.

Tea and coffee Čaj a káva

Czechs usually drink tea with lemon (**s citrónem**). Also popular are rose hip tea (**šípkový čaj**) and chamomile tea (**heřmánkový čaj**). Czechs like their coffee richly brewed, and you will find Turkish-style coffee (**turecká káva**), with coffee grounds left in the bottom of the cup, and Viennese-style coffee (**vídeňská káva**), with the coffee topped with whipped cream, widely available. Cappuccino and espresso are popular, too.

I'd like (a) …	**Chtěl(a) bych …** *khutye(a) bikh*
tea with milk/with lemon	**čaj s mlékem/s citrónem** *chuy sumleh-kem/sutsit-ronem*
black coffee	**černou kávu** *cher-noh kah-vooh*
coffee with milk	**bílou kávu** *bee-loh kah-vooh*
hot chocolate/cocoa	**horkou čokoládu/kakao** *hor-koh choko-lah-dooh/kakao*
cola/lemonade	**kolu/limonádu** *ko-looh/limo-nah-dooh*
fruit juice	**ovocnou šťávu** *ovots-noh shtyah-vooh*
orange/pineapple	**pomerančovou/ananasovou** *pome-run-cho-voh/ana-na-sovoh*
milk shake	**mléčný koktejl** *mleh-chnee kok-teyel*
mineral water	**minerálku** *mine-rahl-kooh*
carbonated/non-carbonated	**s bublinkami/bez bublinek** *zboob-lin-kamih/bez-boob-linek*

MENU READER

dobře upečené	*dob-rzheh oopecheneh*	well-done
dušené	*doo-she-neh*	braised/stewed
dušené v páře	*doo-sheneh fpah-rzheh*	steamed
grilované	*grilovaneh*	grilled
hodně krvavé	*hod-nyeh kur-vaveh*	very rare
kořeněné	*ko-rzhe-nye-neh*	spicy
krvavé	*kur-vaveh*	rare
marinované	*marinovaneh*	marinated
mírně propečené	*meer-nyeh propecheneh*	medium
nakrájené na kostičky	*na-krah-yeneh na-kos-tyich-kih*	diced
na másle	*na-mah-sleh*	sautéed
pečené	*pe-che-neh*	baked/roasted
plněné	*pul-nye-neh*	stuffed
smažené	*sma-zhe-neh*	fried
uzené	*oozeneh*	smoked
vařené	*va-rzhe-neh*	boiled
ve smetaně	*ve-sme-ta-nyeh*	creamed
ve strouhance	*ve-stroh-hun-tseh*	breaded

A

alkoholické nápoje alcoholic drinks
ananas pineapple
angrešt gooseberry
anýz aniseed
anýzovka aniseed liqueur

aperitiv aperitif
arašídy peanuts
artyčok artichoke
aspik jelly
avokádo avocado

B

banán banana
banán v čokoládě chocolate-covered banana
bazalka basil
bažant pheasant
bez kofeinu decaffeinated
biftek steak
bílá with milk/white (coffee)
bílé hrozny white grapes
bílé zelí white cabbage
bílek egg white
bílý chléb white bread
bobkový list bay leaf
boby broad beans
bonbony candy
borůvkové knedlíky blueberry dumplings
borůvkový koláč blueberry pie/tart
borůvky blueberries
borovička brandy
bramboračka thick soup with potatoes and vegetables
bramborák potato pancake
bramborová kaše mashed potato
bramborová polévka potato soup
bramborové hranolky french fries
bramborové knedlíky potato dumplings
bramborové krokety potato croquettes
bramborové taštičky s masitou nádivkou potato ravioli with meat filling
brambory potatoes
brokolice broccoli
broskev peach
brusinky cranberries

brzlík sweetbreads
buchta bun
bůček pork belly
burské oříšky peanuts
bylinková směs mixed herbs
bylinky herbs

C

candát pike perch
celer celery root
celozrnná mouka whole-wheat flour
cemr loin (pork, etc.)
cibule onions
citrón lemon
citrónová šťáva lemon juice
cukety zucchini
cukr sugar
cukrová kukuřice corn
cukroví small sweet pastries
cukrový meloun melon

Č

čaj tea (beverage)
čekanka chicory
černá black (coffee)
černý rybíz black currants
čerstvé datle fresh dates
čerstvé fíky fresh figs
čerstvé ovoce fresh fruit
čerstvý fresh
čerstvý tvaroh fresh curd cheese
červená řepa beets
červené hrozny black grapes
červené zelí red cabbage
červený red (wine)
červený rybíz red currants
česnek garlic
česneková majonéza garlic mayonnaise

česneková omáčka garlic sauce
česneková polévka garlic soup
čevapčiči meatballs
čínské zelí Chinese cabbage
čistý straight [neat]
čočka lentils
čočková polévka lentil soup
čočkový salát lentil salad
čokoláda chocolate

D

datle dates
dezert dessert
dezertní víno dessert wine
divočák/divoký kanec wild boar
domácí home-made
dort cake
drůbež poultry
drůbky giblets
dršťková polévka tripe soup
dršťky tripe
dýně pumpkin
dušená ryba steamed fish
dušená rýže steamed rice
dušené hovězí pot roast
dušené ovoce stewed fruit
dušené telecí maso na víně veal braised in wine
dušený stewed
dvojitý double (a double shot)
džem jam
džin gin
džin s tonikem gin and tonic
džus fruit juice

E

estragon tarragon

F

fíky figs
fazole beans

fazolové klíčky bean sprouts
fenykl fennel
francouzská zálivka vinaigrette
fazolová polévka bean soup

G

garnáti shrimp
granátová jablka pomegranates
gratinovaný gratin/au gratin
grep grapefruit
gril grill
grilované kuře grilled chicken
grilovaný na dřevěném uhlí charcoal-grilled
guláš goulash, stew
gulášová polévka Hungarian goulash soup

H

heřmánkový čaj chamomile tea
hladká mouka flour
hlavní jídla entrées
hlíva ústřičná oyster mushrooms
hodně kořeněný highly seasoned
holoubě pigeon
horká čokoláda hot chocolate
horká voda hot water
horký hot (temperature)
hořčice mustard
houby mushrooms
houska roll
houskový knedlík bread dumpling
hovězí beef
hovězí pečeně roast beef
hovězí tokáň beef in wine and tomato purée
hovězí vývar beef broth
hovězí vývar s játrovými knedlíčky beef broth with liver dumplings

hrachor sugar snap peas
hrachová polévka s uzeným masem pea soup with smoked meat
hranolky french fries
hrášek peas
hrozinky raisins
hrozny/hroznové víno grapes
hruška pear
hřebíček cloves
hřiby ceps (mushrooms)
humr lobster
husa goose

CH

chlazené nápoje cold drinks
chlazený chilled /iced
chléb bread
chlebíček open sandwich
chlupaté knedlíky dumplings with diced smoked meat and sauerkraut
chobotnice octopus
chřest asparagus
chuťovky savories

J

jablečná šťáva apple juice
jablečný mošt cider (non-alcoholic)
jablečný závin apple strudel
jablko apple
jablkový koláč apple pie/tart
jahody strawberries
jarní cibulka spring onions
játra liver
játrová paštika liver pâté
játrové knedlíčky liver balls
jazyk tongue
jehněčí lamb
jehněčí guláš lamb stew
jehněčí kýta leg of lamb

jelínek brandy
jelení venison
jelito black pudding
jemný mild (flavor)
jídelní lístek menu
jídlo dish (meal)
jitrnice white sausage
jogurt yogurt

K

kachna duck
kakao cocoa
kandované ovoce candied fruit
kapary capers
kapoun capon
kapr carp
kapr na černo baked carp in a beer, prune, and vegetable sauce
kapr na česneku carp grilled with butter and garlic
kapr na kmíně carp baked with caraway seeds
kapustová polévka cabbage soup
karafa carafe
karamel caramel
karbanátek fried burger
Karlovarská Becherovka® herb brandy
kaštany chestnuts
káva coffee
kaviár caviar
kečup ketchup
kedlubna kohlrabi
kiwi kiwi fruit
klobásky sausages
kmín caraway
knedlík dumpling
knedlíky s vejci dumpling with scrambled egg
kobliha donut

kohout cockerel
kokos coconut
koktejl milk shake
koláč pie/tart (sweet/savory)
koláček tartlette (sweet/savory)
kompot stewed fruit
konsomé consommé
kopr dill
koroptev partridge
kořeněná klobása spicy sausage
koření seasoning/spices
kořeněný hot/spicy/seasoned
kost bone
kotlety chops
koza goat
kozí sýr goat cheese
krab crab
krájený sliced
králík rabbit
králík na smetaně roast rabbit in rich cream sauce
krekry crackers
krémovitá polévka cream soup
kroketa croquette
kroupy barley
krůta turkey
křen horseradish
křepelka quail
kukuřice corn
kuře chicken
kuře na paprice chicken with creamy paprika sauce
kuřecí játra chicken liver
kuřecí prso breast of chicken
kuřecí vývar chicken broth/soup
kuře pečené s nádivkou roast chicken with stuffing
květák cauliflower
kyselé okurky sour pickles

kýta leg (cut of meat)
kyselé zelí sauerkraut

L

langoš fried dough coated in garlic
led ice
ledvinky kidneys
lehký light (sauce, etc.)
ležák lager
lihoviny spirits
likér liqueur
lilek eggplant
limetta lime
limettová šťáva lime juice
limonáda lemonade
lískové ořechy hazelnuts
lístkové těsto puff pastry
lišky chanterelle mushrooms
lívance small pancakes with plum and cottage cheese, topped with yogurt or sour cream
lívanečky fritters
losos salmon
luštěniny legumes

M

mák poppy seeds
máslo butter
máta mint
majonéza mayonnaise
majoránka marjoram
makový koláč poppy seed cake
makrela mackerel
malé občerstvení snacks
maliny raspberries
mandarínka tangerine
mandle almond
marcipán marzipan
marmeláda jam
maso meat (general)

masová směs na roštu mixed grill
masový a zeleninový vývar meat and vegetable broth
mečoun swordfish
med honey
melasa molasses
meloun watermelon
meruňkové knedlíky apricot dumplings
meruňkovice apricot brandy
meruňky apricots
míchaná zelenina mixed vegetables
míchaný salát mixed salad
minerálka/minerální voda mineral water
místní speciality local specialties
mléko milk
mleté maso ground meat
mletý minced
moravský vrabec stewed pork stuffed with ham, egg, and pickles
moruše mulberry
mořský jazyk sole
moučník dessert
mouka flour
mozeček brains
mrkev carrots
muškátový oříšek nutmeg

N

na česneku in garlic
nadívané olivy stuffed olives
nádivka stuffing
na grilu cooked on a grill
nakládané houby pickled mushrooms
nakládané okurky pickles
nakládaný marinated
na kosti on the bone
nakrájený na plátky sliced

nakyselo sour (taste)
naměkko soft-boiled (eggs)
na oleji in oil
nápojový lístek wine list
na roštu barbecued
na rožni spit-roasted
na špízu skewered
natvrdo hard-boiled (egg)
naťový celer celery
nealkoholické nápoje non-alcoholic/soft drinks
nektarinka nectarine
Niva® blue cheese
nudle noodles
nudle s mákem noodles with poppy seeds, butter, and sugar
nugát nougat

O

obalovaný (ve strouhance) breaded (cutlet, etc.)
oběd lunch
obloha garnish, trimming
obložený chlebíček open sandwich
okoun perch
okurka cucumber
olivy olives
omáčka gravy/sauce
omeleta omelet
oplatky wafers
ořechy nuts
ostrá pepřová omáčka hot pepper sauce
ostružinová marmeláda blackberry jam
ostružinový koláč blackberry pie
ostružiny blackberries
ostrý hot (spicy)
ovesná kaše porridge
ovesné vločky porridge oats

ovoce fruit
ovoce z konzervy canned fruit
ovocná šťáva fruit juice
ovocný koláč fruitcake
ovocný kompot fruit compote
ovocný nápoj fruit drink

P

palačinky pancakes
palačinky s čokoládou pancakes with chocolate sauce
palačinky s ovocem a se zmrzlinou pancakes with fruit and ice cream
pálenka brandy
párek v rohlíku hot dog
párky sausages
paštika pâté
pažitka chives
pečená kachna roast duck
pečená ryba baked fish
pečené brambory roast potatoes
pečené kuře roast chicken
pečeně se slaninou roasted with bacon
pečený baked/roasted
pečivo pastries
perlička guinea fowl
perlivý carbonated
perník gingerbread
petrželka parsley
pfeferonka chili pepper
piškot sponge cake
pivo beer
plátek slice
platýs halibut
plísňový sýr blue cheese
plněné papriky v rajčatové omáčce stuffed peppers in tomato sauce
podmáslí buttermilk

poleva icing
polévka soup
pomazánka z Nivy blue cheese spread
pomeranč orange
pomerančová marmeláda marmalade
pomerančová šťáva/pomerančový džus orange juice
pomfrity french fries
porce portion
pórek leek
pórková polévka leek soup
porstké víno port
pražené arašídy roasted peanuts
pražené mandle roasted almonds
prso/prsíčko breast
předrkmy appetizers
přírodní řízek unbreaded cutlet
pstruh trout
pstruh na másle trout grilled with butter
pudink custard
pudinkový krém cream
punč punch

R

rajčata tomatoes
rajčatová omáčka tomato sauce
rajská polévka tomato soup
rak crayfish
ramstejk rumpsteak
rebarbora rhubarb
rizoto risotto
rohlíky rolls (bread)
rosol jelly
roštěnka sirloin steak
roštěnky na pivě beef and onion stew cooked in beer
rozinky raisins

rozmarýna rosemary
ruláda filet steak
ruské vejce mayonnaise
růžičková kapusta Brussel sprouts
růžový blush [rosé] (wine)
ryba fish
rybí filé fish filet
rybí polévka fish soup
rýže rice

Ř

ředkvička radish
řeřicha cress/watercress
řízek cutlet (esp. veal)

S

s citrónem with lemon
s cukrem with sugar
s ledem on the rocks
s mlékem with milk
salám salami
salát green salad/lettuce
salát ze syrového zelí coleslaw
sardelky anchovies
sardelová pasta anchovy paste
sardinky sardines
sekaná ground beef
selátko suckling pig
sendvič sandwich
sirup syrup
sklenice/sklenička glass
skopové mutton
skopový guláš mutton stew
skořice cinnamon
skotská whisky Scotch whisky
sladký sweet
sladkokyselá omáčka sweet-and-sour sauce
slané mandle salted almonds
slaneček salted herring

slanina bacon
slaný savory/salty
slávky mussels
sleď herring
slepičí vývar s nudlemi chicken broth with vermicelli
slivovice plum brandy
slunečnicová semínka sunflower seeds
smažená ryba fried fish
smažená vejce scrambled eggs
smažené kuře fried chicken
smaženka croquette
smažený kapr carp fried in breadcrumbs
smažený květák cauliflower fried in breadcrumbs
smažený sýr slices of Edam or Gouda fried in breadcrumbs
smažený v těstíčku fried in batter
smažený vepřový řízek Wiener schnitzel
smetana cream
smetanová omáčka white sauce
smetanový creamy
sněhová pusinka meringue
snídaně breakfast
sodová voda soda water
sója soy
solené arašídy salted peanuts
solený salted
specialita dne dish of the day
speciality šéfa kuchyně specialties of the house
srdce heart
srnčí venison
srnčí hřbet dušený na víně saddle of venison braised in wine
stehno leg (cut of meat)

stolní víno table wine
strouhanka breadcrumbs
strouhaný grated
studená jídla cold dishes
studená polévka cold soup
studená voda iced water
studený hot
suchý dry
sůl salt
sultánky sultanas/raisins
sušené datle dried dates
sušené fíky dried figs
sušené švestky prunes
sušenky cookies
svíčková tenderloin (cut of meat)
svíčková na smetaně tenderloin of beef in creamy root vegetable sauce
sýr cheese
syrový raw

Š

šafrán saffron
šalotka shallots
šalvěj sage
šery sherry
šípkový čaj rosehip tea
škubánky s mákem bread dumplings with poppy seeds and sugar
šlehačka whipped cream
šopský salát tomato and cucumber salad with feta cheese
špagety spaghetti
špek spek (bacon)
špekáčky frankfurter
špekové knedlíky se zelim dumplings stuffed with bacon, served with sauerkraut
špenát spinach

šproty sprats (small herrings)
šťáva gravy (meat)/juice (fruit)
štika pike
štrůdl apple strudel
šumivé víno sparkling wine
šumivý fizzy/sparkling (drinks)
šunka ham
šunka od kosti ham on the bone
šunka s vejci ham and eggs
švestkové knedlíky plum dumplings, sieved curd cheese, and sugar
švestky plums

T

tatarský biftek steak tartare
tavený sýr soft cheese
telecí veal
telecí játra veal liver
teplý warm
těsto pastry
těstoviny pasta
těžký full-bodied (wine)
tmavý chléb black bread
tonik tonic water
topinka toast
tresčí játra cod liver
treska cod
třešně cherries
tučný fatty
tuňák tuna
turecká káva Turkish-style coffee
tykev squash
tymián thyme

U

uherský salám Hungarian salami
úhoř eel
umělé sladidlo sweetener

ústřice oysters
utopenci marinated sausage
uzená makrela smoked mackerel
uzená šunka smoked ham
uzenáč smoked herring
uzené maso smoked pork
uzené se zelím a knedlíky smoked pork with sauerkraut and dumplings
uzený bůček smoked pork belly
uzený jazyk smoked tongue
uzený losos smoked salmon
uzený sýr smoked cheese
uzený úhoř smoked eel

V

v těstíčku in batter
vafle waffles
vajíčka eggs
vaječná jídla egg dishes
vanilka vanilla
vanilková zmrzlina vanilla ice cream
vařené brambory boiled potatoes
vařící boiling (water)
večeře dinner
vejce eggs
velmi suchý very dry (wine)
vepřové pork
vepřové klobásky pork sausages
vepřové žebírko stewed rib of pork
vermut vermouth
vídeňská káva Viennese coffee
víno wine
višně morello cherries
vlašské ořechy walnuts
voda water
vuřt sausage
vývar consommé

Z

zajíc hare
zajíc na divoko hare cooked with bacon, onions, and vegetables in red wine
zajíc na smetaně roast hare in rich cream sauce
zákusek cake/dessert
zapékaný gratin/au gratin
zavináče pickled herrings
zázvor ginger
zázvorky ginger cookies
zelí cabbage
zelená paprika green peppers
zelené fazole green beans
zelené fazolky French beans
zelenina vegetables
zeleninová jídla vegetable dishes
zeleninová polévka vegetable soup
zelňačka thick soup with potatoes, sauerkraut, and cream
zelná polévka s klobásou cabbage soup with smoked sausage
zmrzlina ice cream
zmrzlinový pohár (s ovocem) ice-cream sundae (with fruit)
znojemská pečeně slices of roast beef in a pickle sauce
zralý ripe
zvěřina game

Ž

žampiony mushrooms
žebírka ribs
želé jelly
žemle bun
žitný chléb rye bread
žloutek egg yolk

DUTCH

ESSENTIALS

Hello.	**Dag.** *daakh*
Good evening.	**Goedenavond.** *khooder<u>naa</u>vont*
A table for …, please.	**Een tafel voor …, alstublieft.** *ern <u>tah</u>fel foar … alstuw<u>bleeft</u>*
1/2/3/4	**een/twee/drie/vier** *ehn/tway/dree/feer*
Thank you.	**Dank u.** *dank uw*
I'd like to pay.	**Ik wil graag betalen.** *ik vil ghraaghbe<u>taa</u>lern*
Good-bye.	**Dag.** *daakh*

PLACES TO EAT

Café *café*
Amsterdam is famous for its **bruine café's** (brown cafés)—old, dark, and wood-panelled

Cafetaria *café-<u>tah</u>reeah*
Self-service restaurant serving hot and cold food

Broodjeswinkel *<u>brott</u>yes-winkle*
Sandwich shop serving rolls (**broodjes**) with ham, cheese, and fish; reasonably priced

Koffieshop *coffee-shop*
Coffee is brewed strong and served with **koffiemelk**, a thick kind of evaporated milk; be aware that some **koffieshops** (especially in Amsterdam) sell stronger substances than caffeine

Restaurant *resto-<u>rahnt</u>*
Includes: Indonesian, French, Italian, Chinese, Japanese, Turkish, Indian, Thai, and more

Pannekoekhuisje _panneh-kook-heusyeh_

Pancake houses offering a huge range of savory and sweet
pannekoeken and the thinner variety, **flensjes**

Proeflokaal _proof-lokahl_

A place where you can taste and buy different kinds of **jenever**
(Dutch gin), beer, and other alcoholic beverages

Wegrestaurant _veg-restorahnt_

Highway or road restaurant, usually self-service

Snackbar _snackbar_

Quick bites, including favorites such as **patat** (French fries),
kroketten (croquettes) and **bitterballen** (small meatballs)

Theesalon _tay-salon_

Tea shops serving different kinds of tea, **gebak** (pastries), and coffee

MEAL TIMES

Breakfast (**ontbijt**, 7–10 a.m.): Tea or coffee, bread (brown, white,
or currant bread, and **ontbijtkoek**, a sticky sweet ginger cake),
sliced cheese and cold meats, jam, and perhaps a boiled egg
(**gekookt eitje**)

Lunch (**lunch**, 12–2 p.m.): Bread (**boterhammen**) or rolls
(**broodjes**) with cheese and cold meats, pickles (**augurken**),
salad, and fruit

Dinner (**diner**, 6–8 p.m.): Soup, potatoes, meat, and vegetables
followed by fruit, yogurt, etc.

DUTCH CUISINE

Truly Dutch dishes are heavy winter fare, but menus reflect the
extent to which the Dutch have been open to foreign influences
throughout the centuries. Many restaurants have a **menu van de
dag** (set menu), a **toeristenmenu** (tourist menu), a **dagschotel** (dish
of the day), or you can go **à la carte.**

Spicy dishes from Indonesia (a Dutch colony until 1949) are now part of Dutch eating habits. Characteristics are chili condiment (**sambal**), shrimp crackers (**krupuk**), peanuts, coconut, and sweet soy sauce.

FINDING A PLACE TO EAT

Can you recommend a good restaurant?	**Kunt u een goed restaurant aanbevelen?** *kuhnt uw ayn khoot restoarant aanberfaylern*
Is there a/an … near here?	**Is er een … in de buurt?** *is ehr ayn … in der buwrt*
Indonesian restaurant	**Indonesisch restaurant** *indoanaysees restoarant*
inexpensive restaurant	**redelijk geprijsd restaurant** *rayderlik kherprayst restoarant*
restaurant with local dishes	**restaurant met plaatselijke gerechten** *restourant met plaatserlayker kherehkhtern*
vegetarian restaurant	**vegetarisch restaurant** *vaykhertaarees restoarant*
Is there (a/an) … nearby?	**Is er een … in de buurt?** *is ehr ayn … in der burt*
café	**eethuisje** *aythoaisyer*
ice-cream parlor	**ijssalon** *ayssalon*
pizzeria	**pizzeria** *pitseria*

RESERVATIONS

I'd like to reserve a table …	**Ik wil graag een tafel … reserveren.** *ik vil khraakh ayn taaferl … rayzervayrern*
for two	**voor twee personen** *foar tvay persoanern*
for this evening/ tomorrow at …	**voor vanavond/morgen om …** *foar fanaafont/morkhern om*

We'll come at 8:00.	**We komen om acht uur.**
	wer koamern om aght uhr
We have a reservation.	**We hebben gereserveerd.**
	vay hepbern kherayzervayrt

YOU MAY HEAR

Voor hoe laat?	For what time?
Welke naam is het?	What's the name, please?
Roken of niet-roken?	Smoking or non-smoking?
Het spijt me. Het is erg druk./	I'm sorry. We're very busy./
We zitten vol.	We're full.

Could we sit …?	**Kunnen we … zitten?**
	kuhnern vay … zittern
outside	**buiten** *boaitern*
by the window	**bij het raam** *bay het raam*

ORDERING

Waiter!/Waitress!	**Meneer!/Mevrouw!**
	mernayr/mefrow
May I see the wine list, please?	**Mag ik de wijnkaart?**
	makh ik der vaynkaart

YOU MAY HEAR

Wilt u al bestellen?	Are you ready to order?
Wat mag het zijn?	What would you like?
Wat wilt u drinken?	What would you like to drink?
Ik kan … aanbevelen.	I recommend …
We hebben geen …	We don't have …
Eet smakelijk.	Enjoy your meal.

Do you have a set menu?	**Heeft u een dagmenu?** *hayft uw arn dakhmenuw*
Can you recommend some typical local dishes?	**Kunt u wat typisch plaatselijke gerechten aanbevelen?** *kuhnt uw vat teepish plaatslerker kherehkhtern aanberfaylern*
Could you tell me what … is?	**Kunt u me vertellen wat … is?** *kuhnt uw mer fertellern vat … is*
I'd like …	**Ik wil graag …** *ik vil khraakh*
a bottle/glass/carafe of …	**een fles/glas/karaf …** *ayn fles/khlas/karraf*

SPECIAL REQUESTS

With a side order of …	**Met … erbij** *met … ehrbay*
Could I have salad instead of vegetables?	**Mag ik salade in plaats van groenten?** *makh ik salaader in plaats fan khroontern*
Does the meal come with vegetables/potatoes?	**Wordt het geserveerd met groenten/aardappelen?** *vort het khersehrvayrt met khroontern/aardapperlern*
May I have some …?	**Mag ik wat …?** *makh ik vat*
bread	**brood** *broat*
butter	**boter** *boater*
lemon	**citroen** *seetroon*
mustard	**mosterd** *mostert*
pepper	**peper** *payper*
salt	**zout** *zowt*
oil and vinegar	**olie en azijn** *oalee en asayn*
sugar	**suiker** *zoaiker*
artificial sweetener	**zoetjes** *zootyers*

vinaigrette	**slasaus** _slaa_sows
Could you bring a child's seat?	**Heeft u ook een kinderstoeltje?** _hayft uw oak ayn kinderstool_tyer
Where can I change the baby?	**Waar kan ik de baby verschonen?** _vaar kan ik der baybee ferskhoa_nern

GENERAL QUESTIONS

Could I have a(n) ..., please?	**Mag ik een ..., alstublieft?** _makh ik ayn ..., alstuwbleeft_
ashtray	**asbak** _asbak_
cup/glass	**kopje/glas** _kopyer/khlas_
fork/knife	**vork/mes** _fork/mes_
plate/spoon	**bord/lepel** _bort/layperl_
napkin	**servet** _sehrfet_
I'd like (a) ...	**Ik wil graag een ...** _ik vil khraakh ayn_
beer	**biertje** _beertyer_
tea/coffee	**thee/koffie** _tay/koffee_
black/with milk	**zonder melk/met melk** _zonder melk/met melk_
I'd like red/white wine.	**Ik wil graag een rode/witte wijn.** _ik vil khraakh ayn roader/vitter vayn_
bottled/draft beer	**flessebier/getapt bier** _flesserbeer/khertapt beer_
That's all, thanks.	**Dat is genoeg, dank u.** _dat is khernookh, dangk uw_
Where are the restrooms?	**Waar is het toilet?** _vaar is het toilet_

SPECIAL REQUIREMENTS

I can't eat food containing …	**Ik mag geen … eten.** *ik makh khayn … aytern*
salt/sugar	**zout/suiker** *zowt/soaiker*
Do you have any dishes/ drinks for diabetics?	**Heeft u ook gerechten/drankjes voor diabetici?** *hayft uw oak kherehkhtern/ drankyers foar deeabayteesee*
Do you have vegetarian dishes?	**Heeft u vegetarische gerechten?** *hayft uw vaykhertaareeser kherehkhtern*

COMPLAINTS

There must be some mistake.	**Er moet een vergissing zijn.** *ehr moot ayn ferkhissing zayn*
That's not what I ordered.	**Dat is niet wat ik heb besteld.** *dat is neet vat ik hep berstelt*
I asked for …	**Ik heb om … gevraagd.** *ik hep om … kherfraakht*
I can't eat this.	**Dit kan ik niet eten.** *dit kan ik neet aytern*
The meat is …	**Het vlees is …** *het flays is*
overdone	**overgaar** *oaferkhaar*
underdone	**niet gaar** *neet khaar*
too tough	**te taai** *ter taay*
The food is cold.	**Het eten is koud.** *het aytern is kowt*
This isn't fresh.	**Dit is niet vers.** *dit is neet fehrs*
How much longer will our food be?	**Hoe lang duurt het eten nog?** *hoo lang duwrt het aytern nokh*

We can't wait any longer. **We kunnen niet langer wachten.**
We're leaving. **We gaan weg.** *vay kuhnern neet*
langer vakhtern. vay khaan vehkh

PAYING

Tipping: See page 332.

The check, please. **Mag ik de rekening?**
makh ik der raykerning

We'd like to pay **We willen graag apart betalen.**
separately. *vay villern khraakh apart*
bertaalern

It's all together, please. **Alles bij elkaar, alstublieft.**
allers bay elkaar, alstuwbleeft

I think there's a mistake in **Ik geloof dat er een fout in**
this check. **deze rekening zit.** *ik kherloaf*
dat ehr ayn fowt in dayzer
raykerning zit

What is this amount for? **Waar is dit bedrag voor?**
vaar is dit berdrakh foar

I didn't have that. **Dat heb ik niet gehad. Ik had ...**
I had … *dat hep ik neet kherhat. ik hat*

Can I pay with this **Kan ik met deze creditcard**
credit card? **betalen?** *kan ik met dayzer*
kredeetkaart bertaalern

Could I have a receipt, **Mag ik een kwitantie,**
please? **alstublieft?** *makh ik ayn*
kvitantsee, alstuwbleeft

That was a very **Dat was een uitstekende**
good meal. **maaltijd.**
dat vas ayn oaitstaykernder
maaltayt

COURSE BY COURSE

Breakfast Ontbijt

I'd like …	**Ik wil graag …** *ik vil khraakh*
eggs	**eieren** *ayyerern*
boiled/fried/scrambled	**gekookte/gebakken/roereieren** *kherkoakter/kherbakkern/roorayyerern*
fruit juice	**vruchtensap** *fruhkhternsap*
grapefruit/orange	**grapefruit/sinaasappel** *graypfroot/sinaasapperl*
honey	**honing** *hoaning*
jam	**jam** *zhehm*
milk	**melk** *melk*
rolls	**broodjes** *broatyers*
toast	**toost** *toast*

Appetizers Voorgerechten

Erwtensoep *ehrternsoop*
Thick green pea soup with smoked sausage and pork

Russische eieren *ruhsseeser ayyerern*
Boiled egg filled with mayonnaise, garnished with fish and salad

Huzarensla *huhzaarernslaa*
Mixture of potato, raw vegetables, and meat with mayonnaise, garnished with salad, pickles, and hard-boiled egg

Nieuwe haring *neeoower haaring*
Freshly caught, salt-cured herring

gerookte paling	*kheroakter paaling*	smoked eel
mosselen	*mosserlern*	mussels

oesters	_oosters_	oysters
pasteitje	_pastaytyer_	pastry filled with meat or fish (vol-au-vent)
zure haring	_zuwrer haaring_	pickled herring (rollmops)

Soups Soep

Groentensoep (met balletjes) _khroontersoop (met ballertyers)_
Vegetable soup (with tiny meat balls)

Bruine bonen soep _broainer boanern soop_
Brown bean soup; filling winter dish of kidney beans

Erwtensoep _ehrternsoop_
The famous thick Dutch pea soup with pig's knuckle (**met kluif**), pieces of smoked sausage, and bacon—a meal in itself

Sajur lodeh _saayoor lodder_
Indonesian fragrant soup of vegetables and coconut

aardappelsoep	_aardapperlsoop_	potato soup
aspergesoep	_aspehrkhersoop_	asparagus soup
bouillon	_booyon_	consommé
gebonden soep	_kherbondern soop_	cream soup
heldere soep	_helderer soop_	broth
kippesoep	_kipersoop_	chicken soup
koninginnesoep	_koaninginnersoop_	cream of chicken
ossestaartsoep	_osserstaartsoop_	oxtail soup
tomatensoep	_toamaaternsoop_	tomato soup
uiensoep	_oaiyernsoop_	onion soup
vermicellisoep	_vehrmiselleesoop_	clear noodle soup
vissoep	_fissoop_	fish soup

Egg dishes Eiergerechten

boerenomelet	_boorernommerlet_	omelet with potatoes, vegetables, and bacon
gebakken ei	_kherbakkern ay_	fried egg
gekookt ei	_kherkoakt ay_	boiled egg
nasi goreng	_naasee khoareng_	Indonesian fried rice with spices, meat, and a fried egg on top
roereieren met gerookte zalm	_roorayyerern met kheroakter zalm_	scrambled eggs with smoked salmon
spiegeleieren met ham	_speekherlayyerern met ham_	fried eggs and ham
zachte eieren met saus en croutons	_zakhter ayyerern met sows en krootons_	soft-boiled eggs with sauce and croutons

Fish and seafood Vis, schaal- en schelpdieren

forel	_foarel_	trout
garnalen	_kharnaalern_	shrimp
haring	_haaring_	herring
inktvis	_inktfis_	squid
kabeljauw	_kaabelyow_	cod
kreeft	_krayft_	lobster
makreel	_makreel_	mackerel
mosselen	_mosserlern_	mussels
oesters	_oosters_	oysters
paling	_paaling_	eel
sardientjes	_sardeentyers_	sardines
schelvis	_skhelfis_	haddock
schol	_skhol_	plaice

tong	*tong*	sole
tonijn	*toanayn*	tuna
venusschelpen	*veenuhsskhelpern*	clams
zalm	*zalm*	salmon

Gerookte paling *kheroakter paaling*
Smoked eel served on toast or with salad and potatoes

Nieuwe haring *neeoower haaring*
Fresh salted herring in season; traditionally picked up by the tail
and held above the mouth for eating

Haringsla *haaringslaa*
Salad of salted or marinated herring mixed with cold potato,
cooked beetroot, apple, pickles, and mayonnaise

Stokvisschotel *stokfisskhoaterl*
Oven stew of dried cod, potatoes, rice, onions, and mustard

Meat and poultry Vlees en gevogelte

biefstuk	*beefstuhk*	steak
duif	*doaif*	pigeon
eend	*aynt*	duck
fazant	*fasant*	pheasant
gans	*khaans*	goose
haas	*haas*	hare
houtsnip	*howtsnip*	woodcock
kalfsvlees	*kalfsflays*	veal
kalkoen	*kalkoon*	turkey
kip	*kip*	chicken
konijn	*koanayn*	rabbit
kuiken	*koaikern*	spring chicken
lamsvlees	*lamsflays*	lamb

reebout	_raybowt_	venison
rundvlees	_ruhnt_flays	beef
spek	_spek_	bacon
varkensvlees	_farkerns_flays	pork
worstjes	_vorst_yers	sausages

Blinde vinken _blind_er _fink_ern
Veal slices stuffed with chopped veal, onion, and bacon

Wiener Schnitzel _veen_er _shnit_serl
Veal in breadcrumbs served with anchovy, capers, and lemon

Goulash _goo_lash
Hungarian goulash—cubes of beef, veal, or pork in a sauce of tomato, onion, and paprika

Hazepeper _haazer_payper
Raw hare marinated in vinegar, wine, and herbs, stewed in gravy

Jachtschotel _yakht_skhoaterl
"Hunter's stew"—meat casserole with potatoes served with apple sauce

Vegetables Groenten

aardappels	_aard_dapperls	potatoes
andijvie	and_ay_vee	endive
bietjes	_beet_yers	beet
Brussels lof	_bruhs_serls lof	chicory
champignons	shampeen_yons_	mushrooms
erwten	_ehr_tern	peas
knoflook	_knof_loak	garlic
komkommer	kom_kom_mer	cucumber
kool	koal	cabbage
paprika's	_pap_reekas	peppers
(rode, groene)	(_roa_der, _khroo_ner)	(red, green)

rapen	_raapern_	turnips
selderij	_selderay_	celery
sla	_slaa_	lettuce
sperziebonen	_spehrseeboanern_	green beans
uien	_oaiyern_	onions
wortels	_vorterls_	carrots

Stamppot van boerenkool met worst
Stamppot fan boorernkoal met vorst
One-pan dish of kale and potatoes, served with smoked sausage

Hutspot met klapstuk _huhtspot met klapstuhk_
Mashed potatoes, carrots, and onions served with rib of beef

Hete bliksem _hayter blikserm_
"Hot lightning"—potatoes, bacon, and apple with sugar and salt

Bami goreng _baamee khoareng_
Indonesian fried noodles with spices, vegetables, onion, and meat,
served with a fried egg

Gado-gado _khaadoa-khaadoa_
Indonesian _al dente_ mixture of vegetables, cucumber, and tofu
(**tahu**), with peanut sauce and egg

Cheese Kaas

Edammer kaas _aydammer kaas_
Mild, low fat cheese from Edam, sealed in red wax

Goudse kaas _khowtser kaas_
Famous cheese from Gouda, softer than Edam and higher in fat

Friese nagelkaas _freeser naakherlkaas_
From the province of Friesland, made with skimmed milk and cloves

Komijnekaas _koamaynerkaas_
Mild, hard cheese with cumin seeds; also called **Leidse** or **Delftse
kaas**

Dessert Nagerecht

Appeltaart _apperltaart_
Dutch apple tart filled with fruit and spices; served with sweetened, whipped cream (**slagroom**)

Haagse bluf _haakhser bluhf_
Fluffy dessert of sweetened, whipped egg whites with red currant sauce

Pannekoeken _pannerkookern_
Thick pancakes, served in special pancake restaurants (**pannekoekhuisjes**)

Poffertjes _poffertyers_
"Puffed up" tiny pancakes, piled on a plate and sprinkled with sugar icing

Gebak _kherbak_
Custard slice

Chipolatapudding _shipoalaatapuding_
Set pudding of eggs, biscuits, and liqueur

Kwarktaart _kvarktaart_
A light cheesecake

Vla _flaa_
Custard, sold ready-made in the shops in different flavors

Wafels _vaaferls_
Waffles, often served with ice cream and/or syrup

Fruit Fruit

Appelmoes _apperlmoos_
Apple sauce, often served with children's meals

Vruchtenvlaai _fruhkhternflaai_
Fruit flan from Limburg, filled with fruit, such as cherries or strawberries

aardbeien	_aardbayern_	strawberries
appels	_apperls_	apples
druiven	_droaivern_	grapes
frambozen	_framboazern_	raspberries
granaatappels	_khranaatapperls_	pomegranates
kersen	_kehrsern_	cherries
meloen	_meloon_	melon
perziken	_pehrzikern_	peaches
pruimen	_proaimern_	plums
sinaasappels	_sinaasapperls_	oranges

DRINKS

Aperitifs Aperitieven

A popular aperitif (**aperitief** or **borreltje**) is beer or **jenever** (a kind of gin). There is **jonge** (young) **jenever** and **oude** (mature) **jenever**, **bessenjenever** (black currant flavor), **citroenjenever** (lemon), and **berenburg** (Frisian gin). Sherry, port, and vermouth are known by their English names.

Beer Beir/Pils

Heineken, Amstel, and Oranjeboom are the best-known Dutch beers. Ask for **een pilsje** if you want a lager. Alternatively, you could try dark beer (**een donker bier**), light beer (**een licht bier**), draft beer (**getapt bier**), old brown (**oud bruin**), or orange-flavored bitter (**oranjebitter**).

Do you have … beer?   **Heeft u … bier?** _hayft uw … beer_

bottled/draft   **flessebier/getapt**
flesserbeer/khertapt

Wine Win

Can you recommend a ... wine?	**Kunt u een ... wijn aanbevelen?** *kuhnt uw ayn ... vayn aanberfaylern*
red/white/blush [rosé]	**rode/witte/rosé** *roader/vitter/roasay*
dry/sweet/sparkling	**droge/zoete/mousserende** *droakher/zooter/moosserernder*
May I have the house wine?	**Mag ik de huiswijn?** *makh ik der hoaisvayn*
I'd like a corkscrew.	**Ik wil graag een kurketrekker.** *ik vil khraakh ayn kuhrkertrekker*

Spirits and liqueurs Sterke dranken en likeurs

Advocaat *adfoakaat*
The famous Dutch egg liqueur is served with a small spoon, and also combined with whipped cream, ice cream, cherry brandy, or a soft drink. Other Dutch liqueurs are **Half om half** (strong), **Parfait'amour** (fragrant), and **Curaçao** (orange flavor).

Brandewijn *brandervayn* .
Brandy is served with the traditional **Brabantse koffietafel** (generous brunch in the province of Brabant). Popular varieties are **boerenjongens** (with raisins) and **boerenmeisjes** (with apricots).

straight [neat]	**puur** *puwr*
on the rocks [with ice]	**met ijs** *met ays*
with water/tonic water	**met water/tonic** *met vaater/tonnik*
I'd like a single/double ...	**Ik wil graag een enkele/dubbele ...** *ik vil khraakh ayn engkerler/ duhberler*

brandy/gin/whisky/vodka	**cognac/jenever/whisky/wodka**
	konyak/yernayver/wiskee/vodka
Cheers!	**Proost!** _prohst_

Non-alcoholic drinks

Koffie _koffee_

Mid-morning coffee with pastries (**een kopje koffie met gebak**) is a popular time to ask friends to come around. Coffee is drunk with a little **koffiemelk**, a kind of evaporated milk sold in small bottles, or **slagroom**, a sweetened whipped cream also used as a topping on ice cream.

Thee _tay_

Tea is drunk very weak and without milk, sometimes **met citroen** (with lemon). Herbal tea (**kruidenthee**) is also popular.

I'd like (a) …	**Ik wil graag …** _ik vil khraakh_
(hot) chocolate	**(warme) chocolade melk**
	(varmer) shoakoalaader melk
chocolate milk	**chocomel** _shoakoamel_
soft drink	**frisdrank** _frisdrank_
lemonade	**limonade** _limoanaader_
fruit juice	**vruchtensap** _fruhkhternsap_
orange	**sinaasappel** _sinaasapperl_
pineapple	**ananas** _annanas_
mineral water	**mineraalwater** _mineraalvaater_
carbonated	**gazeus/met prik** _khasus/met prik_
non-carbonated	**niet-gazeus/zonder prik**
	neet-khasus/zonder prik
buttermilk	**karnemelk** _karnermelk_

MENU READER

gebakken	*gherbakkern*	baked/fried
gefrituurd	*gherfreetuwrt*	deep-fried
gegrilleerd	*gherghrilayrt*	grilled
gekookt	*gherkoakt*	boiled
gemarineerd	*ghermareenayrt*	marinated
gepaneerd	*gherpanayrt*	breaded
gepocheerd	*gherposhayrt*	poached
gerookt	*gherroakt*	cured/smoked
geroosterd	*gherraostert*	roasted
gesauteerd	*ghersoatayrt*	sautéed
gesmoord	*ghersmoart*	braised
gestoofd	*gherstoaft*	stewed
gestoomd	*gherstoamt*	steamed
gevuld	*gherfuwlt*	stuffed
goed doorbakken	*ghoot doarbakkern*	well-done
in blokjes gesneden	*in blokyers ghersnaydern*	diced
in de oven gebruind	*in der oafern gherbroaint*	oven-browned
kort gebakken	*kort gherbakkern*	rare
met room bereid	*met roam berayt*	creamed
pikant	*peekant*	spicy
redelijk doorbakken	*rayderlayk doarbakkern*	medium
saignant	*saynyant*	rare

48

A

aalbessen red currants
aan de kluif on the bone
aardappel potato
aardappelpuree mashed potato
aardappelsalade potato salad
aardappelsoep potato soup
aardbeien strawberries
abrikozen apricots
advocaat egg liqueur
afgemaakt met seasoned with
alcoholische drank alcoholic drink
amandel almond
amandelgebak almond tart
Amsterdamse ui pickled onion
ananas pineapple
andijvie endive
andijviesla endive salad
anijs aniseed
anijslikeur aniseed liqueur
ansjovis anchovies
aperitief aperitif
appel apple
appelbol apple dumpling
appelflappen apple turnovers
appelmoes apple sauce
appeltaart apple pie/tart
artisjokken artichoke
asperge asparagus
aspergepunten asparagus tips
aspergesoep asparagus soup
au gratin au gratin
aubergine eggplant
augurken pickles

avocado avocado
avondeten tea (mealtime)

B

baars bass/perch
babyinktvis baby squid
babyoctopus baby octopus
balletjes tiny meat balls (in vegetable soup)
bami Chinese/Indonesian noodles
bami goreng fried Chinese/Indonesian noodles
banaan banana
banketletter (almond) pastry letter
basilicum basil
bataat sweet potato
bavarois Bavarian cream
beignets fritters
beschuit Dutch toast
bessen currants
biefstuk steak (pan-fried)
biefstuk tartaar ground steak
biefstuk van de haas porterhouse steak
biefstuk van de rib T-bone steak
bier beer
bieslook chives
bieten beetroot
biscuitjes biscuits
bitterballen breaded meat balls
bladerdeeg puff pastry
blanc-manger blancmange
blankvoorn roach
blauwe druiven black grapes
bleekselderij celery
blikgroenten canned vegetables

blinde vinken meat rolls (veal or beef)
bloedworst black pudding
bloem (plain) flour
bloemkool cauliflower
boerenjongens brandy with raisins
boerenkool kale
boerenmeisjes brandy with apricots
boerenomelet omelet with potatoes, vegetables, and bacon
bolus Chelsea bun
bonen beans
borrel aperitif
borreltjes drinks (alcoholic)
borst breast
borstplaat thick sugar slice
bosbessen blueberries
boter butter
boterbabbelaar butterscotch
boterham sandwich
boterhammen sliced bread
boterkoek butter biscuit
boterletter (almond) pastry letter
bouillon consommé
bourbon bourbon (whisky)
bout leg (cut of meat)
bowl punch
braadstuk roast
Brabantse koffietafel generous brunch
bramen blackberries
brandewijn brandy
brasem bream
brood bread

broodje roll
broodkruimels breadcrumbs
bruine bonen brown beans
bruine bonen soep brown bean soup
Brussels lof chicory

C

caffeïnevrij decaffeinated
cake cake, sponge cake
caraf carafe
caramelpudding crème caramel
cep cep (mushroom)
champignons/champignonhoedjes button mushrooms
chanterelle champignons chanterelle mushrooms
chipolatapudding set pudding of eggs, biscuits, and liqueur
chocolade chocolate
chocomel chocolate milk
citroen lemon
citroengras lemon grass
citroensap lemon juice
cognac brandy
consommé consommé
contre-fillet sirloin steak
corned beef corned beef
courgette zucchini
croquet croquette

D

dadels dates
dagschotel dish of the day
dessert dessert
dessertwijn dessert wine
dille dill

diner dinner
dooier egg yolk
doperwten garden peas
doughnut donut
dragon tarragon
drilpudding jelly
droge wijn dry wine
droog dry
druiven grapes
dubbel double (a double shot)
duif pigeon

E

Edammer kaas Edam cheese
eend duck
eierdooier egg yolk
eieren eggs
eiergerechten egg dishes
eigengemaakt home-made
eiwit egg white
erwten peas
erwtensoep pea soup

F

fazant pheasant
filet filet
filterkoffie freshly brewed coffee
flamberen flaming [flambé]
flensjes thin small pancakes
fles bottle
flessebier bottled beer
foeli mace
forel trout
frambozen raspberries
fricandeau fricandeau (meat with sauce)

Friese nagelkaas cheese with cloves
frisdrank soft drink

G

gado-gado Indonesian mixture of vegetables, cucumber, and tofu
gans goose
garnalen shrimp
garnering garnish, trimming
gazeus carbonated (drinks)
gebak(jes) pastries
gebakken (in de pan) fried
gebakken (oven) baked
gebakken kip fried chicken
gebarbecued barbecued
gebonden soep cream soup
gebraden braised
gecorseerd full-bodied (wine)
gedroogd dried
gedroogde dadels dried dates
gedroogde pruimen dried prunes
gedroogde vijgen dried figs
geflambeerd flaming [flambé]
gegratineerd gratin
gegrilleerde kip grilled chicken
gehakt ground meat
gehaktballetjes meat balls
geit goat
geitenkaas goat cheese
gekoeld chilled (wine, etc.)
gekonfijte vruchten candied fruit
gekookt eitje boiled egg
gekookte aardappels boiled potatoes
gekruid seasoned

gele sperciebonen butter beans

gemarineerd in azijn marinated in vinegar

gember ginger

gemengd assorted, mixed

gemengde grill mixed grill

gemengde groenten mixed vegetables

gemengde kruiden mixed herbs

gemengde noten assorted nuts

gemengde salade mixed salad

geraspt grated

gerookte paling smoked eel

gerookte zalm smoked salmon

geroosterd brood toast

geroosterde aardappels roast potatoes

geroosterde kip roast chicken

gestoofd fruit stewed fruit

gestoomd steamed

gestoomde vis steamed fish

getapt bier draft beer

gevogelte fowl

gevuld met stuffed with

gevulde olijven stuffed olives

gezouten salted

gezouten pinda's salted peanuts

glas glass

goelasj goulash

granaatappelen pomegranates

griesmeelpudding semolina pudding

grill grill

groene erwten garden peas

groene paprika's green peppers

groene salade green salad

groentebouillon vegetable broth

groenten vegetables (general)

groentensoep vegetable soup

grog grog, hot toddy

Goudse kaas Gouda cheese

guave guava

H

Haagse bluf dessert of whipped egg white with red currant sauce

haan cock

haas hare

hachee hash

halve fles half bottle

hamlap pork steak

hanekammensoep chanterelle soup

hapjes snacks

hapjes vooraf appetizers

hard hard-boiled (egg)

harde kaas hard cheese

harder grey mullet

haring herring

haringsla salad of salted or marinaded herring

hart heart

hartig savory

havermoutpap porridge

hazelnoten hazelnuts

hazepeper jugged hare

heet hot (temperature)

heet water hot water

heilbot halibut

heldere soep clear soup

hersens brains

hete bliksem dish of potatoes, bacon, and apple

hete pepersaus hot pepper sauce
Hollandse biefstuk Dutch steak
honing honey
hoorntjes cream horn
hopjes coffee caramel/toffee
houtsnip woodcock
huiswijn house wine
hutspot stew made of mashed potatoes with carrots and onions or with kale
hutspot met klapstuk mashed potatoes, carrots, and onions served with rib of beef
huzarensla mixture of potato, raw vegetables, and meat with mayonnaise

I

ijs ice, ice cream
ijsgekoeld iced (drink)
ijswater iced water
in beslag in batter
in beslag gebakken fried in batter
in de pan gebakken vis fried fish
in knoflook in garlic
in olie in oil
in oven gebakken vis baked fish
in plakjes gesneden sliced
ingeblikte vruchten canned fruit
inktvis squid
inwendige organen giblets

J

jachtschotel meat casserole with potatoes
jam jam
jenever gin

jeneverbessen juniper berries
jong geitevlees kid (goat)
jonge eend duckling
jus gravy

K

kaas cheese
kaasplank cheese board
kabeljauw cod
kalfskarbonaden veal chops
kalfsoester scallop
kalfsvlees veal
kalkoen turkey
kammosselen scallops
kaneel cinnamon
kappertje caper
kapucijners marrowfat peas
karaf carafe
karbonades chops
karnemelk buttermilk
karwij caraway
kastanjes chestnuts (sweet)
katenspek smoked bacon
kaviaar caviar
kekers chickpeas
kersen cherries
kerstomaatje cherry tomato
kervel chervil
kievitsbonen kidney beans
kievitseieren lapwing's eggs
kip chicken
kip en gevogelte poultry
kippeborst breast of chicken
kippenlever chicken liver
kippensoep chicken broth, soup
kiwivrucht kiwi fruit

klapstuk beef rib
kluif pig's knuckle (bone)
knakworst frankfurter
knoedel dumpling
knoflook garlic
knoflookmayonaise garlic mayonnaise
knoflooksaus garlic sauce
knolraap rutabaga
knolselderij celery root
koekjes cookies
koffie coffee
kokkelschelp cockle
kokos coconut
kokosmakarons coconut macaroon
komijn cumin
komijnekaas cheese with cumin seeds
komkommer cucumber
komkommersalade cucumber salad
konijn rabbit
koninginnesoep cream of chicken
kool cabbage
koolrabi kohlrabi
koolsla coleslaw
koriander coriander
korstdeeg shortcrust pastry
koteletten chops, cutlets
koud cold
koud buffet cold buffet
koud gerecht cold dish
koude drankjes cold drinks
koude soep cold soup
krab crab

kreeft lobster
krentenbrood currant bread
kroepoek shrimp crackers
krokant crisp
kroketten croquettes
kropsla lettuce
kruiden herbs
kruidnagels cloves
kruisbes gooseberry
kuiken spring chicken
kwarktaart light cheesecake
kwartelvlees quail
kweegelei quince jelly
kwetsen damson

L

lamsbout leg of lamb
lamsstoofschotel lamb stew
lamsvlees lamb
laurierblad bay leaf
lekkerbekje fried breaded filet of haddock
lende loin
lendebiefstuk filet, rump steak
lendevlees loin (pork)
lente-uitjes spring onions
lever liver
licht light (sauce)
likeur liqueur
limoen lime
limoensap lime juice
limonade lemonade
limonadesiroop fruit drink
linzen lentils
loempia spring roll

lofsla salad of raw chicory rings
lopend buffet buffet

M

machtig rich (sauce)
maïs sweet corn
makreel mackerel
mandarijn tangerine
marmelade marmalade
marsepein marzipan
mayonaise mayonnaise
melk milk
meloen melon
menu menu
menu van de dag menu of the day
met balletjes with tiny meat balls (in vegetable soup)
met citroen with lemon
met ijs on the rocks [with ice]
met koolzuur carbonated
met melk white/with milk (coffee)
met prik carbonated (drinks)
met suiker with sugar
met water/tonic with water/tonic water
mie noodles
mierikswortel horseradish
milkshake milk shake
mineraalwater mineral water
moerbei mulberry
moorkop chocolate éclair
mosselen mussels
mosterd mustard
mousserend sparkling
mousserende wijn sparkling wine
munt mint

muntthee mint tea

N

nasi goreng Indonesian rice dish with egg
nectarine nectarine
niertjes kidneys
niet-alcoholische dranken non-alcoholic drinks
nieuwe haring freshly caught, salt-cured herring
noga nougat
nootmuskaat nutmeg

O

octopus octopus
oesters oysters
oesterzwammen oyster mushrooms
oliebollen donut ball
olijven olives
omelet omelet
ontbijt breakfast
ontbijtgranen cereal
op houtskool geroosterd charcoal-grilled
op ijs on the rocks
ossehaas tenderloin
ossestaart ox
ossestaartsoep oxtail soup

P

paddestoelen field mushrooms
paling eel
pannekoeken pancakes
paprika's peppers

parelhoen guinea fowl
passievrucht passion fruit
pastei pie
pasteideeg pastry
pasteitje vol-au-vent
pastinaken parsnips
patat french fries
patates frites french fries
pâté pâté
patrijs partridge
peer pear
pekelvlees sliced salted meat
pens tripe
peper pepper
perzik peach
peterselie parsley
peultjes sugar peas
pikant worstje spicy sausage
pils lager
pinda's peanuts
pindasaus peanut sauce
pittabrood pita bread
pittig sharp (flavor)
plaatselijke specialiteit local speciality
plak slice
poffertjes tiny puffed-up pancakes
pompoen pumpkin
poon sea robin [gurnard fish]
portie portion
prei leeks
prinsessenbonen haricot beans
pruimen plums, prunes
pure whisky straight [neat] whisky
puur straight [neat]

R

raap turnip
rabarber rhubarb
radijs radish
rammenas winter radish
rapen turnips
rauw raw
reebout venison
rettich rettich (white radish-related, carrot-shaped vegetable)
ribstuk rib
rijp ripe
rijst rice
risotto risotto
rivierkreeft crayfish
rode kool red cabbage
rode peper chili pepper
roerei scrambled egg
rog ray
roggebrood rye bread
rollade rolled meat
romig creamy
rood red (wine)
rookvlees sliced smoke-dried beef
room cream
roomijs ice cream
roomsoep cream soup
rosbief roast beef
rosé blush [rosé] (wine)
rozemarijn rosemary
rozijnen raisins
rum rum
rundvlees beef
russische eieren hard-boiled egg filled with mayonnaise

saffraan saffron

sajur lodeh Indonesian soup of vegetables and coconut

salade salad

salie sage

sap juice

sardientjes sardines

saté meat on skewers

saucijzebroodje sausage roll

saucijzen sausages

saus sauce

savooiekool savoy cabbage

schaaldieren crustaceans

schapekaas ewe's milk cheese

schapevlees mutton

schelpdieren shellfish

schelvis haddock

schenkel shank (top of leg)

schimmelkaas blue cheese

schnitzel veal/pork cutlet

schol plaice

schorseneer salsify, oyster plant

schotel dish

Schotse Whisky Scotch whisky

schouderstuk shoulder (meat cut)

schuimgebak meringue

schuimig foamy

selderij celery

sinaasappel orange

sinaasappelsap orange juice

siroop syrup

sjalots shallots

sla lettuce

slagroom sweet whipped cream

slakken snails

slasaus vinaigrette

snijbonen sliced green beans

snoepjes candy

soep soup

soesjes choux pastry

specerijen spices

specialiteiten van de chef-kok specialties of the house

speenvarken suckling pig

spek bacon

spekpannekoeken bacon pancakes

spelletje game

sperziebonen green beans

spiegelei fried egg

spiesjes met skewered

spijkerrog skate

spinazie spinach

spitskool oxheart cabbage

sprits Dutch short biscuit

sprotten sprats

spruitjes Brussel sprouts

spuitwater soda water

stamppot one-pan dish with vegetables and mashed potatoes

sterk strong (flavor)

sterk gekruid highly seasoned

sterke dranken spirits

stervrucht star fruit

stokbrood french bread, baguette

stokvis hake

stokvisschotel oven stew of dried cod

stoofschotel casserole, stew

strandgapers clams

stroop treacle, molasses
stuk van de rib T-bone steak
suiker sugar
suikerglazuur icing
sultanarozijnen sultanas

T

taart tart (sweet, savory)
taartje tartlette (sweet, savory)
tafelwijn table wine
tafelzuur pickles
tahoe tofu, bean curd
tarbot turbot
tartaartje ground steak
tarwebloem wholewheat flour
taugé bean spouts
thee tea
tijm thyme
timbaaltje timbale (chopped meat or fish in a pastry shell)
tomaten tomatoes
tomatenketchup tomato ketchup
tomatensaus tomato sauce
tomatensoep tomato soup
tompoes custard slice
tong tongue, sole (fish)
tonic tonic water
tonijn tuna
toost toast
tostie toasted sandwich
touristenmenu tourist menu
tournedos filet steak (thick, round)
truffels truffles
tuinbonen broad beans
tuinkers cress

tulband turban-shaped fruit cake

U

uien onions
uiensoep onion soup
uitsmijter lunchtime snack of bread, ham, and fried eggs

V

van de haas tenderloin (cut of meat)
vanille vanilla
varkenshaasje pork tenderloin
varkenskarbonaden pork chops
varkenspootjes pigs' feet
varkensvlees pork
varkensworstjes pork sausages
veenbes cranberry
vegetarisch vegetarian
venkel fennel
venusschelpen clams
vermicellisoep clear noodle soup
vermout vermouth
vers fresh
vers fruit fresh fruit
verse dadels fresh dates
verse kwark fresh-curd cheese
verse vijgen fresh figs
vet fatty
vijgen figs
vis fish
viskroketten fish fingers
vissoep fish soup
vla custard
vlaai fruit tart
vlees meat
vleesbouillon meat broth

vogelnestje bird's nest (edible)

vruchtendrank fruit drink

vruchtensap fruit juice

vruchtenvlaai fruit flan from the province of Limburg

WXYZ

wafels waffles

walnoten walnuts

warme chocolademelk hot chocolate

waterkastanjes water chestnuts

waterkers watercress

watermeloen watermelon

wentelteefjes french toast

Wiener Schnitzel breaded veal slices

wijn wine

wijnkaart wine list

wijting whiting

wild zwijn wild boar

wilde eend wild duck (mallard)

witlof chicory

witlofsla chicory salad

witte bonen white/baked beans

witte druiven white grapes

witte kool white cabbage

witte saus white sauce

worstjes sausages

wortelsalade raw grated carrot

worteltjes carrots

yoghurt yogurt

zacht mild (flavor)

zacht gekookt soft-boiled (eggs)

zachte kaas soft cheese

zalm salmon

zandgebak shortbread, shortcake

zeebaars sea bass

zeebarbeel red mullet

zeebliek whitebait

zeebrasem sea bream

zeeduivel monkfish

zeekat cuttlefish

zeepaling conger eel

zeer droog very dry (wine)

zeevis, schaal- en schelpdieren seafood

zelfrijzend bakmeel self-rising flour

zoet sweet

zoet-zure saus sweet and sour sauce

zoete rode paprika's sweet red peppers

zoete wijn sweet wine

zoetjes sweetener

zoetwatervis freshwater fish

zonder plain

zonder melk black (coffee)

zonder prik non-carbonated

zout salt

zoutwatervis salt-water fish

zult brawn

zure bom big pickle

zure haring pickled herring, rollmops

zuring sorrel

zuur sour (taste)

zuurkool sauerkraut

zwaardvis swordfish

zwarte bessen black currants

zwezeriken sweetbreads

FRENCH

ESSENTIALS

Hello.	**Bonjour.**	*bawngzhoor*
Good evening.	**Bonsoir.**	*bawngswar*
A table for...	**Une table pour...**	*ewn tabler poor*
1/2/3/4	**un/deux/trois/quatre**	*ang/dur/trwa/katr*
Thank you.	**Merci.**	*mehrsee*
The check, please.	**L'addition, s'il vous plaît.**	
	ladeesyawng seel voo pleh	
Good-bye.	**Au revoir.**	*oa rervwar*

PLACES TO EAT

Auberge *oabehrzh*
An inn, often in the country; serves full meals and drinks

Bistrot *beestroa*
Varies from a café, selling drinks and basic food, to a more picturesque restaurant, with traditional cuisine; usually not expensive

Brasserie *brasserree*
Large café serving good, simple food and drinks, often offering a **plat du jour** (dish of the day)

Buffet *bewfeh*
In principal train stations; the food is generally good

Café/bar *kafay/bar*
On virtually every street corner; coffee and drinks served, sometimes light meals, too; beer, wine, and liquor are available but not fancy cocktails

Crêperie *krepehree*
Offers snacks of light pancakes with various fillings

Restaurant *restoarang*
Classified by stars, forks, and knives and endorsed by everyone
including travel agencies and gastronomic guilds

Restoroute *restoaroot*
Just off a highway; table and/or cafeteria service available

Rôtisserie *roateessree*
Often linked with a **charcuterie** (delicatessen)

Routier *rootyay*
Roughly equivalent to a roadside diner; the food is simple but can
be surprisingly good if you happen to hit upon the right place

MEAL TIMES

Le petit déjeuner *ler pertee dayzhurnay*
Breakfast: 7–10 a.m. Traditionally just bread, butter, jam, a croissant,
and **un petit noir** (small black coffee), tea or hot chocolate.

Le déjeuner *ler deayzhurnay*
Lunch: 12–2 p.m. Don't have time for a leisurely meal? Try a
restaurant offering a **plat du jour** (single dish of the day) or light salad.

Le dîner *ler deenay*
Dinner is usually served late, from 8–10 p.m. The French are likely
to linger over their meal, so service may seem on the slow side.

FRENCH CUISINE

Apart from the many regional specialties, you can sample **haute
cuisine** (sophisticated dishes made according to time-honored
recipes) or **nouvelle cuisine** (a more refined preparation enhancing
the delicate flavors of the food).
Most restaurants display a menu (**la carte**) outside. Besides ordering
à la carte, you can order a fixed price menu—**le menu (à prix fixe)**.

FINDING A PLACE TO EAT

Can you recommend a good restaurant?	**Pouvez-vous nous recommander un bon restaurant?** *poovay voo noo rerkommahngday ang bawng restoarahng*
Is there a … restaurant near here?	**Y a-t-il un restaurant … près d'ici?** *ee ateel ang restoarahng … preh deessee*
traditional local	**local traditionnel** *lokal tradeessyonell*
inexpensive	**bon marché** *bawng marshay*
vegetarian	**végétarien** *vayzhaytaryang*
Where can I find a …?	**Où puis-je trouver …?** *oo pweezh troovay*
café	**un café** *ang kafay*
fast-food restaurant	**un fast-food** *ang fast food*
tea room	**un salon de thé** *ang salawng der tay*
pizzeria	**une pizzeria** *ewn peetzehreea*
steak house	**un restaurant-grill** *ang restoarahng greel*

RESERVATIONS

I'd like to reserve a table for 2.	**Je voudrais réserver une table pour deux personnes.** *zher voodray rayzehrvay ewn tabl poor dur pehrsonn*
For this evening/ tomorrow at …	**Pour ce soir/demain à … heures.** *poor ser swar/dermang a … urr*
We'll come at 8:00.	**Nous viendrons à huit heures.** *noo vyangdrawng a weeturr*
A table for 2, please.	**Une table pour deux, s'il vous plaît.** *ewn tabl poor dur seel voo pleh*

| We have a reservation. | **Nous avons réservé.** |
| | *noo zavawng rayzehrvay* |

| **C'est à quel nom, s'il vous plaît?** | What's the name, please? |
| **Je regrette. Il y a beaucoup de monde/nous sommes complets.** | I'm sorry. We're very busy/full. |

Could we sit …?	**Pouvons-nous nous asseoir …?**
	poovawng noo noo zaswar
outside	**dehors** *der or*
in a non-smoking area	**dans une zone non-fumeur**
	dahng zewn zon nawng fewmurr
by the window	**près de la fenêtre** *preh der la fernetr*

ORDERING

Waiter!/Waitress!	**Monsieur!/Mademoiselle!**
	murssyew/madmwazel
May I see the wine list, please?	**Puis-je avoir la carte des vins, s'il vous plaît?** *pweezh avwar la karter day vang seel voo pleh*

Vous désirez commander?	Are you ready to order?
Qu'est-ce que vous prendrez?	What would you like?
Je vous recommande/conseille …	I recommend …
Est-ce que vous voulez … avec?	Would you like … with that?
Nous n'avons pas de …	We haven't got …
Bon appétit.	Enjoy your meal.

Do you have a set menu?	**Avez-vous un menu à prix fixe?** *avay voo zang mernew a pree feex*
Can you recommend some typical local dishes?	**Pouvez-vous recommander des spécialités régionales?** *poovay voo rerkommahngday day spaysyaleetay rayzhyonal*
Could you tell me what … is?	**Pourriez-vous me dire ce qu'est …?** *pooryay voo mer deer ser keh*
What's in it?	**Qu'y a-t-il dedans?** *kee ateel derdahng*
I'd like …	**Je voudrais …** *zher voodray*
a bottle/glass/ carafe of …	**une bouteille/un verre/ une carafe de …** *ewn bootay/ang verr/ewn karaf de*

SPECIAL REQUESTS

With a side order of …	**Avec … comme accompagnement.** *avek … ko makawngpahnmahng*
Could I have salad instead of vegetables, please?	**Est-ce que je pourrais avoir une salade à la place des légumes?** *ess ker zher pooray avvar ewn salad a la plass day laygewm*
Does the meal come with vegetables/ potatoes?	**Le plat est-il servi avec des légumes/ pommes de terre?** *ler pla eteel sehrvee avek day laygewm/pom der tehr*
Do you have any sauces?	**Avez-vous des sauces?** *avay voo day soass*
May I have some …?	**Puis-je avoir …?** *pwee zhavwar*
bread	**du pain** *dew pang*
butter	**du beurre** *dew burr*
ice	**des glaçons** *day glassawng*

lemon	**du citron** *dew seetrawng*	
mustard	**de la moutarde** *der la mootard*	
pepper	**du poivre** *dew pwavr*	
salt	**du sel** *dew sel*	
seasoning	**de l'assaisonnement** *der lassayzonmahng*	
sugar	**du sucre** *dew sewkr*	
(artificial) sweetener	**de l'édulcorant** *der laydewlkorahngt*	
vinaigrette	**de la vinaigrette** *der la veenaygret*	
Could we have a child's seat, please?	**Pourrions-nous avoir une chaise haute (pour bébé)?** *pooryawng noo avvar ewn shezer oat (poor baybay)*	
Where can I nurse/ change the baby?	**Où est-ce que je peux allaiter/ changer le bébé?** *oo ess ker zher pur aletay/shahngzhay ler baybay*	

GENERAL QUESTIONS

Could I have a(n) (clean) …, please?	**Pourriez-vous m'apporter … (propre)?** *pooryay voo maportay … (propr)*	
ashtray	**un cendrier** *ang sahngdryay*	
cup/glass	**une tasse/un verre** *ewn tass/ang vehr*	
fork/knife	**une fourchette/un couteau** *ewn foorshett/ang kootoa*	
napkin	**une serviette** *ewn sehrvyett*	
plate/spoon	**une assiette/une cuillère** *ewn assyett/ewn kweeyehr*	
I'd like a cup of …	**Je voudrais une tasse de …** *zher voodray ewn tass der*	
tea/coffee	**thé/café** *tay/kafay*	
black/with milk	**noir/au lait** *nwar/oa leh*	

65

F
R
E
N
C
H

I'd like a ... of red/white wine.	**Je voudrais ... de vin rouge/blanc.** *zher voodray ... der vang roozh/blahng*
carafe/bottle/glass	**une carafe/une bouteille/un verre** *ewn karaf/ewn bootay/ang vehr*
Do you have ... beer?	**Avez-vous de la bière ...?** *avay voo der la byehr*
bottled/draft	**en bouteille/pression** *ahng bootay/pressyawng*
That's all, thanks.	**C'est tout, merci.** *seh too mehrsee*
Where are the restrooms?	**Où sont les toilettes?** *oo sawng lay twalett*

SPECIAL REQUIREMENTS

I mustn't eat food containing ...	**Je ne dois pas manger de plats contenant ...** *zher ner dwa pa mahngzhay der pla kawngtnahng*
salt/sugar	**du sel/du sucre** *dew sel/dew sewkr*
Do you have meals/drinks for diabetics?	**Avez-vous des repas/boissons pour diabétiques?** *avay voo day rerpa/ bwassawng poor dyabayteek*
Do you have vegetarian meals?	**Avez-vous des repas végétariens?** *avay voo day rerpa vayzhaytaryang*

COMPLAINTS

That's not what I ordered.	**Ce n'est pas ce que j'ai commandé.** *ser neh pa ser ker zhay kommahngday*
I asked for ...	**J'ai demandé ...** *zhay dermahngday*
The meat is ...	**La viande est ...** *la vyahngd eh*
overdone	**trop cuite** *tro kweet*
underdone	**pas assez cuite** *pa zassay kweet*
The food is cold.	**La nourriture est froide.** *la nooreetewr eh frwad*

How much longer will our food be?	**Il y en a encore pour combien de temps?** *eel yahng na ahngkor poor kawnbyang der tahng*
We can't wait any longer. We're leaving.	**Nous ne pouvons plus attendre. Nous partons.** *noo ner poovawng plew atahngdr. noo partawng*

PAYING

Tipping: See page 332.

The check, please.	**L'addition, s'il vous plaît.** *ladeesyawng seel voo pleh*
We'd like to pay separately.	**Nous voudrions payer séparément.** *noo voodryawng payay sayparaymahng*
It's all together, please.	**Tous les repas ensemble, s'il vous plaît.** *too lay repa ahngsahngbl seel voo pleh*
I think there's a mistake in this check.	**Je crois qu'il y a une erreur sur l'addition.** *zher krwa keel ee a ewn ehrurr sewr ladeesyawng*
What is this amount for?	**Que représente ce montant?** *ker reprayzahngt ser mawngtahng*
I didn't have that. I had …	**Je n'ai pas pris ça. J'ai pris …** *zher nay pa pree sa. zhay pree*
Can I pay with this credit card?	**Puis-je payer avec cette carte de crédit?** *pweezh payay avek set kart der kraydee*
Could I have a receipt?	**Puis-je avoir un reçu?** *pweezh avwar ang rersew*
That was a very good meal.	**C'était un très bon repas.** *sayteh ang treh bawng repa*

COURSE BY COURSE

Breakfast Petit déjeuner

I'd like some …	**Je voudrais …** *zher voodray*
eggs	**des œufs** *day zur*
fried/scrambled	**au plat/brouillés** *oa plah/brooyay*
grapefruit juice	**un jus de pamplemousse** *ang zhew der pangplermoos*
honey	**du miel** *dew myel*
jelly/jam	**de la confiture** *der lah kawngfeetewr*
marmalade	**de la marmelade** *der lah marmerlad*
milk	**du lait** *dew lay*
orange juice	**un jus d'orange** *ang zhew dorahngzh*
rolls	**des petits pains** *day pertee pang*
toast	**du pain grillé** *dew pang greeyay*

Appetizers Hors-d'œuvre

Andouille(tte) *angdooy(ett)*
Seasoned, aromatic sausage made from tripe, served grilled or fried

Bouchée à la reine *booshay ah lah ren*
Pastry filled with creamed sweetbreads and mushrooms

Pâté *patay*
Liver purée, such as **pâté de campagne; pâté de foie gras**
indicates a fine paste of duck or goose liver, often with truffles
(**truffé**); **pâté en croûte** is in a pastry crust

Quenelles *kernel*
Light dumplings made of fish, fowl, or meat, served with a velvety
sauce; the best known are **quenelles de brochet**, made of pike

Quiche *keesh*
Open-faced tart with a filling of cheese, vegetables, meat, or seafood;
quiche lorraine is garnished with bacon

Soups Potages et soupes

Soups appear on menus in various forms: **bouillon, consommé, crème, potage, soupe,** and **velouté.** Look for these specialties:

à l'ail	*ah lay*	garlic
à l'œuf	*a lurf*	with a raw egg
à l'oignon	*ah lonyawng*	French onion
à la bière	*a la byehr*	beer with chicken stock and onions
aïgo bouïdo	*aeegoa bweedoa*	garlic soup (*Prov.*)
au cresson	*oa kressawn*	watercress
au pistou	*oa peestoo*	vegetable (*Prov.*)/basil
au porto	*oa portoa*	with port wine
aux choux	*oa shoo*	cabbage
bilibi	*beeleebee*	fish and oyster
bisque	*beesk*	seafood stew/chowder
bonne femme	*bon fam*	potato, leek, and sometimes bacon
bouillabaisse	*booyabess*	fish and seafood soup (*Mars.*)
Célestine	*saylesteen*	with chicken and noodles
Colbert	*kolbehr*	with poached eggs, spring vegetables
Condé	*kawngday*	mashed red beans
Crécy	*krehsee*	carrots and rice
de Pélous	*der payloo*	crab with tomatoes
de poisson	*der pwassawn*	small fish, simmered and puréed
de volaille	*der volay*	chicken
du Barry	*dew baree*	cream of cauliflower
garbure	*garbewr*	cabbage soup, often with pork or goose
julienne	*zhewlyen*	shredded vegetables
Parmentier	*parmahngtyay*	potato
pot-au-feu	*po toa fur*	meat and vegetable stew

Fish and seafood Poissons et fruits de mer

You'll recognize: **carpe, crabe, harengs, maquereau, perche, sardines, saumon, scampi, sole, truite, turbot.**

escargots	*eskargoa*	snails
huîtres	*weetr*	oysters
morue	*morew*	cod
moules	*mool*	mussels
thon	*tawng*	tuna

Bar aux herbes en chemise *bar oazerb ahng shermeez*

Bass stuffed with spinach and herbs, wrapped in lettuce and poached in white wine

Cotriade *kotreeyad*

Assorted fish soup/stew with shellfish, onion, carrots, potatoes, garlic, Calvados, and white wine (*Brittany*)

Homard à l'américaine *oma rah lamayreeken*

Sautéed diced lobster, flamed in cognac and then simmered in wine, aromatic vegetables, herbs, and tomatoes

Meat Viandes

I'd like some …	**Je voudrais …** *zher voodreh*	
bacon	**du lard** *dew lar*	
beef	**du bœuf** *dew burf*	
chicken	**du poulet** *dew pooleh*	
duck	**du canard** *dew kanar*	
goose	**de l'oie** *der lwah*	
ham	**du jambon** *dew zhahngbawng*	
lamb	**de l'agneau** *der lahnyo*	
pork	**du porc** *dew por*	
rabbit	**du lapin** *dew lapang*	
sausages	**des saucisses** *day soasseess*	
steak	**du steak** *dew stek*	
veal	**du veau** *dew voa*	

Meat Cuts Morceaux de viande

contre-filet	*kawngtre feeleh*	loin strip steak
côte de bœuf	*koat der burf*	T-bone steak
côtelettes	*koaterlet*	chops
entrecôte	*ahngtrerkoat*	rib or rib-eye steak
escalope	*eskalop*	cutlet
filet	*feeleh*	filet steak
gigot	*zheegoa*	leg
médaillon	*maydahyawng*	tenderloin steak
rognons	*roñawng*	kidneys
tournedos	*toornerdoa*	tenderloin of T-bone steak

Meat dishes Plats de viande

Blanquette de veau *blawnket der voa*
Veal stew in a white sauce with onions and mushrooms

Bœuf bourguignon *burf boorgeenyawng*
A rich beef stew with vegetables, braised in red Burgundy wine

Canard à l'orange *kahnahrah lorahngzh*
Duck braised with oranges and orange liqueur

Cassoulet toulousain *kassoolay tooloozang*
A casserole of white beans, pork, sausages and preserved goose

Civet *seevay*
Game stew, with wine, onions and blood sauce; e.g., **civet de lièvre** (jugged hare)

Coq au vin *ko koa vang*
Chicken stewed with onion, mushroom, bacon in a red wine sauce; e.g. **coq au Chambertin** (chicken in Chambertin [wine])

Couscous *kooskoos*
Arab dish based on cracked wheat; with vegetables and meat

Lapin à la flamande *lahpang a la flamawnd*
Marinated rabbit, braised potatoes, carrots, cabbage, turnip, bacon and sausage, simmered in beer (*Belg.*)

Ragoût *ragoo*
Meat stew, generally served in a delicate gravy with vegetables; for example **ragoût de bœuf** (beef stew)

Vegetables Légumes

You'll recognize: **artichaut, carottes, concombre, lentilles, oignons, radis, tomates.**

haricots verts	*areekoa vehr*	french (green) beans
laitue	*lehtew*	lettuce
petits pois	*pertee pwah*	peas

Champignons *shahngpeenyawng*
Button mushrooms; common wild varieties include: **bolets** (boletus), **cèpes** (flat), **chanterelle** (aromatic), **morille** (sweet)

Pommes (de terre) *pom (der tehr)*
Potatoes; **allumettes** (matchsticks), **dauphine** (mashed and deep-fried), **duchesse** (mashed), **en robe des champs** (in their skins), **frites** (fries), **gaufrettes** (waffles), **mignonettes** (fries), **paille** (straws), **pont-neuf** (straight cut)

Truffes *trewf*
Truffles: highly prized fungus with a heavy, musky flavor; the black truffle of Périgord is regarded as the supreme delicacy

Chou rouge à la flamande *shoo roo zhah lah flamangd*
Red cabbage, cooked with apples, onions, red wine, and vinegar (*Belg.*)

Chou fassum *shoo fassang*
Cabbage stuffed with rice, eggs, cheese, and ground meat (*Prov.*)

Salads Salades

The French will save a side salad until the end of their main course.

salade composée	*salad kawngpoazay*	mixed salad
salade de foies de volaille	*salad der fwa der volay*	lettuce with chicken livers
salade russe	*salad rewss*	diced vegetables
salade de thon	*salad der tawng*	tuna salad
salade verte	*salad vehrt*	green salad

Salade antiboise *salad awngteebwaz*
Fish, anchovy filets, green peppers, beets, rice, and capers in vinaigrette

Salade niçoise *salad neeswaz*
Riviera salad with tuna, anchovies, olives, and vegetables

Cheese Fromages

With almost 400 French cheeses, there are plenty to suit any palate.

mild	**beaumont, belle étoile, boursin, brie, cantal, coulommiers, mimolette, Port-Salut, reblochon, saint-paulin, tomme**
sharp, tangy	**bleu de Bresse, brousse, camembert, livarot, maroilles, munster, pont-l'évêque, roquefort, vacherin**
goat's milk	**bûcheron, cabécou, crottin de Chavignol, rocamadour, st-marcellin, valençay**
Swiss cheeses	**beaufort, comté, emmental, gruyère**

Croque-monsieur *krok mersyur*
Toasted ham and cheese sandwich

Croûte au fromage *kroot oa fromazh*
Hot, melted cheese served over a slice of toast, sometimes with ham and topped with a fried egg

Fromage blanc *fromazh blahng*
Fresh white cheese to be eaten with sugar or with pepper and salt

Raclette *raklet*
Firm cheese grilled until the surface begins to melt; the melting cheese is then scraped off on to a warmed plate and eaten with cold meat, boiled potatoes, pickles, and pickled pearl onions

Dessert Desserts

Crêpe *krep*
Thin pancake; **à la confiture** (with jelly); **au sucre** (with sugar); **normande** (with Calvados and cream); **suzette** (simmered in orange juice and cream)

Diplomate *deeplomat*
Molded custard dessert with crystallized fruit and lined with sponge cake fingers steeped in liqueur

Sabayon *sabayawng*
Creamy dessert of egg yolks, wine, sugar, and flavoring

Tarte Tatin *tart tartang*
Hot caramelized apples with crust on top and served with vanilla ice cream, **chantilly** (whipped cream), or **crème anglaise** (custard)

DRINKS

Beer Bière
Beer is to the Belgians what wine is to the French, and it is often served in its own type of glass. Look for the following types:

Bière blanche (white beer)
Cloudy and honeyish, e.g., *Hoegaarden, Kwak*

Bière blonde (lager)
Light, Pilsener-style, e.g., *Jupiler, Lamot, Stella Artois*

Bière brune (red beer)
Refreshing and sour, e.g., *Rodenbach*

Bières trappistes (abbey beers)
Dark and full bodied, e.g., *Chimay, Orval*

Gueuze (blended Lambic beers)
e.g., *Kriek* (cherry), *Frambozen* (raspberries), *Faro* (sugar)

Lambic (wheat beer)
e.g., *Kronenbourg, Pelforth,* and *Kanterbräu* (French) and
Cardinal and *Hürlimann* (Swiss)

Wine Vins

French cuisine and wine are inseparable components that complement
each other. The wine waiter (**le sommelier**) will offer advice and a tip
is appreciated for this service. Grape varieties:

red: **Cabernet-Sauvignon, Carignan, Cinsaut, Gamay,
        Grenache, Merlot, Mourvedre, Pinot Noir, Syrah**

white: **Chardonnay, Chenin Blanc, Gewurztraminer, Muscadet,
        Muscat, Riesling, Sauvignon Blanc, Sémillon**

I'd like a corkscrew.   **Je voudrais un tire-bouchon.**
                          zher voodray ang teer booshwang

Cheers!   **Santé!** *sawntay*

Reading the label

**AC (appellation contrôlée)
/AOC** highest quality wine
blanc white
brut dry
cépage grape variety
château wine-making estate
côte/coteaux slope/hills
crémant sparkling
cru superior growth
demi-sec medium dry/sweet
doux sweet
millésime vintage
**mis en bouteilles dans nos
caves** bottled in our cellars

mis en bouteilles par bottled by
mousseux sparkling/frothy
rosé rosé
rouge red
sec dry
VDQS good quality regional
wine
vignoble vineyard
vin de garde wine to lay down
to mature
vin de pays local wine; less
strict quality control than AC
vin de table table wine
vin ordinaire table wine

Non-alcoholic drinks

France offers a wide choice of mineral waters. You'll also have no trouble finding your favorite soft drinks or sodas.

I'd like …	**Je voudrais …**	*zher voodray*
(hot) chocolate	**un chocolat (chaud)**	*ang shokolah (shoa)*
coke/lemonade	**un coca/une limonade**	*ang koka/ewn leemonad*
milkshake	**un frappé**	*ang frapay*
mineral water	**de l'eau minérale**	*der loa meenayral*
carbonated	**gazeuse**	*gazurz*
non-carbonated	**non gazeuse**	*nawng gazurz*
tonic water	**un Schweppes**	*ang shweps*

Un café *ang kafay*

Coffee can be served: **au lait** (with milk); **complet** (with bread, rolls, butter, and jam); **crème** (with cream); **décaféiné/sans caféine** (decaffeinated); **frappé** (shaken, iced); **noir** (black); **soluble** (instant).

Un jus de fruits *ang zhoo der frwee*

Common fruit juices are **jus d'orange** (orange), **jus de poire** (pear), **jus de pomme** (apple), and **jus de tomate** (tomato).

Un thé *ang tay*

Tea can be drunk the British way, **au lait** (with milk), but it is more usual to have it **au citron** (with lemon), **à la menthe** (mint), **glacé** (iced) or **nature** (black). **Tisane** (herbal tea) is a popular alternative.

MENU READER

à la vapeur	*a la vapurr*	steamed
au four	*oa foor*	baked
bouilli	*booyee*	boiled
braisé	*brezay*	braised
coupé en dés	*koopay ahng day*	diced
en ragoût	*ahng ragoo*	stewed
épicé	*aypeessay*	spicy
farci	*farsee*	stuffed
frit (dans la friture)	*free (dahng la freetewr)*	(deep) fried
fumé	*fewmay*	smoked
grillé	*greeyay*	grilled
mariné	*mareenay*	marinated
pané	*panay*	breaded
poché	*poshay*	poached
rôti	*roatee*	roasted
sauté	*soatay*	sautéed
velouté de ...	*velootay der*	creamed
bleu	*blur*	very rare
saignant	*senyahng*	rare
à point	*a pwang*	medium
bien cuit	*byang kwee*	well-done

A

à la, à l', au, aux in the manner of, as in, with
à l'étouffée stewed
à la croque au sel served raw with vinaigrette and salt
abricot apricot

agneau lamb
aiglefin (églefin) haddock
aïgo bouïdo garlic soup (*Prov.*)
aiguillettes de canard au vinaigre filet of duck in raspberry vinegar
ail garlic
aïoli garlic mayonnaise

alose shad (fine textured fish with delicate flesh)

alouette lark

alouettes sans têtes stuffed small rolled veal cutlets

amandes almonds

américaine white wine, brandy, garlic, shallots, tomatoes, shrimp, or lobster flavoring

amuse-gueule savory biscuits, crackers; appetizers

ananas pineapple

anchois anchovies

anchoïade purée of unsalted anchovies in olive oil (*Prov.*)

andouille(tte) tripe sausage

aneth dill

anglaise boiled or steamed vegetables; breaded and fried

anguille eel

anguille au vert eel flavored with sorrel, sage, and parsley (*Belg.*)

anis aniseed

A.O.C. officially recognized wine

apéritifs aperitifs

artichaut artichoke

asperges asparagus

aspic (meat or fish in) aspic

assaisonnement seasoning

assiette anglaise assorted cold cuts

assiette de charcuterie selection of cold meat

attente: 15 min waiting time: 15 minutes

au bleu (especially for trout) poached when it's fresh

au choix choice of …

au citron with lemon

au four baked

au gril grilled

au lait with milk

aubergine eggplant

avec de l'eau gazeuse with (seltzer) water

avec des glaçons on the rocks

B

baguette thin loaf of French bread

ballon a glass

bar sea bass

bar aux herbes en chemise stuffed sea bass

barbue brill (fish like a turbot)

barquette small boat-shaped pastry shell garnished with fruit

basilic basil

bâtard small French bread stick

baudroie angler

bavarois Bavarian cream cakes

béarnaise creamy sauce of vinegar, egg, white wine, shallots, tarragon

bécasse woodcock

bécassine snipe

béchamel white sauce

beignet fritter, generally filled with fruit, vegetables, or meat

betterave beet

beurre butter

beurre blanc butter, shallots, vinegar, white wine

beurre noir browned butter, vinegar, and/or lemon juice

bière beer

bière blonde/brune light/dark beer

bière en bouteilles bottled beer

bière sans alcool non-alcoholic beer

bifteck beef steak

bigarade with oranges

bigorneaux winkles
biscuit de Savoie sponge cake
biscuits cookies
biscuits apéritifs appetizers, snacks
biscuits salés crackers
bisque seafood chowder/stew
bisque d'écrevisses crayfish chowder/stew
bisque de homard lobster chowder/stew
blanc white (wine); breast (chicken)
blanchaille herring
blanquette de veau veal in cream sauce
bleu very rare; blue (cheese); boiled fresh (fish)
bœuf beef
bœuf bourguignon wine beef stew
bœuf mode beef chunks with carrots and onions in red wine
bœuf salé corned beef
boissons drinks
boisson non alcoolisée soft drink/soda
bolets boletus mushrooms
bombe molded ice cream mousse
bordelaise sauce of mushrooms, red wine, shallots, beef marrow (*Bord.*)
bouchée à la reine sweetbreads in pastry
boudin blood sausage/black pudding
bouillabaisse seafood soup (*Mars.*)
bouilleture d'anguilles eel cooked in cream (*Anjou*)
bouilli boiled; boiled beef
bouillon bouillon
bouillon de poulet chicken bouillon
boulettes (de viande) meatballs
bourguignonne red wine, herbs, button mushrooms, shallots

bourride fish chowder/stew (*Prov.*)
brandade de morue creamed salt cod
brème bream (fish)
brioche bun
brioche au sucre bun with sugar
(à la) broche (on a) skewer
brochet pike
brochette skewered kebab
brugnon nectarine
brut very dry (wine)
bûche de Noël Christmas log
bulots large whelks (seafood)

C

cabillaud (fresh) cod
cabri kid goat
cacahuètes peanuts
cade chickpea cake (*Riv.*)
café coffee
café au lait coffee with milk
café complet coffee with bread, rolls, butter, and jam
café crème coffee with cream
café décaféiné decaffeinated coffee
café frappé blended cold coffee
café noir black coffee
café sans caféine decaffeinated coffee
café soluble instant coffee
caille quail
calissons ground almonds and marzipan (*Aix*)
cal(a)mars squid
calvados apple brandy (*Norm.*)
canard (sauvage) (wild) duck
canard à l'orange duck in orange
canard laqué Peking duck
caneton duckling
caneton à la rouennaise duckling in red wine sauce (*Norm.*)

cannelle cinnamon
câpres capers
carafe carafe
carbonnade charcoal-grilled meat
carbon(n)ade flamande beef slices and onions in beer *(Belg.)*
caricoles sea snails *(Belg.)*
carottes carrots
carpe carp
carré d'agneau rack of lamb
carré braisé à la niçoise braised loin with vermouth and lemon peel
carrelet plaice (flat fish)
casse-croûte sandwich, snack
cassis black currants; black currant liqueur
cassoulet toulousain beef and pork casserole
céleri(-rave) celeriac
cèpes flap mushrooms
céréales cereal
cerf venison (red deer)
cerfeuil chervil
cerises (noires) (black) cherries
cervelas type of sausage
cervelle brains
chabichou cheese of cow's and goat's milk
champignons (de Paris) mushrooms
chantilly whipped cream
chapon capon
charcuterie cold cuts; assorted pork products
charlotte fruit dessert in mold
Chartreuse herb liqueur
chasseur wine, mushrooms, onions, shallots, herbs
chateaubriand double filet steak (tenderloin of porterhouse steak)
chaud hot
chaud-froid dressing with gelatin

chaudrée fish and seafood stew
chausson aux pommes apple turnover
chevreuil venison/roe deer
chichifregi roll donuts *(Riv.)*
chicorée endive/chicory
chips potato chips
chocolat (chaud) (hot) chocolate
chocolat froid cold chocolate
chocolatine chocolate puff pastry
chou (rouge) (red) cabbage
chou rouge à la flamande red cabbage in red wine *(Belg.)*
chou fassum stuffed cabbage *(Prov.)*
chou-fleur cauliflower
chou-fleur au gratin cauliflower with white cheese sauce
choucroute sauerkraut
choucroute garnie sauerkraut, sausages, and cured pork
choux de Bruxelles brussels sprouts
ciboulette chives
citron lemon
citron pressé lemon juice
citron vert lime
civet game stew
clafoutis fruit in pancake batter
clous de girofle clove
cochon de lait suckling pig
(en) cocotte pot-roasted
cœurs d'artichaut artichoke hearts
cognac brandy
colonel lemon (water ice) doused with vodka
communard red wine and black currant liqueur
compris(e) included
concombre cucumber

confit preserves
confiture jam
congolais coconut cake
consommé consommé
consommé à l'œuf consommé with a raw egg
consommé au porto consommé with port wine
consommé Célestine consommé with chicken and noodles
consommé Colbert consommé with poached eggs, spring vegetables
contre-filet loin strip steak
coq au vin chicken in red wine
coq de bruyère woodgrouse
coquelet à l'estragon spring chicken with tarragon sauce
coquilles St-Jacques scallops
coriandre coriander
cornichons pickles
corsé full-bodied (wine)
côte rib
côte de bœuf T-bone steak
côtelettes chops
cotriade fish soup (*Britt.*)
cou d'oie farci stuffed goose neck
coulis soup; creamy sauce
coupe (glacée) ice cream dessert
courgette zucchini
couronne ring-shaped loaf
couscous Arab cracked wheat dish
couvert silverware
crabe crab
crème cream
crème anglaise custard equivalent
crème brûlée custard with crispy caramel topping
crème caramel caramel pudding
crème Chantilly whipped cream
crème d'asperges cream of asparagus

crème de bolets cream of boletus mushrooms
crème de volaille cream of chicken
crème pâtissière cream with butter
crêpe pancake
crêpe à la confiture pancake with jam
crêpe au sucre pancake with sugar
crêpe dentelle thin biscuity pancake (*Britt.*)
crêpe normande pancake with Calvados and cream
crêpe suzette large, thin pancakes simmered in orange juice and flambéed with orange liqueur
crépinette flat seasoned sausage
cresson watercress
crevettes shrimp
croissants flaky crescent rolls
croquembouche caramel-coated pastry puff
croque-madame a croque-monsieur with an egg on top
croque-monsieur toasted ham and cheese sandwich
crottin de Chavignol goat's cheese
croustade filled pie/pastry shell
croûte au fromage melted cheese on toast, with ham and topped by a fried egg
cru raw; system of grading wine
crudités mixed raw vegetable salad
crustacés shellfish
cuisses de grenouilles frog's legs
cuit à la vapeur steamed
cuit au bleu poached when fresh
cul de veau à l'angevine veal rump in rich sauce with vegetables (*Loire*)
cumin caraway

D

dartois jam pastry
dattes dates
daube de bœuf beef stew with tomatoes and olives (*Prov.*)
daurade sea bream (fish)
décaféiné decaffeinated
délice dessert specialty of the chef
délimité de qualité supérieure superior quality (wine)
demi-bouteille a half bottle
demi-poulet grillé half a roasted chicken
dessert desserts
diable hot-pepper sauce
diabolo menthe mint cordial
dinde turkey
dinde aux marrons turkey with chestnuts
dindonneau young turkey (cock)
diplomate molded dessert
doux sweet (wine)
dur hard (egg)
duxelles with mushrooms

E

eau (chaude) (hot) water
eau minérale mineral water
eau minérale gazeuse carbonated mineral water/seltzer
eau minérale non gazeuse non-carbonated mineral water
échalote shallot
éclair au chocolat/café long cake filled with chocolate/coffee cream
écrevisses crayfish
émincé de bœuf aux morilles beef stew with morels
emporter, à to take out
en chemise baked in waxed paper

en saison in season
endives endive
entrecôte rib/rib-eye steak
entrées first course/appetizer
entremets small dish served before cheese; dessert
épaule shoulder
épaule braisée aux marrons braised shoulder with chestnuts
éperlans smelts/spaling (small fish)
épices spices
épinards spinach
escalope cutlet
escalope à la crème veal cutlet cooked with cream
escalope viennoise breaded veal cutlet
escargots snails
espadon swordfish
estouffade de bœuf beef stew
estragon tarragon
expresso espresso

F

faisan pheasant
far sweet batter pudding, often with dried fruit (*Britt.*)
farces stuffing, liver and truffles
faux-filet sirloin steak
fenouil fennel
féra lake salmon
fèves broad beans
ficelle thin breadstick
figues figs
filet filet steak
filet mignon au poivre vert meat with green pepper sauce
financière Madeira wine, truffles, olives, mushrooms
fines herbes mixture of herbs

flageolets small kidney beans

flamiche savory cheese pie with leeks or onions

flan custard tart

florentin thin crust of almonds and dark chocolate

(à la) florentine with spinach

foie liver

foie de veau grillé à la moutarde grilled calf's liver with mustard and breadcrumbs

foie gras goose or duck liver

fond d'artichaut artichoke heart

fondue melted cheese dip (*Switz.*)

fondue bourguignonne meat fondue with different sauces

fondue chinoise thinly sliced meat plunged into simmering stock

forestière with mushrooms, shallots, and white wine

fougasse flat loaf with anchovies, olives, cheese (*Prov.*)

(au) four baked

fraises strawberries

framboises raspberries

frappé chilled, iced; milkshake

fricassée braised meat in sauce

frigousse casserole of chicken, bacon, and chestnuts (*Britt.*)

frisée curly lettuce

frites french fries

friture de mer small fish, generally deep fried, eaten like fries

froid cold

fromage cheese

fromage blanc fresh white cheese

fromage blanc à la crème fresh white cheese served with cream

fromage de chèvre goat's cheese

fruits fruit

fruits confits candied fruit

fruits de mer seafood

fruits frais fresh fruits

fruits secs dried fruit

G

galette flat, plain cake/crêpe

galette complète crêpes filled with egg, ham, and cheese

ganses small fried cakes topped with sugar (*Prov.*)

garbure cabbage soup, with pork or goose

garniture au choix choice of vegetable accompaniment

gâteau cake

gâteau au chocolat chocolate cake

gâteau Bigarreau sponge cake with praline filling

gâteau breton rich pound cake

gâteau de riz rice pudding

gâteau de semoule semolina pudding

gâteau lyonnais chocolate and chestnut cake

gaufres waffles

(à la) gelée in aspic

génoise light cake

gibelotte de lapin rabbit stew in wine sauce

gibier game

gigot leg of lamb

gigot à la bretonne roast leg of lamb with dried beans

gin-tonic gin and tonic

gingembre ginger

glace ice cream

glace à la fraise/à la vanille strawberry/vanilla ice cream

glacé iced, glazed

goujon gudgeon (freshwater fish)

grand veneur sauce for game

(au) gratin browned with bread-crumbs or cheese
gratin dauphinois sliced potatoes gratinéed with milk, cream, and garlic
gratin de queues d'écrevisses baked crayfish tails
gratinée au four baked with cheese and ham
grattons grilled pork fat (*Lyon*)
grenadine red fruit syrup
grillades grilled meat
grive thrush
grondin gurnard (firm fleshed fish)
groseilles red currants
groseilles à maquereau goose-berries

H

hachis Parmentier shepherd's pie
hareng herring
haricots blancs haricot beans, white kidney beans
haricots verts french (green) beans
(aux) herbes with herbs
hollandaise egg yolks, butter, vinegar
homard lobster
homard à l'américaine sautéed lobster
homard thermidor lobster gratinéed with cheese
hors-d'œuvre appetizers
hors-d'œuvre variés assorted appetizers
huîtres oysters

I

île flottante meringue in custard
(à l')indienne (in) curry sauce

J

jambon ham
jambon de Bayonne raw, salty ham
jambon-beurre sandwich with ham and butter
jambonneau cured pig's knuckle
jardinière cooked assorted vegetables
jarret knuckle
Joconde almond sponge
julienne thinly sliced vegetables
jus (fruit) juice
jus d'orange orange juice
jus de fruits fruit juice
jus de pamplemousse grapefruit juice
jus de poire pear juice
jus de pomme apple juice
jus de tomate tomato juice

K

Kig-Ha-Farz mixture of pork, beef, vegetables, and buckwheat (*Britt.*)
kir white wine with black currant liqueur
kir royal champagne and black currant liqueur
kirsch cherry liqueur
kouing-aman crisp butter cake (*Britt.*)

L

lait milk
laitue lettuce
lamproie lamprey (fish)
langouste spiny (rock) lobster
langoustines Dublin bay scampi
langue tongue

lapin rabbit
lapin à la flamande marinated rabbit (*Belg.*)
lard bacon
laurier bay leaf
léger light (wine)
légumes vegetables
lentilles lentils
lièvre wild hare
limonade soft drink/soda
liqueur liqueur
(à la) lorraine braised in red wine with red cabbage
lotte burbot (firm white flesh fish)
lotte de mer anglerfish, monkfish
loup sea bass
(à la) lyonnaise sautéed with onions

M

madère with Madeira wine
magret de canard filet breast of fattened duck (*Dord.*)
maïs corn
maison homemade
maître d'hôtel headwaiter
mandarine tangerine
manons chocolate filled with fresh cream (*Belg.*)
maquereau mackerel
marc grape spirit
marcassin young wild boar
marchand de vin wine merchant
marinière white wine, mussel broth thickened with egg yolks
marjolaine marjoram; layered nut cake
marrons chestnuts
matelote (d'anguilles) fish (esp. eel) stew with wine (*Tours, Anjou*)
médaillon tenderloin steak

melon melon
menthe mint
menthe à l'eau mint syrup with water
menu à prix fixe set menu
menu gastronomique gourmet menu
menu touristique choice of dishes for each course, for a fixed price
meringue meringue
merlan whiting
méthode champenoise in the champagne style
meunière brown butter, parsley, lemon juice
miel honey
(à la) milanaise with Parmesan and noisette butter
milhassou sweet, cornmeal pudding
milkshake milkshake
mille-feuille flaky pastry with cream filling (napoleon)
(à la) mode in the style of, esp. local recipe
moelle bone marrow
molle, pâte soft (cheese)
mollet soft (egg)
mont-blanc chestnut dessert with whipped cream
morilles morels (mushrooms)
Mornay cheese sauce
mortadelle Bologna sausage
morue cod
moules mussels
moules marinière mussels simmering in white wine with shallots, thyme, and parsley
mousse au chocolat chocolate mousse
mousse de foie light liver pâté

mousseline mayonnaise with cream; puréed raw fish with cream
mousseux sparkling (wine)
moutarde mustard; mustard sauce
mûres mulberries, blackberries
muscade nutmeg
myrtilles blueberries

N

nature plain; black (tea)
navets turnips
nectar d'abricot apricot juice
(à la) niçoise with garlic, anchovies, olives, onions, and tomatoes
Noilly Prat® a French vermouth
noir black (coffee/tea)
noisette hazelnut; boneless round piece of meat
noisette de porc aux pruneaux pork tenderloin/filet with prunes and cream (*Loire*)
noix walnuts
noix de coco coconut
noix de muscade nutmeg
(à la) normande mushrooms, eggs, and cream sauce
nouilles noodles

O

œufs eggs
œuf à la coque boiled egg
œuf dur hard-boiled egg
œufs Argenteuil eggs on tartlet with asparagus and cream sauce
œufs à la Bruxelles eggs with braised chicory and cream sauce
œufs à la diable deviled eggs
œufs à la neige meringue on custard
œufs au bacon bacon and eggs

œufs au jambon ham and eggs
œufs au plat fried eggs
œufs brouillés scrambled eggs
œufs mimosa hard-boiled eggs served with mayonnaise
oie goose
oignons onions
olives olives
omble (chevalier) char (delicate, flavorful fish)
omelette (nature) (plain) omelet
omelette au fromage cheese omelet
omelette au jambon ham omelet
omelette aux champignons mushroom omelet
omelette aux fines herbes herb omelet
onglet prime cut of meat
opéra chocolate and nut cake
orange orange
orangeade orangeade
origan oregano
ormeaux abalones (chewy shellfish)
ortolan ortolan bunting

P

pain bread
pain au chocolat flaky pastry filled with chocolate
pain au levain leaven bread
pain aux raisins snail-shaped bun with raisins
pain blanc/bis white/brown bread
pain complet/intégral whole-wheat bread
pain d'épices gingerbread (*Dijon*)
pain de seigle rye bread
pain de son bran bread
pain grillé toast

paillasson fried, sliced potatoes (*Lyon*)

palourdes clams

pamplemousse grapefruit

panaché selection; shandy

panbagna/pan bagnat tuna and salad sandwich (*Riv.*)

pannequet parcel shaped crêpe

(en) papillote baked in grease-proof paper

parfait glacé frozen dessert

Paris-Brest pastry ring with cream

(à la) parisienne with mushrooms in white wine sauce

Parmentier with potatoes

pastèque watermelon

pastis aniseed-based drink (*Prov./Midi*); flaky apple pie (*Dord.*)

pâté molded pastry case; liver and pork purée

pâtes pasta

pâtes fraîches fresh pasta, noodles

pâtisseries pastries

paupiettes de veau Valentino veal "birds" stuffed with asparagus, with tomato sauce

(à la) paysanne containing vegetables

pêche peach

perche perch

perdreau young partridge

perdrix partridge

Périgueux with goose or duck liver purée and truffles

Pernod® aniseed flavored aperitif

persil parsley

petit déjeuner breakfast

petit four small cake

petit noir espresso

petit pain roll

petit pain au cumin roll with caraway seeds

petit pain aux pavots roll with poppy seeds

petit salé aux lentilles pork breast with lentils

petit-suisse thick fromage frais (fresh curd cheese) eaten with sugar or jam

petits pois peas

petits trianons chocolate fudge bars

pieds feet

pieds (et) paquets stuffed sheep's feet (*Mar.*)

pigeon pigeon

pigeonneau squab

pignons buttery croissants with pine-nuts (*Prov.*)

pilaf rice boiled in a bouillon with onions

piment pimiento

pintade guinea fowl

pintadeau young guinea cock

pissaladière type of pizza made with onions and anchovies (*Prov.*)

pistou vegetable and pasta soup; garlic and fresh basil paste (*Riv.*)

plaque de chocolat chocolate bar

plat (du jour) dish (of the day)

plateau plate

plat principal main course

plie plaice (flat fish)

poire pear

poire à la Condé hot pear on bed of vanilla-flavored rice

poire Belle-Hélène pear with vanilla ice cream and chocolate sauce

poireaux leeks

pois mange-tout string-peas

poissons fish

poivrade pepper sauce

poivre pepper
poivrons sweet peppers
polenta polenta
pomme apple
pommes de terre potatoes
pommes allumettes potato match-sticks
pommes dauphine potato mashed in butter and egg yolks, mixed in seasoned flour and deep-fried
pommes duchesse potato mashed with butter and egg yolks
pommes en robe des champs potatoes in their skins
pommes frites french fries
pommes mousseline mashed potatoes
pommes nature boiled, steamed potato
pommes nouvelles new potatoes
pommes vapeur steamed, boiled potato
pompes à l'huile cake flavored with orange flower water or aniseed (*Riv.*)
porc pork
porto port; with port wine
pot-au-feu beef stew with vegetables
potage soup
potage à l'ail garlic soup
potage au cresson watercress soup
potage bilibi fish and oyster soup
potage bonne femme potato, leek, and sometimes bacon soup
potage Condé mashed red bean soup
potage du Barry cream of cauliflower
potage julienne shredded vegetable soup
potage Parmentier potato soup
potiron pumpkin
poularde fattened pullet

poule stewing fowl
poule au pot stewed chicken with vegetables
poulet chicken
poulet créole chicken in white sauce with rice
poulet Marengo chicken in white wine
poulet rôti roast chicken
poulette with butter, cream, and egg yolks
poulpes octopus
pour deux personnes for two
poussin spring chicken
praires clams
pressé fresh (juice)
pression draft beer
profiterole filled pastry
(à la) provençale onions, tomatoes, garlic
pruneaux prunes
prunes plums
pudding à la Reine bread pudding with lemon, cream, and apricot
puits d'amour pastry shell with liqueur-flavored custard
purée de pommes de terre mashed potatoes

Q

quatre-quarts pound cake
quenelles dumplings
quiche savory open-faced tart

R

raclette melted cheese dish
radis radishes
ragoût meat stew
raie ray
raifort horseradish

raisin (blanc/noir) (white/black) grapes
raisins secs raisins
ramequin small cheese tart
râpé grated
rascasse fish used in bouillabaisse
ratatouille vegetable casserole
ravigote vinegar sauce with eggs, capers, and herbs
religieuse au chocolat/café puff cake with chocolate/coffee filling
rémoulade sauce flavored with mustard and herbs
réserve du patron house wine
rhubarbe rhubarb
rhum rum
Ricard® aniseed-flavored aperitif
rillettes pâté, usually of duck
rillettes de porc minced pork served chilled in earthenware pots
rillons chunky pieces of pork (hors-d'œuvre)
ris de veau veal sweetbreads
riz rice
rognons kidneys
romarin rosemary
rosbif roast beef
rosé rosé (wine)
rosette dried sausage (*Lyon*)
rouge red (wine)
rouget red mullet
rouille pink, garlic mayonnaise
rouilleuse white wine sauce, thickened with blood

S

sabayon creamy dessert
sablé au beurre type of shortbread
sacristains pastry straws with sugar or cheese topping
safran saffron

saint-cyr baked meringue with frozen chocolate mousse
saint-honoré choux cake with cream
saint-pierre nutty, sweet-flavored fish
salade salad
salade composée mixed salad
salade au cabécou goat-cheese salad (*Dord.*)
salade chiffonnade shredded lettuce and sorrel in melted butter
salade de foies de volaille lettuce with chicken livers
salade de museau de bœuf marinated headcheese
salade de thon tuna salad
salade niçoise tuna, anchovies, black olives, tomatoes, and rice
salade russe diced vegetable salad in mayonnaise
salade verte green salad
sandre pike perch, zander
sandwich sandwich
sandwich au fromage cheese sandwich
sandwich au jambon ham sandwich
sanglier wild boar
sans glaçon straight
sarcelle teal (a duck)
sardines sardines
sauces sauces
sauce bleue vinaigrette with blue cheese (roquefort type)
sauce diable sauce with cayenne, shallots, pepper
sauce Périgueux rich Madeira sauce with cognac and truffles
saucisse sausage
saucisse de Francfort frankfurter

saucisse de Morteau type of pork sausage to cook
saucisse de Strasbourg Strasbourg (pork) sausage, knackwurst
saucisson cold sausage
saucisson brioché large sausage in a bun (*Lyon*)
sauge sage
saumon salmon
savarin sponge cake in rum
scallopini breaded veal cutlets
scampi shrimp
Schweppes® tonic water
sec dry (wine)
sel salt
selon arrivage when available
selon grosseur/grandeur (s.g.) price according to size
sirop syrup
socca chickpea cake, eaten hot (*Nice*)
sole sole
sorbet sherbet
soubise onion-cream sauce
soufflé light fluffy dish with browned egg whites
soufflé au Grand Marnier soufflé made of orange liqueur
soufflé Rothschild vanilla-flavored soufflé with candied fruit
soupe soup
soupe à la bière beer soup with chicken stock and onions (*Belg.*)
soupe à l'oignon French onion soup
soupe au pistou vegetable soup with pesto sauce (*Prov.*)
soupe aux choux cabbage soup
soupe de Pélous crab soup with tomatoes, saffron, and bread

soupe de poisson small fish, simmered with tomatoes and saffron, then puréed and sieved
soupe du jour soup of the day
spécialités locales local specialties
steak beef steak
steak au poivre steak with cracked black pepper
steak tartare raw ground filet with egg, capers, and parsley
steak-frites steak and french fries
sucre sugar
supplément/en sus extra charge
suprême thickened chicken broth
suprême de volaille chicken breast in cream sauce
sur commande made to order

T

tablier de sapeur pig's feet/fried tripe in breadcrumbs
tajine lamb with almonds and sultana raisins
tapenade spicy mousse of olives and anchovies (*Prov.*)
tartare mayonnaise flavored with mustard and herbs
tarte à la brousse type of cheese cake (*Corsica*)
tarte à la cannelle blueberry-cinnamon flan
tarte au citron meringuée lemon meringue pie
tarte au fromage cheese tart
tarte aux pommes apple tart
tarte de blettes tart with ground chard leaves, cheese, dried currants
tarte frangipane almond cream tart
tarte Tatin upside down apple tart

tartelette small tart
tartine buttered bread with jam, marmalade, or honey
tarte tropézienne rich cake filled with crème pâtissière
tasse de thé cup of tea
tellines small triangular shellfish seasoned with garlic and parsley (*Riv.*)
terrine sliced pâté
tête de nègre meringue cake covered with dark chocolate
thé tea
thé à la menthe mint tea
thé au citron tea with lemon
thé au lait tea with milk
thé glacé iced tea
thé nature black tea
thon tuna
thym thyme
tian de courgettes zucchini custard (*Riv.*)
(en) timbale cooked in a pastry case or mold
tisane herbal tea
tomates tomatoes
tomate aux crevettes tomato filled with shrimp and mayonnaise (*Belg.*)
tourain/tourin soup (*Dord.*)
tournedos tenderloin of T-bone steak
tournedos Rossini beef in Madeira wine sauce
tourte layer cake
tourteau fromager goat cheesecake
tranche slice
tripes à la mode de Caen baked tripe with Calvados

triple sec orange liqueur
truffes truffles
truite trout
truite saumonée salmon trout
turbot turbot

V

vacherin glacé ice-cream cake
veau veal
velouté de tomates cream of tomato
velouté de volaille cream of chicken
veloutée thickened chicken or meat stock
verre a glass
verre de lait a glass of milk
verte mayonnaise with spinach, watercress, herbs
viande meat
viande séchée des Grisons cured dried beef
vin wine
vinaigrette oil and vinegar dressing
vin du pays local wine
vin ordinaire table wine
volaille fowl, poultry
V.S.O.P. cognac aged over 5 years

WXY

waterzooi de poulet chicken in white wine (*Belg.*)
xérès sherry
yaourt/yoghourt yogurt

GERMAN

Hello.	**Hallo.** *hahlo*
Good evening.	**Guten Abend.** *gooten ahbend*
A table for …	**Ein Tisch für …** *ayn tish fewr*
2/3/4.	**zwei/drei/vier.** *tsvai/dry/feer*
The check, please.	**Die Rechnung, bitte.** *dee rekhnoong bitteh*
A receipt, please.	**Eine Quittung, bitte.** *ayneh queetoong bitteh*
Thank you.	**Danke.** *dahnkeh*
Good-bye.	**Auf Wiedersehen.** *owf veederzayn*

PLACES TO EAT

Beisel *byzel*
The Austrian equivalent to a **Gasthaus**

Bierhalle *beerhalleh*
Beer hall; serving hot dishes, salads, and pretzels

Bierstube *beershtoobeh*
Equivalent to a bar, though the atmosphere may be very different

Café *kahfay*
Coffee shop offering pastries, snacks, and drinks

Gasthaus/Gasthof *gahsthouse/gahsthoaf*
Inn, usually in the country, offering home cooking

Konditorei *kondeeto-rye*
Pastry shop, often with a café

Milchbar *milkhbar*
Bar serving milk drinks with pastries; called **Milchstübl** in some regions

Raststätte *rahstshtetteh*
Roadside restaurant; called **Rasthof** in Austria; with lodging and
service-station facilities

Ratskeller *rahtskeller*
Restaurant in the cellar of the town hall (often an historic building)

Restaurant *restoroang*
Up-scale establishments with a menu to match, ranging from local
specialties to international cuisine; also called **Gaststätte**

Schnellimbiss *shnelimbiss*
Snack bar; the principal fare is beer and sausages; a sausage stand
(Würstchenstand) is similar

Weinstube *vineshtoobeh*
Cozy restaurant where you can order simple hot dishes and snacks

MEAL TIMES

Frühstück *frewshtewk*
Breakfast: 7–10 a.m. You'll be offered cold meats, cheeses, pâtés,
jams, and marmalades, accompanied by a variety of breads, together
with tea, coffee, or hot chocolate. Boiled eggs are also popular.

Mittagessen *mittahgessen*
Lunch: 11:30 a.m.–2 p.m. Many Germans eat their main meal in
the middle of the day and most restaurants will offer their set
menus **(Menü** or **Gedeck)** at midday as well as in the evening. If
you want something smaller, look under **Kleine Gerichte**.

Abendessen/Abendbrot *ahbentessen/ahbentbroat*
Dinner: consists of a variety of bread with cold meats, cheeses, and
maybe salad. You'll be able to get a full menu in restaurants which
tend to serve between 6:30 and 9:30 p.m; larger restaurants may
serve until 10 or 11 p.m.

Most restaurants will offer several fixed-price menus **(Tagesgedeck)**
at different price points. These usually change every day and provide

typical German dishes at a reasonable price. Or you can choose from the à la carte menu **(Speisekarte)**. Service is included.

It's quite common to drink beer with most meals, but if you want to try some of the local wine ask for **eine Flasche** (bottle), **eine halbe Flasche** (half-bottle) or **eine Karaffe** (carafe).

FINDING A PLACE TO EAT

Can you recommend a good restaurant?	**Können Sie ein gutes Restaurant empfehlen?** *kurnen zee ayn gootess restorroang empfaylen*
Is there a(n) … restaurant near here?	**Gibt es hier in der Nähe ein … Restaurant?** *gipt ess heer in dehr naieh ayn … restorroang*
traditional local	**traditionelles gutbürgerliches** *traditsionehles gootbewrgerlikhes*
inexpensive	**preiswertes** *pricevayrtes*
vegetarian	**vegetarisches** *veghetahrishes*
Where can I find a(n) …?	**Wo finde ich …?** *voa findeh ikh*
sausage stand	**einen Würstchenstand** *aynen vewrstkhenshtant*
fast-food restaurant	**einen Schnellimbiss** *aynen shnelimbis*
ice-cream parlor	**eine Eisdiele** *ayneh icedeeleh*
pizzeria	**eine Pizzeria** *ayneh pizzeria*

RESERVATIONS

I'd like to reserve a table for 2.	**Ich möchte einen Tisch für zwei Personen bestellen.** *ikh murkhteh aynen tish fewr tsvay pehrzoanen behshtelen*
For this evening/ tomorrow at …	**Für heute Abend/Morgen um …** *fewr hoyteh ahbent/morgen oom*
We'll come at 8:00.	**Wir kommen um acht Uhr.** *veer kommen oom akht oor*

| We have a reservation. | **Wir haben einen Tisch bestellt.** |
| | *veer hahben aynen tish behshtelt* |

YOU MAY HEAR	
Ihr Name, bitte?	What's the name, please?
Es tut mir leid.	I'm sorry.
Wir sind völlig ausgebucht.	We're completely booked.

Could we sit …?	**Können wir … sitzen?**
	kurnen veer … sitsen
outside	**im Freien** *im fryhen*
by the window	**am Fenster** *ahm fenster*
smoking/non-smoking	**Raucher/Nichtraucher**
	rowkher/nikhtrowkher

ORDERING

Waiter/waitress!	**Bedienung!** *behdeenoong*
Excuse me, please!	**Entschuldigen Sie, bitte!**
	entshuldiggen zee bitteh
The wine list, please.	**Die Weinkarte, bitte.**
	dee vinekarteh bitteh

YOU MAY HEAR	
Bitte schön?	Can I help you?
Haben Sie gewählt?	Are you ready to order?
Was nehmen Sie?	What would you like?
Ich empfehle Ihnen …	I recommend …
… haben wir nicht.	We don't have …
Guten Appetit.	Enjoy your meal.
Hat's geschmeckt?	Did you like it?

Do you have a set menu?	**Haben Sie ein Menü?** *hahben zee ayn maynew*
Can you recommend some typical local dishes?	**Können Sie etwas typisch Deutsches empfehlen?** *kurnen zee etwas tewpish doytshes empfaylen*
Could you tell me what … is?	**Können Sie mir sagen, was … ist?** *kurnen zee meer zahgen vahs … ist*
What is in it?	**Was ist darin?** *vahs ist dahrin*
I'd like …	**Ich hätte gern …** *ikh hetteh gehrn*
I'll have …	**Ich nehme …** *ikh naymeh*
a bottle/glass/ carafe of …	**eine Flasche/ein Glas/eine Karaffe …** *ayneh flasheh/ayn glahs/ayneh karaffeh*

SPECIAL REQUESTS

Could I have … without …?	**Kann ich … ohne … haben?** *kahn ikh … oaneh … hahben*
Could I have salad instead of vegetables, please?	**Kann ich bitte Salat statt Gemüse haben?** *kahn ikh bitteh zahlaht shtat gemewzeh hahben*
Does the meal come with vegetables/ potatoes?	**Ist Gemüse/Sind Kartoffeln bei dem Essen dabei?** *ist gemewzeh/sint kartoffeln by dem essen dahby*
Do you have any sauces?	**Haben Sie Soßen?** *haben zee zoassen*
May I have some …?	**Könnte ich etwas … haben?** *kurnteh ikh etvahs … haben*
bread	**Brot** *broat*
butter	**Butter** *bootter*
ice	**Eis** *ice*
lemon	**Zitrone** *tsitroaneh*

mustard	**Senf** *zenf*
pepper	**Pfeffer** *pfefer*
salt	**Salz** *sahlts*
seasoning	**Würze** *vewrtseh*
sugar	**Zucker** *tsooker*
artificial sweetener	**Süßstoff** *sewsshtof*
Could we have a child's seat, please?	**Können wir bitte einen Kinderstuhl haben?** *kurnen veer bitteh aynen kindershtool hahben*
Where can I feed/ change the baby?	**Wo kann ich das Baby füttern/wickeln?** *voa kahn ikh das baby fewttern/vikeln*

GENERAL QUESTIONS

Could I/we have (a/an) …, please?	**Kann ich/Können wir bitte … haben?** *kahn ikh/kurnen veer bitteh … hahben*
ashtray	**einen Aschenbecher** *aynen ahshenbekher*
cup/glass	**eine Tasse/ein Glas** *ayneh tahseh/ayn glahs*
fork/knife	**eine Gabel/ein Messer** *ayneh gahbel/ayn messer*
napkin	**eine Serviette** *ayneh zehrvietteh*
plate/spoon	**einen Teller/Löffel** *aynen teller/lurfel*
I'd like …	**Ich hätte gern …** *ikh hetteh gehrn*
hot chocolate	**heiße Schokolade** *highseh shokolahdeh*
coffee	**Kaffee** *kafay*
black/with milk	**schwarz/mit Milch** *shvarts/mit milkh*
tea	**Tee** *tay*
I'd like a … of red/ white wine.	**Ich hätte gern … Rotwein/Weißwein.** *ikh hetteh gehrn … roatvine/vicevine*

bottle	**eine Flasche** *ayneh flahsheh*
glass	**ein Glas** *ayn glahs*
Nothing more, thanks.	**Nichts mehr, danke.**
	nikhts mair dahnkeh
Where is the	**Wo sind die Toiletten?**
restroom?	*voa sint dee twaletten*

SPECIAL REQUIREMENTS

I can't eat food	**Ich darf nichts essen, was … enthält.**
containing …	*ikh darf nikhts essen vahs … enthehlt*
salt/sugar	**Salz/Zucker** *salts/tsooker*
Do you have meals/	**Haben Sie Gerichte/Getränke für**
drinks for diabetics?	**Diabetiker?** *hahben zee gerikhteh/*
	getrehnkeh fewr deeahbayticker
Do you have	**Haben Sie vegetarische Gerichte?**
vegetarian meals?	*haben zee veghetahrisheh gerikhteh*

COMPLAINTS

That's not	**Das habe ich nicht bestellt.**
what I ordered.	*dahs hahbeh ikh nikht beshtelt*
I asked for …	**Ich wollte …** *ikh volteh*
The meat is …	**Das Fleisch ist …** *das flysh ist*
overdone	**zu stark gebraten** *tsoo shtark gebrahten*
underdone	**zu roh** *tsoo roa*
too tough	**zu zäh** *tsoo tsay*
The food is cold.	**Das Essen ist kalt.** *das essen ist kahlt*
This isn't fresh.	**Das ist nicht frisch.** *das ist nikht frish*
How much longer	**Wie lange dauert unser Essen noch?**
will our food be?	*vee lahngeh dowert unzer essen nokh*

PAYING

Tipping: See page 332.

The check, please.	**Zahlen, bitte.** *tsahlen bitteh*
We'd like to pay separately.	**Wir möchten getrennt bezahlen.** *veer murkhten getrent betsahlen*
It's all together, please.	**Alles zusammen, bitte.** *ahless tsoozahmen bitteh*
I think there's a mistake in this bill.	**Ich glaube, Sie haben sich verrechnet.** *ikh glowbeh zee hahben zikh fehrrekhnet*
What is this amount for?	**Wofür ist dieser Betrag?** *voafewr ist deezer betrahg*
I didn't have that. I had …	**Das hatte ich nicht. Ich hatte …** *das hatteh ikh nikht. ikh hatteh*
Can I pay with this credit card?	**Kann ich mit dieser Kreditkarte bezahlen?** *kahn ikh mit deezer kredeetkarteh betsahlen*
Could I have a receipt?	**Kann ich eine Quittung haben?** *kahn ikh ayneh kvittoong hahben*
That was a very good meal.	**Das Essen war sehr gut.** *das essen vahr zayr goot*

COURSE BY COURSE

Breakfast Frühstück

No trip to Germany would be complete without sampling some bread: **Weißbrot** (white), **Vollkornbrot** (whole grain), **französisches Weißbrot/Baguette** (French), **Zwiebelbrot** (onion), **Rosinenbrot** (raisin), **Roggenbrot** (rye).

I'd like …	**Ich hätte gern …** *ikh hetteh gehrn*
rolls	**Brötchen** *brudkhen*

toast	**Toast** *toast*	
cereal	**Müsli/Cornflakes** *mewslee/cornflakes*	
cheese	**Käse** *kehzeh*	
cold meats	**Aufschnitt** *owfshnit*	
eggs	**Eier** *eyer*	
boiled egg	**ein gekochtes Ei** *ayn gekokhtes eye*	
fried eggs	**Spiegeleier** *shpeegeleyer*	
scrambled eggs	**Rühreier** *rewreyer*	
honey	**Honig** *hoanikh*	
jam	**Marmelade** *marmeladeh*	
milk	**Milch** *milkh*	
orange juice	**Orangensaft** *orangshenzahft*	

Appetizers Vorspeisen

Aufschnittplatte *owfshnitplaheh*
Assorted cold cuts served with pickles and bread

Bauernomelett *bowernomlett*
Diced bacon and onion omelet

Fleischpastete *flyshpastehteh*
Meat paté

Matjesfilet nach Hausfrauenart *matyehsfillay nakh howsfrowenart*
Filets of herring with apples and onions

Russische Eier *roosisheh eyer*
Hard-boiled eggs with mayonnaise

Stolzer Heinrich *stoalzer hinerikh*
Fried pork sausage in beer sauce (*Bavarian*)

Soups Suppen

Backerbsensuppe *bakehrpsenzuppeh*		type of split-pea soup
Bauernsuppe *bowernzuppeh*		cabbage and frankfurter soup

Champignonsuppe _shampinyongzuppeh_	mushroom soup
Erbsensuppe _ehrpzenzuppeh_	pea soup
Flädlesuppe _flehdlehzuppeh_	broth with pancake strips
Gemüsesuppe _ghemewsehzuppeh_	vegetable soup
Gulaschsuppe _goolashzuppeh_	spiced soup of stewed beef
Hühnerbrühe _hewnerbreweh_	chicken broth
Leberknödelsuppe _laborknurdelzuppeh_	liver-dumpling soup
Nudelsuppe _noodlezuppeh_	noodle soup
Ochsenschwanzsuppe _oxenshvantszuppeh_	oxtail soup
Tomatensuppe _tomahtenzuppeh_	tomato soup

Fish and seafood Fisch und Meeresfrüchte

You'll recognize **Hering, Karpfen,** and **Makrele**.

Dorsch	_dorsh_	young cod
Forelle	_forelleh_	trout
Garnelen	_garnaylen_	shrimp
Kabeljau	_kahbelyow_	cod
Lachs	_laks_	salmon
Languste	_lahngoosteh_	crayfish
Muscheln	_musheln_	clams/mussels
Salm	_zalm_	salmon
Scholle	_sholleh_	plaice/flounder
Tintenfisch	_tintenfish_	squid, octopus

Meat Fleisch

Rindfleisch	_rintflysh_	beef
Hähnchen	_hainkhen_	chicken
Ente	_enteh_	duck

Schinken	*shinken*	ham
Lammfleisch	*lammflysh*	lamb
Schweinefleisch	*shwinehflysh*	pork
Kaninchen	*kahneenkhen*	rabbit
Würste	*vewrsteh*	sausages
Truthahn	*troothahn*	turkey
Kalbfleisch	*kahlpflysh*	veal
Reh	*ray*	venison

To find out what type of cut you'll be getting, look to the end of the word: the meat comes first (e.g. **Schweine-)**, followed by the cut (-**kotelett**).

-braten	*brahten*	joint, roast
-brust	*broost*	breast
-hachse/haxe	*hahkseh*	shank
-herz	*herts*	heart
-kotelett	*kotlett*	cutlet, chop
-klößchen	*klurskhen*	little dumplings
-leber	*layber*	liver
-schnitzel	*shnitsel*	cutlet
-zunge	*tsungeh*	tongue

Meat Dishes Fleischgerichte

Eisbein	*icebine*	pickled pig's knuckle
Faschiertes	*fahsheertes*	ground meat
Fleischkäse	*flyshkehzeh*	meatloaf
Gehacktes	*ghehahktes*	ground meat
Kalbshaxen	*kahlpshahksen*	roast shank of veal
Leberkäse	*layberkaizeh*	type of meatloaf
Wiener Schnitzel	*veener shnitsel*	breaded veal cutlet

Bauernschmaus sauerkraut with bacon, smoked pork, sausages, dumplings, potatoes (*Austrian*)

Berner Platte sauerkraut or green beans with pork chops, bacon and beef, sausages, tongue, ham (*Swiss*)

Holsteiner Schnitzel breaded veal cutlet topped with fried egg, garnished with vegetables and accompanied by bread and butter, anchovies, mussels, and smoked salmon

Kohlroulade cabbage leaves stuffed with ground meat

Maultaschen ravioli filled with meat, vegetables, and seasoning

Rouladen slices of beef or veal filled, rolled, and braised (in gravy)

Sauerbraten beef roast, marinated with herbs, braised in a rich sauce

Schlachtplatte platter of various sausages and cold meats

Sausages Würste

Bierwurst	*beervoorst*	pork and beef, smoked
Blutwurst	*blootvoorst*	blood sausage
Bockwurst	*bokvoorst*	large frankfurter
Bratwurst	*brahtvoorst*	pork, fried or grilled
Fleischwurst	*flyshvoorst*	mildly seasoned, popular with children
Jagdwurst	*yahgtvoorst*	smoked pork, similar to salami
Leberwurst	*laybervoorst*	liver sausage
Katenrauchwurst	*kahtenrowkhvoorst*	country-style, smoked
Regensburger	*raygensboorger*	highly spiced, smoked
Rotwurst	*roatvoorst*	blood sausage
Weißwurst	*vicevoorst*	veal and bacon with parsley and onion
Zervelatwurst	*tservehlahtvoorst*	similar to salami
Zwiebelwurst	*tsveebelvoorst*	pork and onion

Side dishes Beilagen

Kartoffeln *kartoffeln* potatoes, which may appear as:
Bratkartoffeln/Röstkartoffeln (fried), **Rösti** (hash-brown),
Kartoffelbrei/-püree (mashed), **Kartoffelsalat** (potato salad),
Salzkartoffeln (boiled)

Klöße/Knödel *klursseh/knurdel* dumplings—often served with
soups or meat dishes; varieties: **Grießklöße** (semolina),
Kartoffelklöße (potato), **Leberknödel** (liver), **Mehlklöße** (flour),
Nockerl (small), **Semmelknödel** (Bavarian bread dumplings);
dumplings are called **Klöße** in northern Germany, but **Knödel** in
the south

Teigwaren *tiegwaaren* pasta; some varieties include **Nudeln**
(noodles), **Spätzle,** and **Knöpfli** (types of gnocchi)

Vegetables Gemüse

You'll recognize these vegetables: **Brokkoli, Karotten,
Sauerkraut, Sellerie, Tomaten.**

Blumenkohl	*bloomenkoal*	cauliflower
Bohnen	*boanen*	beans
Erbsen	*ehrpsen*	peas
Gurke	*goorkeh*	cucumber
Karfiol	*karfioal*	cauliflower
Kopfsalat	*kopfzahlaht*	head of lettuce
Mohrrüben	*moarrewben*	carrots
Zwiebeln	*tsveebeln*	onions
gemischter Salat	*gemishter zahlaht*	mixed salad
grüner Salat	*grewner zahlaht*	green salad
Rettichsalat	*rettichzahlaht*	white radish salad
Rotkrautsalat	*roatkrowtzahlaht*	red cabbage salad
Tomatensalat	*tomahtenzahlaht*	tomato salad

Kohl/Kraut *koal/krowt* cabbage; variations: **Grünkohl** (kale), **Krautsalat** (cole-slaw), **Rotkohl/-kraut** (red cabbage), **Sauerkraut** (pickled, shredded cabbage), **Weißkohl/-kraut** (white cabbage)

Pilze *piltseh* mushrooms; varieties: **Champignons** (white) and **Pfifferlinge** (chanterelle)

Cheese Käse

hard cheeses	(mild)	**Allgäuer Bergkäse** (like Swiss cheese), **Appenzeller, Räucherkäse** (smoked), **Tilsiter**
	(sharp)	**Handkäse, Harzer Käse, Schabzieger**
soft cheeses	(mild)	**Allgäuer Rahmkäse, Altenburger** (goat's milk cheese), **Edelpilz** (blue cheese), **Frischkäse** (curd cheese), **Kümmelkäse** (with caraway seeds), **Sahnekäse** (cream cheese), **Schichtkäse**
Swiss cheeses	(mild)	**Emmentaler, Greyerzer**

Fruit Obst

You'll recognize: **Apfel, Banane, Mandarine, Melone, Aprikosen, Datteln, Kokosnuss, Orange, Rhabarber**.

Apfelsine	*ahpfelzeeneh*	orange
Birne	*beerneh*	pear
rote/schwarze Johannisbeeren	*roateh/shvartseh yohahnisbayren*	red/black currants
Kirschen	*keershen*	cherries
Pflaumen	*pflowmen*	plums, prunes
Zitrone/Limone	*tsitroaneh/limoaneh*	lemon/lime
Zwetschgen	*tsvetshgen*	plums

Dessert Nachtisch

Apfelkuchen	*ahpfelkookhen*	apple tart
Dampfnudeln	*dampfnoodeln*	sweet dumplings
gemischtes Eis	*gemishtes ice*	mixed ice cream
Germknödel	*gehrmknurdel*	sweet dumpling
Obstsalat	*oabstzahlaht*	fruit salad
Rote Grütze	*roateh grewtseh*	red berry compote
Zwetschgenkuchen	*zvetshgenkookhen*	plum tart

Ice cream Eis

Some common flavors are **Erdbeereis** (strawberry), **Schokoladeneis** (chocolate), **Vanilleeis** (vanilla).

A … portion, please.	**Eine … Portion, bitte.**	
	ayneh … portsioan bitteh	
small	**kleine** *klineh*	
medium/regular	**mittlere/normale** *mitlereh/normahleh*	
large	**große** *groaseh*	

DRINKS

Beer Bier

For easy ordering, ask for **Bier vom Fass** (draft beer). To be more specific, ask for **ein Helles** (light beer) or **ein Dunkles** (dark beer).

Alkoholfreies Bier: alcohol-free

Altbier: high hops content; similar to British ale

Berliner Weiße mit Schuss: pale beer with a shot of raspberry syrup

Bockbier, Doppelbock, Starkbier: high alcoholic and malt content

Export: pale, higher in alcohol and less bitter than Pilsener

Hefeweizen/Hefeweißbier: pale, brewed from wheat

Kölsch: golden and light, brewed in Cologne

Kulmbacher Eisbock: highest alcohol content of all German beer

Malzbier: dark and sweet, very low in alcohol

Pilsener (Pils): pale and strong with an aroma of hops

Radlermaß/Alsterwasser: lager shandy (beer with lemonade)

Weißbier: light, brewed from wheat grain

Wine Wein

The Association of German Wine Estates (VDP) acts as a quality control and ensures that wines carrying the VDP label are of superior quality. The wine seal **(Weinsiegel)** on the neck of the wine bottle is color-coded for easy recognition: yellow seal for dry **(trocken),** green for medium-dry **(halbtrocken),** and red for sweet **(lieblich).**

Kabinett: light, dry wine

Spätlese: riper, more full-bodied, often sweeter

Auslese: slightly dry wine, richer than Spätlese

Beerenauslese: slightly sweet wine, honeyed and rich

Trockenbeerenauslese: sweet, dessert wine

Eiswein: intensely sweet, fairly scarce and expensive

Tafelwein: table wine; lowest quality

Qualitätswein bestimmter Anbaugebiete: medium quality

Qualitätswein mit Prädikat: highest quality wine

I'd like a corkscrew.   **Ich hätte gern einen Korkenzieher.**
ikh hetteh gehrn aynen korken-tseer

Other drinks

You'll recognize **Cognac, Rum, Wodka, Whisky.** Other drinks you may want to order include **Apfelwein** (fermented cider), **Bowle** (punch), **Glühwein** (mulled wine), **Portwein** (port), **Weinbrand** (brandy).

More common are liqueurs and brandies:

Schnaps *shnapps*

The generic term for spirits/brandies. Varieties: **Apfel-schnaps** (apple); **Birnenschnaps** (pear); **Bommerlunder** (caraway-flavored brandy); **(Doppel)Korn** (aqua vitae); **Dornkaat/Steinhäger** (similar to gin); **Heidelbeergeist** (blueberry brandy); **Kirschwasser** (cherry brandy); **Obstler** (fruit brandy); **Zwetschgen-wasser** (plum brandy); **Träsch** (pear and apple brandy); **Weizenkorn** (aqua vitae)

Likör *likur*

Liqueur: **Aprikosenlikör** (apricot), **Eierlikör** (eggnog), **Himbeerlikör** (raspberry), **Kirschlikör** (cherry), **Kümmel** (caraway-flavored)

Cheers!	**Prost!** *prohst*

Non-alcoholic drinks

You'll have no trouble finding your favorite soft drinks or sodas. Also popular is **Kaffee und Kuchen** (coffee and cakes) in the afternoon.

I'd like …	**Ich hätte gern …** *ikh hetteh gehrn*
hot chocolate	**eine heiße Schokolade** *ayneh highseh shokolahdeh*
(a glass of) milk	**(ein Glas) Milch** *(ayn glahs) milkh*
mineral water	**Mineralwasser** *meenehrahlvasser*
carbonated	**mit Kohlensäure** *mit koalenzoyreh*
non-carbonated	**ohne Kohlensäure** *oaneh koalenzoyreh*
fruit juice	**Fruchtsaft** *frookhtzaft*
coffee	**Kaffee** *kafay*
tea	**Tee** *tay*

MENU READER

Back-	*bahk*	baked
blutig	*blootick*	rare/underdone
durchgebraten	*doorkgehbrahten*	well-done
frittiert	*freeteert*	deep-fried
gebacken	*gehbahken*	baked
(im schwimmenden Fett)		
gebacken	*gehbahken*	deep-fried
(in der Pfanne) gebraten	*gehbrahten*	fried
(im Ofen) gebraten	*gehbrahten*	roasted
gedämpft	*gehdempft*	steamed
gefüllt	*gehfewlt*	stuffed
gegrillt	*gehgrilled*	grilled/broiled
gekocht	*gehkokt*	boiled
geräuchert	*gehroyshert*	smoked
geschmort	*gehshmort*	braised
geschwenkt	*gehshwenkt*	sautéed
mariniert	*mariniert*	marinated
paniert	*pahniert*	breaded
-spießchen	*shpeesken*	skewered
überbacken	*ewerbahken*	oven-browned
vom Rost	*vom rost*	grilled/broiled

A

Aal eel
Aalsuppe eel soup
Abendbrot supper
Abendessen dinner

alkoholfrei non-alcoholic
alkoholfreies Bier non-alcoholic beer
alkoholfreies Getränk non-alcoholic drink

alle Preise inklusive Bedienung und Mehrwertsteuer (MwSt.) service charge and VAT (sales tax) included

Allgäuer Käsesuppe cheese soup from the Allgäu

Alsterwasser beer with lemonade

Altbier similar to British ale

Ananas pineapple

Anis aniseed

Aperitif aperitif

Apfel apple

Apfelcreme apple cream dessert

Apfelkuchen apple tart

Apfelküchlein apple fritters

Apfelsaft apple juice

Apfelschnaps apple brandy

Apfelsine orange

Apfelsinensaft orange juice

Apfelstrudel apple strudel

Apfelwein cider

Appetithäppchen canapés

Aprikosen apricots

Aprikosenlikör apricot liqueur

... Art ...-style

Auberginen eggplant

auf Bestellung made to order

-auflauf soufflé

Aufschnitt(platte) cold cuts

auf Vorbestellung advance order

Auslese wine classification

Austern oysters

B

Bachsaibling brook trout

Backerbsensuppe type of pea soup

Backpflaumen prunes

Baguette French bread

Banane banana

Barsch freshwater perch

Basilikum basil

Basler Mehlsuppe flour soup with grated cheese (Swiss)

Bauernomelett diced bacon and onion omelet

Bauernschmaus sauerkraut with meats, dumplings/potatoes

Bauernsuppe cabbage and frankfurter soup

(deutsches) Beefsteak hamburger

Beerenauslese wine classification

Beilagen accompaniments

belegtes Brot open-face sandwich

Berliner jelly donut

Berliner Weiße pale beer

Berner Platte sauerkraut or green beans with meat

Bete beet

Bethmännchen marzipan balls

Beuschel veal with lemon sauce

Bienenstich honey-almond cake

Bier beer

Bierwurst smoked pork and beef sausage

Birne pear

Birnen, Bohnen & Speck pears, green beans, and bacon

Birnenschnaps pear brandy

Bismarckhering pickled herring with onions

blau boiled in bouillon

Blaubeer-Kaltschale chilled blueberry soup

Blaubeeren blueberries

Blaukraut red cabbage

Blindhuhn Westphalian vegetable stew
Blumenkohl cauliflower
Blutwurst blood sausage
Bockbier strong beer
Bockwurst large frankfurter
Bohnen beans
Bohnensuppe bean soup with bacon
Bommerlunder caraway-flavored brandy
Borretsch borage
Bouillon clear soup
Bowle punch
Brachse/Brasse bream
Brandwein brandy
Brat- roast
-braten joint, roast
Bratkartoffeln fried potatoes
Bratwurst fried pork sausage
Brechbohnen string beans
Brokkoli broccoli
Brombeeren blackberries
Brot bread
Brötchen rolls
-brust breast
Bückling kipper
Buletten meat patties
Bündnerfleisch cured beef
Butterkuchen butter crumble cake
Butterreis buttered rice

C

Cayenne-Pfeffer cayenne pepper
Champignons white mushrooms
Champignonsuppe mushroom soup

Chicorée chicory, endives
Christstollen Christmas fruitcake
Cornichons small pickles
-creme pudding
Cremeschnitte napoleon/millefeuille
Curryreis curried rice

D

Dampfnudeln sweet dumplings
Datteln dates
Dill dill
Doornkaat German gin, juniper-berry brandy
Doppelbock strong beer
(Doppel)Korn grain-distilled liquor, similar to whisky
Doppelrahm-Frischkäse cream cheese
Dorsch cod
dunkles Bier dark beer

E

Edelpilz blue cheese, similar to Stilton
Egli perch
Eier eggs
Eierlikör eggnog
Eierspeisen egg dishes
Eintopfgerichte stews
Eis/-eis ice cream
Eisbein pickled pig's knuckle
Eistee iced tea
Eiswein wine classification
Endivien curly endive
Endiviensalat curly endive salad

Endpreise einschließlich Service und Mehrwertsteuer service and VAT included
Ente duck
Erbsen peas
Erbsensuppe pea soup
Erdbeeren strawberries
Erdnüsse peanuts
Espresso espresso coffee
Essig vinegar
Essiggurken pickles
Estragon tarragon
Export strong, pale beer

F

falscher Hase meatloaf
Fasan pheasant
Faschiertes ground meat
Feigen figs
Felchen kind of trout
Fenchel fennel
Filetsteak beef steak
Fisch fish
Fischbeuschelsuppe fish roe and vegetable soup
Fischfrikadellen fish croquettes
Fischgerichte fish dishes
Fischsuppe fish soup
Fisolen green beans
Flädlesuppe broth with pancake strips
Fleisch (gerichte) meat (dishes)
Fleischkäse type of meatloaf
Fleischklößchen meatballs
Fleischpastete type of meatloaf
Fleischsalat diced meat salad with mayonnaise

Fleischwurst mildly seasoned sausage
Fondue bread dipped into melted cheese
Forelle trout
Frankfurter Würstchen frankfurter
französisches Weißbrot French baguette
Fridattensuppe broth with pancake strips
Frikadellen meat patties
frisch geräucherte Gänsebrust auf Toast freshly smoked breast of goose on toast
Frischkäse cream cheese
Früchtetee fruit tea
Fruchtjogurt fruit yogurt
Fruchtsaft fruit juice
Frühstück breakfast
für unsere kleinen Gäste children's meals
für zwei Personen for two

G

Gans goose
Gänseleberpastete goose liver pâté
Garnelen shrimp
Gebäck pastries
gebrühter Weißkrautsalat parboiled white cabbage coleslaw
Geflügel poultry
gehackt diced
Gehacktes ground meat
gekochtes Ei boiled egg
Gelbwurst mildly seasoned sausage
Gelee jelly/jam
gemischter Salat mixed salad

gemischtes Gemüse mixed vegetables

Gemüse vegetables

Gemüse nach Wahl choice of vegetables

Germknödel sweet dumpling

Geröstete hash-brown potatoes

Geschnetzeltes chopped veal in wine sauce

Geselchtes salted and smoked meat, usually pork

gespickter Hirsch larded venison

Getränke drinks

Gewürz spice

Glace/-glace ice cream

Glühwein mulled wine

glutenfreies Brot gluten-free bread

Götterspeise fruit jelly

Grießbrei cream of wheat

Grießklöße semolina dumplings

Grießnockerlsuppe semolina-dumpling soup

grüne Bohnen green beans

grüner Salat green salad

Grünkohl kale

Gugelhupf pound cake

Gulasch gulash; chunks of beef stewed in a rich paprika gravy

Gulaschsuppe spiced soup of stewed beef

Gurken cucumber

H

-hachse shank

Hackbraten meatloaf

Hackepeter spiced pork tartare

Haferbrei oatmeal

Hähnchen chicken

halbfester Käse medium-hard cheese

halbtrocken medium-dry

Hammelfleisch mutton

hart hard

Hase hare

Haselnüsse hazelnuts

Hauptgerichte main courses

Häuptlsalat lettuce salad

hausgemacht homemade

-haxe shank

Hecht pike

Hefeklöße yeast dumplings

Hefekranz ring-shaped cake of yeast dough, with almonds and sometimes candied fruit

Hefeweizen pale beer

Heidelbeeren blueberries

Heidelbeergeist blueberry brandy

Heidschnucken mutton from the Lüneburg Heath

Heilbutt halibut

heiß hot

heißer Apfelwein hot apple cider

helles Bier light beer

-hendl chicken

Hering(salat) herring (salad)

-herz heart

Himbeeren raspberries

Himbeerlikör raspberry brandy

hohe Rippe roast ribs of beef

Holsteiner Schnitzel breaded veal cutlet topped with fried egg

Honig honey

Honigkuchen honey biscuits

Hoppel-Poppel scrambled eggs with diced sausages or bacon

Huhn chicken

Hühnerbrühe chicken broth
Hummer lobster
Hummerkrabben large shrimp
Hüttenkäse cottage cheese

I

Imbiss snacks
Ingwer ginger

J

Jagdwurst smoked pork sausage, similar to salami
Jakobsmuscheln scallops
Jogurt yogurt
Johannisbeersaft currant juice

K

Kabeljau cod
Kabinett wine classification
Kaffee coffee
Kaffeesahne cream
Kaisergranate kind of shrimp
Kaiserschmarren shredded pancake with raisins and syrup
Kakao hot chocolate
Kalbfleisch veal
Kalbshaxen roast shank of veal
Kalbsleber veal liver
kalt cold
Kaltschale chilled fruit soup
Kaninchen rabbit
Kapaun capon
Kapern capers
Karamel caramel
Karfiol cauliflower

Karotten carrots
Karpfen carp
Kartoffelauflauf potato casserole
Kartoffelbälle potato balls
Kartoffelbrei mashed potatoes
Kartoffelchips potato chips
Kartoffelklöße potato dumplings
Kartoffelkroketten potato croquettes
Kartoffelmus mashed potatoes
Kartoffeln potatoes
Kartoffelpuffer potato fritters
Kartoffelsalat (mit Speck) potato salad (with bacon)
Kartoffelstock mashed potatoes
Kartoffelsuppe potato soup
Käse cheese
Käsebrett/Käse nach Ihrer Wahl cheese selection
Käseschnitte open, melted cheese sandwich
Käsestangen cheese sticks
Käsewähe hot cheese tart
Kasseler Rippenspeer smoked pork chops
Katenrauchwurst country-style, smoked sausage
Kekse cookies
Kerbel chervil
-keule haunch
Kirschcreme cherry cream dessert
Kirschen cherries
Kirschlikör cherry liqueur
Kirschwasser cherry brandy
kleine Mahlzeiten light meals/snacks
Klöße dumplings

Knoblauch garlic
Knödel dumplings
Knödelsuppe dumpling soup
Knöpfli kind of gnocchi
koffeinfreier Kaffee decaffeinated coffee
Kognak brandy
Kohl cabbage
Kohlrabi kohlrabi
Kohlroulade cabbage leaves stuffed with ground meat
Kokosnuss coconut
Kompott/-kompott stewed fruit, compote
Königinpastete diced meat and mushrooms in puff-pastry
Königinsuppe soup with beef, sour cream, and almonds
Königsberger Klopse meatballs in white caper sauce
Kopfsalat lettuce
-kotelett chop
Krabben shrimp
Kraftbrühe beef consommé
Kräuter herbs
Kräutersalz herb-flavored salt
Kräutertee herb tea
(roher) Krautsalat coleslaw
Krautstiel white beet
Krautwickel braised cabbage rolls
Krebs river crayfish
Kren horseradish
Krenfleisch pork served with shredded vegetables and horseradish
Kresse watercress
Kuchen/-kuchen cake

Kulmbacher Eisbock strong beer
Kümmel caraway; caraway-flavored liquor
Kürbis pumpkin
Kutteln tripe

L

Labkaus ground/marinated corned beef, pickles, beets, smelts, and herring served with mashed potatoes and fried eggs
Lachs salmon
Lammfleisch lamb
Languste spiny lobster
Lauch leeks
Laugenbrötchen pretzel rolls
Leber liver
Leberkäse type of meatloaf
Leberknödel liver dumplings
Leberknödelsuppe liver-dumpling soup
Leberwurst liver sausage
Lebkuchen gingerbread
Leckerli ginger biscuits
leicht light
Leipziger Allerlei peas, carrots, and asparagus
Lenden- filet of beef (tenderloin)
Lendenstück loin
lieblich sweet
Likör liqueur
Limette lime
Limonade soda
Limone lemon
Linsen lentils
Linsensuppe lentil soup
Lorbeer bay leaf

M

Maibowle white wine punch, flavored with sweet woodruff
Mais sweet corn
Maispoularde corn-fed chicken
Majoran marjoram
Makrele mackerel
Makronen macaroons
Malzbier low-alcohol beer
Mandarine tangerine
Mandeln almonds
Marillen apricots
Marmelade jam
Märzen strong beer
Masthühnchen chicken
Matjesfilet nach Hausfrauenart herring filets
Matjeshering salted young herring
Maultaschen type of ravioli
Meeresfrüchte seafood
Meerrettich horseradish
Mehlklöße flour dumplings
Mehlnockerln small dumplings
Melone melon
Mettwurst spicy smoked pork sausage
Milch milk
Milchkaffee coffee with milk
Milchmixgetränk milk shake
Mineralwasser mineral water
mit Ei with egg
mit Eis on the rocks/with ice
mit Kohlensäure carbonated
mit Milch with milk
mit Sahne with cream
mit Zitrone with lemon

mit Zucker with sugar
Mittagessen lunch
mittel medium
Mohnbrötchen poppy seed rolls
Mohrrüben carrots
Mokka mocha; coffee-flavored
Muscheln clams/mussels
Muskatblüte mace
Muskatnuss nutmeg

N

Nachspeisen/Nachtisch desserts
Nelke clove
Nieren kidneys
Nockerl small dumpling
Nudeln noodles
Nudelsuppe noodle soup
Nürnberger Bratwurst fried veal and pork
Nürnberger Rostbratwurst Nuremberg-style pork sausage
Nuss- nut-flavored
Nüsse nuts

O

Obst fruit
Obstler fruit brandy
Obstsalat fruit salad
Ochsenschwanzsuppe oxtail soup
ohne Kohlensäure non-carbonated
Öl oil
Oliven olives
Omelett(e) omelet
Orangeade orangeade
Orangen oranges

Orangenmarmelade orange marmalade

Orangensaft orange juice

P

Palatschinken pancakes with a jam or cream cheese filling

Pampelmuse grapefruit

Paradeiser tomatoes

Pellkartoffeln potatoes boiled in their skins, then peeled

Petersilie parsley

Petersilienkartoffeln parsley potatoes

Pfeffer pepper (ground)

Pfefferkörner peppercorns

Pfefferminze peppermint

Pfefferpotthast spicy meat and onion casserole

Pfifferlinge chanterelle mushrooms

Pfirsich peach

Pflaumen plums, prunes

Pflümli(wasser) plum brandy

Pharisäer coffee with rum and whipped cream

Pichelsteiner Eintopf meat and vegetable stew

pikant pungent/hot

Pickelsteiner casserole with horseradish, garlic, salsify

Pilsener pilsener

Pilze mushrooms

Piment all-spice

-plätzli cutlet

Pökelfleisch salted meat

Pommes frites french fries

Porree leek

Portwein port

Poulet chicken

Preiselbeeren cranberries

Presskopf pork headcheese

Printen honey biscuits

Prinzessbohnen thick stringbeans

pur straight (neat)

-püree creamed

Q

Quark dairy product similar to plain yogurt

Quitte quince

R

Raclette melted cheese with potatoes and pickles

Radieschen radishes

Radlermaß beer with lemonade

Räucheraal smoked eel

Räucherhering smoked herring

Rebhuhn partridge

Regensburger highly spiced, smoked sausage

Reh(pastete) venison paté

Reibekuchen potato pancake

reif ripe

Reis rice

Reisgerichte rice dishes

Rettichsalat white radish salad

Rhabarber rhubarb

Ribisel currants

Rindfleisch beef

Rindswurst grilled beef sausage

Rippensteak rib steak

Rochen ray
Roggenbrot rye bread
Rohschinken cured ham
Rollmops pickled herring
Rosenkohl brussels sprouts
Rosinen raisins
Rosinenbrot raisin bread
Rosmarin rosemary
Rösti hash browns
Röstkartoffeln fried potatoes
Rotbarsch red sea-bass
Rote Grütze red berry compote
rote Beete beet
rote Johannisbeeren red currants
Rotkohl red cabbage
Rotkrautsalat red cabbage salad
Rotwurst blood sausage
Rouladen slices of rolled and braised beef or veal
Rüben beet
-rücken back
Rüdesheimer Kaffee coffee with brandy and whipped cream
Rüebli carrots
Rühreier scrambled eggs
Rum rum
Russische Eier hard-boiled eggs with mayonnaise

S

Safran saffron
saisonbedingt seasonal
Salate salads
Salbei sage
Salm salmon
Salz salt
Salzgurke pickled cucumber
Salzkartoffeln boiled potatoes
Sardinen sardines
Sauerbraten marinated, braised beef
Sauerkirsch-Kaltschale chilled sour cherry soup
Sauerkraut sauerkraut
Sauerkraut und Rippchen sauerkraut and ribs
Schalotten shallots
scharf piquant/hot
Schellfisch haddock
Schillerlocke pastry cornet with vanilla cream filling
Schillerwein type of rosé
Schinken ham
Schinkenröllchen mit Spargel rolled ham filled with asparagus
Schlachtplatte platter of various sausages and cold meats
Schlesisches Himmelreich smoked pork loin cooked with mixed dried fruits
Schmelzkäse spreadable cheese
Schnaps strong spirit or brandy
Schnecken snails
Schnepfe wood cock
Schnittlauch chives
Schnitzel cutlet
(heiße) Schokolade hot chocolate
Schokoladen- chocolate …
Scholle plaice
Schupfnudeln rolled potato noodles
schwarze Johannisbeeren black currants
schwarzer Kaffee black coffee
Schwarzwälder Kirschtorte Black Forest cake

Schwarzwurzeln salsify
Schweinefleisch pork
Schweinekamm pork shoulder
Schweinekotelett pork chop
Schweinshaxe knuckle of pork
Seebarsch sea bass
Seebutt brill
Seehecht hake
Seezunge sole
sehr trocken extra dry
Sekt sparkling wine
selbstgemacht homemade
Sellerie celery
Selleriesalat celeriac root salad
Semmelknödel Bavarian bread dumplings
Semmelsuppe dumpling soup
Senf mustard
Seniorenmenü senior citizens' meals
Serbische Bohnensuppe spiced bean soup
Sesambrötchen sesame seed rolls
Soleier eggs pickled in brine
Spanferkel suckling pig
Spargel(spitzen) asparagus (tips)
Spätlese wine classification
Spätzle kind of noodle
Speck bacon
Speckknödel bread dumplings with bacon
Spekulatius almond cookies
Spezialität des Hauses specialty of the house
Spezialitäten der Region local specialties
Spiegeleier fried eggs

Spiegeleier mit Schinken/Speck ham/bacon and eggs
Spinat spinach
Sprotten sprats
Stachelbeeren gooseberries
Starkbier strong beer
Steckrüben turnips
Steinbutt turbot
Steinhäger juniperberry brandy
Steinpilze wild yellow mushrooms
Steinpilze Försterinnenart mushrooms forestiere
Stolzer Heinrich sausage in beer
Stör sturgeon
Strammer Max bread with ham, fried eggs, and maybe onions
Streichkäse spreadable cheese
Streuselkuchen coffee cake with crumble topping
Stückchen pastries
Sülze headcheese
Sülzkotelett pork chops in aspic
Suppen soups
süß sweet
Süßspeisen desserts
Süßstoff artificial sweetener

T

Tafelspitz mit Meerrettich boiled beef with horseradish cream sauce
Tagesgedeck set menu of the day
Tagesgericht dish of the day
Taube pigeon, squab
Tee tea
Teewurst soft, spreadable sausage

Teig dough
Teigwaren pasta
Teilchen pastries
Teltower Rübchen baby turnips
Thymian thyme
Tintenfisch squid/octopus
Tomaten tomatoes
Tomatenketchup ketchup
Tomatensaft tomato juice
Tomatensalat tomato salad
Tomatensuppe tomato soup
Topfbraten pot roast
Topfenstrudel flaky pastry filled with vanilla-flavored cream cheese, rolled and baked
Torte/-torte layer cake
Töttchen Westphalian sweet and sour veal stew
Träsch pear and apple brandy
Trauben grapes
Traubensaft grape juice
trocken dry
Trockenbeerenauslese wine classification
Truthahn turkey

U

ungarisch Hungarian
unser Küchenchef empfiehlt … the chef recommends …

V

Vanille vanilla
VDP (Verband Deutscher Prädikats- & Qualitäts Weingüter) officially recognized wine
Vollkornbrot whole grain bread
Vollmilch whole milk
vollmundig full-bodied
Vorspeisen appetizers/starters

W

Wacholder juniper
Wachsbohnen yellow wax beans
Wachtel quail
Waldmeister sweet woodruff
Walnüsse walnuts
warme Getränke hot beverages
Wasser water
Wassermelone watermelon
weich soft
Wein wine
Weinbrand brandy
Weincreme wine cream dessert
Weintrauben grapes
weiß white
Weißbier pale, light beer
Weißbrot white bread
weiße Bohnen white beans
Weißherbst type of rosé

Weißkohl/-kraut white cabbage
Weißwurst veal and bacon
sausage with parsley and onion
Weizenkorn wheat-distilled
liquor, similar to whisky
Wermut vermouth
Whisky whisky
Wiener Schnitzel breaded veal
cutlet
Wienerli Vienna-style frankfurter
Wild game
Wildschwein wild boar
Windbeutel cream puff
Wirsing savoy cabbage
Wodka vodka
Würste sausages
Wurstplatte assorted cold cuts
Würze seasoning
würzig aromatic

Z

Zander (giant) pike-perch
Zervelat(wurst) pork, beef, and
bacon sausage
Zimmertemperatur room
temperature
Zimt cinnamon
Zitrone lemon
**zu allen Gerichten servieren
wir …** all meals are served with …

Zucchetti zucchini
Zucker sugar
Zuckererbsen young green peas
Zunge/-zunge tongue
Zungenwurst blood sausage with
pieces of tongue and diced fat
Zuschlag extra charge/supplement
Zwetschgen plums
Zwetschgenkuchen plum tart
Zwetschgenwasser plum brandy
Zwiebelbrot onion bread
Zwiebeln onions
Zwiebelsuppe onion soup
Zwiebelwurst liver and onion
sausage
Zwischengerichte for the small
appetite

GREEK

ESSENTIALS	
Hello.	Χαίρετε. *kherete*
Good evening.	Καλησπέρα. *kaleespera*
A table for ..., please.	Ένα τραπέζι για ..., παρακαλώ. *ena trapezee ya ..., parakalo*
1/2/3/4	έναν (μια)/δύο/τρεις/τέσσερις *enan/THeeo/trees/teserees*
Thank you.	Ευχαριστώ. *efkhareesto*
I'd like to pay.	Θα ήθελα να πληρώσω. *tha eethela na pleeroso*
Good-bye.	Αντίο. *andeeo*

PLACES TO EAT

Restaurants that display tourist menus, or fixed price menus, will usually provide good value meals. But if you wish to sample truly Greek food you should seek out more ethnic restaurants. Here you can often select your meal, particularly fish, from a display in the kitchen and even talk to the chef about how you want it cooked.

Ταβέρνα *taverna*

The most common eating place; prices are reasonable, and you will find a good selection of **mezeTHes** (appetizers) and **mayeerefta** (baked or stewed snacks), as well as **tees oras** (meat and fish)

Εστιατόριο *esteeatoreeo*

General term for restaurant; more expensive than tavernas

Ψαροταβέρνα *psarotaverna*

A fish taverna, usually found on the islands and in coastal areas; specializing in fish (**psaree**) and seafood (**thalaseena**)

Ψησταριά *pseestareea*

Like a taverna but specializes in grilled meat (always cooked **sta karvoona**, charcoal grilled)

Μεζεδοπωλείο *mezeтнopoleeo*

Specializes in **mezeтнes** (appetizers), which can be incredibly substantial and filling; served with wine, beer, or **oozo** (ouzo, an anise-flavored aperitif)

Ουζερί *oozeree*

A traditional establishment, where you can enjoy an ouzo with a few **mezeтнes**—traditionally, **khtapoтнee** (octopus), **elee-es** (olives), **antzooyes** (anchovies), and **feta** (feta cheese)

Σουβλατζίδικο *soovlatzeeтнeeko*

The Greek answer to fast food; serving grilled skewered meat (**soovlakee**) or **yeeros** (gyros) in pita bread (**peeta**) with tomatoes, onions, and **tzatzeekee** (tzatziki)

MEAL TIMES

Breakfast πρωινό *proeeno*

Usually just a strong sweet cup of coffee (**varee ghleeko**) in the morning, followed by another one at work between 10 and 11 a.m., maybe with a pastry

Lunch μεσημεριανό *meseemeryano*

Eaten from 2–3 p.m., but most restaurants will serve until 4 p.m.

Dinner βραδυνό *vraтнeeno*

Normally at 9 or 10 p.m.; it's not unusual to find restaurants serving food until midnight or later

GREEK CUISINE

The emphasis is on fresh meat, fish, vegetables, and fruit,
flavored with a delicate combination of herbs and spices found
in abundance in the Greek mountains. Some of the food you can
taste today in the Greek islands probably does not differ much
from what the ancient Greeks enjoyed 2,500 years ago, albeit
with Turkish and Italian influences.

FINDING A PLACE TO EAT

Can you recommend a good restaurant?	Μπορείτε να μας συστήσετε ένα καλό εστιατόριο; *boreete na mas seesteesete ena kalo esteeatoreeo*
Is there a(n) ... near here?	Υπάρχει ... εδώ κοντά; *eeparkhee...eτнo konda*
traditional local restaurant	ένα τοπικό παραδοσιακό εστιατόριο *ena topeeko paraτнoseeako esteeatoreeo*
inexpensive restaurant	ένα φτηνό εστιατόριο *ena fteeno esteeatoreeo*
Where can I find a(n) ...?	Πού μπορώ να βρω ...; *poo boro na vro*
souvlaki/gyros stand	ένα σουβλατζίδικο *ena soovlatzeeτнeeko*
café	μια καφετέρια *mia kafeteria*
fast-food restaurant	ένα φαστ φουντ *ena "fast food"*
pizzeria	πιτσαρία *peetsareea*
pastry shop	ένα ζαχαροπλαστείο *ena zakharoplasteeo*

RESERVATIONS

I'd like to reserve a table for 2 this evening at ...	Θα ήθελα να κλείσω ένα τραπέζι για δύο απόψε στις ... *tha eethela na kleeso ena trapezee ya тнeeo apopse stees*
We'll come at 11:00.	Θα έρθουμε στις έντεκα. *tha erthoome stees endeka*
We have a reservation.	Έχουμε κλείσει τραπέζι. *ekhoome kleesee trapezee*
Could we sit ...?	Μπορούμε να καθήσουμε ...; *boroome na katheesoome*
over there/outside	εκεί/έξω *ekee/ekso*
in a non-smoking area	σε μια περιοχή για μη καπνίζοντες *se mia pereeokhee ya mee kapneezondes*
by the window	κοντά στο παράθυρο *konda sto paratheero*
Smoking or non-smoking?	Καπνίζοντες ή μη καπνίζοντες; *kapneezondes ee mee kapneezondes*

ORDERING

Waiter!/Waitress!	Γκαρσόν!/Δεσποινίς! *garson/тнespeenees*
May I see the wine list, please?	Μπορώ να δω τον κατάλογο κρασιών, παρακαλώ; *boro na тнo ton katalogho kraseeon, parakalo*
Do you have a set menu?	Υπάρχει μενού α λα κάρτ; *eeparkhee menoo a la kart*

Can you recommend some typical local dishes?	Μπορείτε να μας συστήσετε τυπικά παραδοσιακά πιάτα; *boreete na mas seesteesete teepeeka paraTHoseeaka piata*
Could you tell me what ... is?	Μπορείτε να μου πείτε τι είναι το ...; *boreete na moo peete tee eene to*
What's in it?	Τί έχει μέσα; *tee ekhee mesa*
I'll have ...	Θα πάρω ... *tha paro*
a bottle/glass/carafe of ...	ένα μπουκάλι/ένα ποτήρι/μια καράφα ... *ena bookalee/ena poteeree/ mia karafa*

SPECIAL REQUESTS

Could I have a salad instead of vegetables, please?	Μπορώ να πάρω σαλάτα αντί λαχανικά, παρακαλώ; *boro na paro salata andee lakhaneeka, parakalo*
Does the meal come with vegetables/potatoes?	Το φαγητό σερβίρεται με λαχανικά/πατάτες; *to fayeeto serveerete me lakhaneeka/patates*
Do you have any sauces?	Έχετε σάλτσες; *ekhete saltses*
May I have some ...?	Μπορώ να έχω λίγο ...; *boro na ekho leegho*
ice	πάγο *pagho*
bread	ψωμί *psomee*
butter	βούτυρο *vooteero*
lemon	λεμόνι *lemonee*

mustard	μουστάρδα *moostarTHa*
pepper	πιπέρι *peeperee*
salt	αλάτι *alatee*
seasoning	αλατοπίπερο *alatopeepero*
sugar	ζάχαρη *zakharee*
artificial sweetener	ζακχαρίνη *zak-khareenee*
vinaigrette	λαδόξιδο *laTHokseeTHo*
olive oil	ελαιόλαδο *eleolaTHo*
Could we have a child's seat, please?	Μπορούμε να έχουμε ένα παιδικό κάθισμα; *boroome na ekhoome epapeTHeeko katheezma*
Where can I feed/ change the baby?	Πού μπορώ να ταΐσω/αλλάξω το μωρό; *poo boro na taeeso/alakso to moro*

GENERAL QUESTIONS

Could I have a(n) (clean) ..., please?	Μπορώ να έχω μια (καθαρό/καθαρή) ... παρακαλώ; *boro na ekho mia (katharo/ katharee) ... parakalo*
ashtray	σταχτοδοχείο *stakhtoTHokheeo*
cup/glass	φλυτζάνι/ποτήρι *fleetzanee/poteeree*
fork/knife	πηρούνι/μαχαίρι *peeroonee/makheree*
napkin	πετσέτα *petseta*

plate/spoon	πιάτο/ένα κουτάλι *piato/ena kootalee*
I'd like (a) ...	Θα ήθελα ... *tha eethela ...*
beer	μια μπύρα *mia beera*
(hot) chocolate	μια ζεστή σοκολάτα *mia zestee sokolata*
coffee/tea	ένα καφέ/ένα τσάι *ena kafe/ena tsaee*
black/with milk	σκέτο/με γάλα *sketo/me ghala*
fruit juice	ένα χυμό φρούτων *ena kheemo frooton*
mineral water	ένα εμφιαλωμένο νερό *ena emfeealomeno nero*
red/white wine	άσπρο/κόκκινο κρασί *aspro/ kokeeno krasee*
Nothing more, thanks.	Τίποτε άλλο, ευχαριστώ. *teepote alo, efkhareesto*
Where's the restroom?	Πού είναι η τουαλέττα; *poo eene ee tooaleta*

SPECIAL REQUIREMENTS

I mustn't eat food containing ...	Δεν πρέπει να φάω φαγητό που περιέχει ... *THen prepee na fao* *fayeeto poo peree-ekhee*
flour/fat	αλεύρι/λίπος *alevree/leepos*
salt/sugar	αλάτι/ζάχαρη *alatee/zakharee*
Do you have meals for diabetics?	Έχετε φαγητά για διαβητικούς; *ekhete fayeeta ya* *THeeaveeteekoos*

Do you have vegetarian meals?	Έχετε φαγητά για χορτοφάγους; _ekhete fayeeta ya khortofaghoos_

COMPLAINTS

There must be some mistake.	Πρέπει να έγινε κάποιο λάθος. _prepee na eyeene kapeeo lathos_
That's not what I ordered.	Δεν παρήγγειλα αυτό. _THen pareengeela afto_
I asked for ...	Ζήτησα ... _zeeteesa_
The meat is ...	Το κρέας είναι ... _to kreas eene ..._
overdone	πολύ ψημένο _polee pseemeno_
underdone	όχι καλά ψημένο _okhee kala pseemeno_
too tough	πολύ σκληρό _polee skleero_
The food is cold.	Το φαγητό είναι κρύο. _to fayeeto eene kreeo_
This isn't fresh.	Αυτό δεν είναι φρέσκο. _afto THen eene fresko_
How much longer will our food be?	Πόση ώρα ακόμη θα κάνει το φαγητό; _posee ora akomee tha kanee to fayeeto_

PAYING

Tipping: See page 332.

I'd like to pay.	Θα ήθελα να πληρώσω. _tha eethela na pleeroso_
We'd like to pay separately.	Θα πληρώσουμε ξεχωριστά. _tha pleerosoome ksekhoreesta_

It's all together.	Όλοι μαζί. _olee ma_ζee
What is this amount for?	Τί είναι αυτό το ποσό; _tee eene af_to to po_so_
I didn't have that. I had ...	Δεν πήρα αυτό. Πήρα ... тнen _peera af_to. _peera_
Can I pay with this credit card?	Μπορώ να πληρώσω με αυτήν την πιστωτική κάρτα; _boro_ na plee_roso_ me af_teen_ teen peestotee_kee _karta_
Could I have a tax [VAT] receipt, please?	Μπορώ να έχω απόδειξη με ΦΠΑ, παρακαλώ; _boro_ na _ekho_ apoтнeeksee me fee-pee-a, paraka_lo_
That was a delicious meal.	Ήταν ένα πολύ νόστιμο γεύμα. _eetan ena polee nosteemo yevma_

COURSE BY COURSE

Breakfast Πρωινό

I'd like …	Θα ήθελα ... tha _eethela_
fruit juice	ένα χυμό φρούτων _ena_ khee_mo frooton_
jam	μαρμελάδα marme_la_тнa
yogurt (with honey)	γιαούρτι (με μέλι) ya_oortee_ (me _melee_)
milk	γάλα _ghala_
rolls	ψωμάκια pso_makeea_

ελιές (γεμιστές)	*elee-es (yemeestes)*	(stuffed) olives
κρύο κρέας	*kreeo kreas*	cold meat
πατέ	*pate*	pâté
πεπόνι	*peponee*	melon
ποικιλία ορεκτικών	*peekeeleea orekteekon*	assorted appetizers
ρέγγα (καπνιστή)	*renga (kapneestee)*	(smoked) herring
καλαμαράκια	*kalamarakeea*	baby squid fried in batter
μαρίδα τηγανητή	*mareeтна teeghaneetee*	whitebait fried in batter

Ντολμαδάκια *dolmaтнakeea*
Vine leaves stuffed with rice and onions and flavored with dill

Ταραμοσαλάτα *taramosalata*
Dip made from fish roe blended with bread, olive oil, lemons, and onions

Τζατζίκι *tzatzeekee*
A dip of yogurt, garlic, cucumber, and olive oil

Σπανακόπιττα *spanakopeeta*
Filo pastry pies filled with spinach, feta cheese, and eggs

Κεφτεδάκια *kefteтнakeea*
Fried meat balls containing onions, bread crumbs, and herbs

Soups Σούπες

κοτόσουπα	*koto<u>soopa</u>*	clear chicken soup
ρεβύθια	*reve<u>etheea</u>*	chickpea soup
σούπα αυγολέμονο	*<u>soopa</u> avgho<u>lemono</u>*	soup with rice, eggs, and lemon juice
πατσάς	*pat<u>sas</u>*	tripe soup
σούπα φακές	*<u>soopa</u> fa<u>kes</u>*	lentil soup
τοματόσουπα	*toma<u>to</u>soopa*	tomato soup
ταχινόσουπα	*takhee<u>no</u>soopa*	"tahini" (sesame seed) soup
φασολάδα	*faso<u>la</u>тнa*	bean soup with tomatoes and parsley
χορτόσουπα	*khor<u>to</u>soopa*	vegetable soup
κακαβιά	*kakav<u>ya</u>*	fish stew with tomatoes

Κρεατόσουπα *krea<u>to</u>soopa*
Meat soup, sometimes thickened with egg and lemon

Ψαρόσουπα *psa<u>ro</u>soopa*
Fish soup thickened with egg and lemon, often with white rice

Τραχανάς *trakha<u>nas</u>*
Cracked wheat soup

Egg dishes/Omelets Πιάτα αυγών/Ομελέτες

I'd like an omelet.	Θα ήθελα μια ομελέττα. *tha <u>ee</u>thela mia omele<u>ta</u>*
eggs	αυγά *av<u>gha</u>*
soft-boiled	μελάτα *me<u>la</u>ta*
hard-boiled	σφικτά *sfeekh<u>ta</u>*

fried	τηγανητά (μάτια)	*teeghanee<u>ta</u> (<u>ma</u>teea)*
poached	ποσέ	*po<u>se</u>*
cheese omelet	ομελέττα με τυρί	*ome<u>le</u>ta me tee<u>ree</u>*
ham omelet	ομελέττα με ζαμπόν	*ome<u>le</u>ta me zam<u>bon</u>*

Fish and seafood Ψάρι και θαλασσινά

Don't miss the boiled fish (scorpion fish, grouper, and blackfish are the best). A soup made from fish broth and thickened with egg and lemon (**afgholemono**) is eaten first, followed by the fish itself and vegetables with mayonnaise. Smaller fish are eaten fried in olive oil (**teeghaneeta**) or grilled over charcoal (**pseeta**).

αντζούγιες	*an<u>tzoo</u>yes*	anchovies
αστακός	*asta<u>kos</u>*	lobster
γαρίδες	*gha<u>ree</u>THes*	shrimp
γλώσσα	*<u>ghlo</u>sa*	sole
καβούρι	*ka<u>voo</u>ree*	crab
καλαμάρι	*kala<u>ma</u>ree*	squid
κέφαλος	*<u>ke</u>falos*	mullet
μπακαλιάρος	*bakalee-<u>a</u>ros*	fresh cod
μπακαλιάρος παστός	*bakalee<u>a</u>ros pas<u>tos</u>*	salted cod
μπαρμπούνι	*bar<u>boo</u>nee*	red mullet
μύδια	*<u>mee</u>THya*	mussels
ξιφίας	*ksee<u>fee</u>as*	swordfish
σαρδέλλα	*sar<u>THe</u>la*	sardines
σουπιά	*soo<u>pia</u>*	cuttlefish
στρείδια	*<u>stree</u>THya*	oysters
σφυρίδα	*sfee<u>ree</u>THa*	grouper

τόννος	*tonos*	tuna
χέλι	*khelee*	eel
χταπόδι	*khtapoTHee*	octopus

Αστακός *astakos*
Lobster, often served with oil and lemon sauce or garlic mayonnaise

Γαρίδες με φέτα/σαγανάκι *ghareeTHes me feta/saghanakee*
Shrimp with onions, tomatoes, and seasonings, baked with feta

Χταπόδι κρασάτο *khtapoTHee krasato*
Octopus stewed in wine sauce

Ψάρι μαρινάτο *psaree mareenato*
Mullet, sole, or mackerel, fried and served with a wine sauce

Meat and poultry Κρέας και πουλερικά

βοδινό	*voTHeeno*	beef
χοιρινό	*kheereeno*	pork
μοσχάρι	*moskharee*	veal
αρνί	*arnee*	lamb
ζαμπόν	*zambon*	ham
κατσικάκι	*katseekakeè*	goat
κοτολέτες	*kotoletes*	cutlets
λουκάνικα	*lookaneeka*	sausages
μπριζόλα βοδινή /χοιρινή	*breezola voTHeenee/ heereenee*	beef/pork steak
μυαλό	*mialo*	brains
νεφρά	*nefra*	kidneys
συκώτι	*seekotee*	liver

φιλέτο	*feeleto*	filet
γαλοπούλα	*ghalopoola*	turkey
κοτόπουλο	*kotopoolo*	chicken
κουνέλι	*koonelee*	rabbit
πάπια	*papia*	duck
φασιανός	*faseeanos*	pheasant
χήνα	*kheena*	goose

Αρνάκι εξοχικό *arnakee eksokheeko*
Spiced lamb and potatoes baked in parchment (sometimes in filo pastry)

Γιουβέτσι *yoovetsee*
Meat (usually lamb) with Greek pasta baked in the oven with tomatoes

Κοντοσούβλι *kondosoovlee*
Skewered pork or lamb, well seasoned and cooked over charcoal

Μελιτζανάτο *meleetzanato*
Beef or veal stewed with tomatoes and eggplant

Μουσακάς *moosakas*
Layers of eggplant and ground meat topped with bechamel sauce

Μπιφτέκι *beeftekee*
A Greek "beefburger": ground meat with breadcrumbs, onions, and herbs grilled over charcoal, topped with grilled cheese or egg

Vegetables and legumes Λαχανικά και όσπρια

Vegetables (**lakhaneeka**) and beans (**ospreea**) often tend to be mixed or cooked with meat or fish. Vegetarians should ask for **ena fayeeto poo na meen ekhee kre-as** ("a dish that has no meat").

αγγούρι	*angooree*	cucumber
αγκινάρες	*angeenares*	artichokes
αρακάς	*arakas*	peas
καρότα	*karota*	carrots
κολοκύθια	*kolokeetheea*	zucchini
κουνουπίδι	*koonoopeeтнее*	cauliflower
κουκιά	*kookeea*	broad beans
κρεμμύδια	*kremeeтнуа*	onions
λάχανο	*lakhano*	cabbage
κόκκινο λάχανο	*kokeeno lakhano*	red cabbage
μανιτάρια	*maneetarya*	mushrooms
μαρούλι	*maroolee*	lettuce
μελιτζάνες	*meleetzanes*	eggplant
μπάμιες	*bamee-es*	okra
ντομάτες	*domates*	tomatoes
πατάτες	*patates*	potatoes
πιπεριές	*peeperyes*	peppers
πιπεριές πράσινες	*peeperyes praseenes*	green peppers
πράσα	*prasa*	leeks
ρύζι	*reezee*	rice
σέλινο	*seleeno*	celery
σπαράγγια	*sparangeea*	asparagus

σπανάκι	*spanakee*	spinach
φασολάκια φρέσκα	*fasolakeea freska*	green beans
ρεβύθια	*reveetheea*	chickpeas
φακές	*fakes*	lentils
φασόλια γίγαντες	*fasoleea yeeghandes*	butter beans

Fruit Φρούτα

ανανάς	*ananas*	pineapple
αχλάδι	*akhlaтнee*	pear
βερύκοκο	*vereekoko*	apricot
δαμάσκηνο	*тнamaskeeno*	plum
γκρέιπφρουτ	*"grapefruit"*	grapefruit
καρπούζι	*karpoozee*	watermelon
κεράσι	*kerasee*	cherry
λεμόνι	*lemonee*	lemon
μήλο	*meelo*	apple
μπανάνα	*banana*	banana
πεπόνι	*peponee*	melon
πορτοκάλι	*portokalee*	orange
μανταρίνι	*mantareenee*	tangerine
ροδάκινο	*roтнakeeno*	peach
σταφύλι	*stafeelee*	grape
σύκο	*seeko*	fig
χουρμάς	*khoormas*	date

Cheese Τυρί

φέτα *feta*
Popular crumbly salted white cheese made from goat's milk

γραβιέρα *ghravy-era*
A Swiss-style cheese; the best come from Crete and Dodoni (*Ipiros*)

κασέρι *kaseree*
Light, yellow cheese, rich in cream with a soft texture

κασκαβάλι *kaskavalee*
Yellow cheese, very creamy and rich

μανούρι *manooree*
Similar to cottage cheese; a tasty dessèrt when mixed with honey

Desserts/Pastries Επιδόρπια/Γλυκά

Greeks rarely eat dessert after their meal. Sweets are usually eaten
after the afternoon siesta and accompanied by a strong cup of coffee.

γρανίτα	*ghraneeta*	sherbet
καραμέλες	*karameles*	candy
καρυδόπιτα	*kareeτΗopeeta*	walnut cake
κρέμα καραμελέ	*krema karamele*	caramel custard
μηλόπιτα	*meelopeeta*	apple pie
παγωτό	*paghoto*	ice cream
ρυζόγαλο	*reezoghalo*	rice pudding
φρουτοσαλάτα	*frootosalata*	fruit salad
λουκούμι	*lookoomee*	Turkish delight

γαλακτομπούρεκο *ghalaktobooreko*
Flaky pastry filled with custard and steeped in syrup

κατάιφι *kata-eefee*
Shredded pastry roll filled with nuts and steeped in syrup

κοπεγχάγη *kopenkhaghee*
Filo pastry filled with almonds, orange juice, and cinnamon

μπακλαβάς *baklavas*
Baklava; a flaky pastry with a nut filling

χαλβάς *khalvas*
Halva; sesame seed paste and sugar

DRINKS

Aperitifs Απεριτίφ

The usual aperitif is ouzo (**oozo**). Your drink will be served with a few savory **mezeTHes**, such as octopus, pieces of cheese, and olives.

I'd like an ouzo.   Θα ήθελα ένα ούζο. *tha eethela ena oozo*

Beer Μπύρα

Do you have ... beer?	Έχετε ... μπύρα;	*ekhete ... beera*
bottled	εμφιαλωμένη	*emfee-alomenee*
draft	βαρελίσια	*vareleeseea*
light/dark	ξανθή/μαύρη	*ksanthee/mavree*

Wine Κρασί

Among the top rated are the red wines from the Averof vineyards and the Athos Peninsula. Porto Carras in Chalkidiki and Achaea Clauss in northwest Peloponnisos produce excellent wines at affordable prices. Also well known is the sweet muscat from Samos and Mavrodaphni. A type of typically Greek wine that takes some getting used to is retsina, essentially a white wine containing pine resin.

Wine is usually produced locally; if you ask for house wine (**krasee varel<u>ee</u>seeo**), a restaurant owner will bring you a carafe of his very own wine, made from grapes from his few square meters of vineyard.

I'd like a bottle of red/ blush [rosé]/white wine.	Θα ήθελα ένα μπουκάλι κόκκινο/ροζέ/ άσπρο κρασί. *tha <u>ee</u>thela <u>e</u>na book<u>a</u>lee kokeeno/roze/aspro kras<u>ee</u>*
a carafe	μια καράφα *mia kar<u>a</u>fa*
a liter	ένα λίτρο *<u>e</u>na l<u>ee</u>tro*
dry/sweet	ξηρό/γλυκό *ksee<u>ro</u>/ghl<u>ee</u>k<u>o</u>*
light/full-bodied	ελαφρύ/δυνατό *elaf<u>ree</u>/THeen<u>a</u>to*
chilled	παγωμένο *pagh<u>o</u>meno*
a corkscrew	ένα τιρμπουσόν *<u>e</u>na teermboos<u>on</u>*
Cheers!	Στην υγειά σας *stin iyi<u>a</u> sas*

Other alcoholic drinks

Note that brandy is **kon<u>ee</u>ak** and rum is **r<u>oo</u>mee**—other spirits are known by their English names (whisky, vodka, gin, etc.).

straight [neat]	σκέτο *sk<u>e</u>to*
on the rocks	με πάγο *me p<u>a</u>gho*
and soda	και σόδα *ke s<u>o</u>THa*
glass	ένα ποτήρι *<u>e</u>na pot<u>e</u>ree*
bottle	ένα μπουκάλι *<u>e</u>na book<u>a</u>lee*

κίτρο *k<u>ee</u>tro*
A sweet liqueur, with a citrus flavor; found on the island of Naxos

Μεταξά *metaksa*
A Greek brandy (from three to seven stars, indicating quality)

κουμ-κουάτ *koom-kooat*
Orange-colored brandy made from tiny oranges (*Corfu*)

Non-alcoholic drinks

The most popular drink in the summer is **frape,** iced coffee shaken
with or without milk and sugar. Freshly squeezed juices are also
widely consumed. Tap water is drinkable almost everywhere, but if
you prefer you can get bottled water (**emfeealomeno**).

coffee	ένα καφέ	*ena kafe*
instant	ένα Νεσκαφέ	*ena neskafe*
Greek	ελληνικό	*eleeneeko*
black	σκέτο	*sketo*
with cream/milk	με κρέμα/γάλα	*me krema/ghala*
tea	ένα τσάι	*ena tsaee*
with milk/lemon	με γάλα/με λεμόνι	*me ghala/me lemonee*
iced tea	ένα παγωμένο τσάι	*ena paghomeno tsaee*
fruit juice	ένα χυμό φρούτων	*ena kheemo frooton*
mineral water	ένα μεταλλικό νερό	*ena metaleeko nero*
carbonated/	αεριούχο/χωρίς ανθρακικό	

MENU READER

This Menu Reader gives listings of common food types and dishes.
The Greek words are shown in large type to help you identify the basic
ingredients making up a dish from a menu that has no English. Note that
tavernas rarely have menus, but you could ask the waiter to write down the
dish if you don't understand what's on offer.

του φούρνου	too _foorno_	baked
της σχάρας	tees _skharas_	barbecued, grilled
βραστός	vras_tos_	boiled
λαδερό	la_THero_	cooked in olive oil
τηγανητός	teeghanee_tos_	fried
μαρινάτος	maree_natos_	marinated
ποσέ	po_se_	poached
ψητό	psee_to_	roasted, baked
παστός	pas_tos_	salted
μαγειρευτό	mayeere_fto_	stewed
γιαχνί	yakh_nee_	stewed in tomato sauce
κρασάτο	kra_sato_	stewed in wine
γεμιστό	yemee_sto_	stuffed

Meat and poultry

κρέας	_kreas_	meat (general)
βοδινό	voTHee_no_	beef
χοιρινό	kheeree_no_	pork
κουνέλι	koo_nelee_	rabbit

αρνί	*ar<u>nee</u>*	lamb
κοτόπουλο	*ko<u>to</u>poolo*	chicken
πάπια	*<u>pa</u>pia*	duck
κιμάς	*kee<u>mas</u>*	ground meat
περιστέρι	*peree<u>ste</u>ree*	pigeon
μυαλό	*mia<u>lo</u>*	brains
κατσικάκι	*katsee<u>ka</u>kee*	goat
χήνα	*<u>khee</u>na*	goose

Fish

ψάρι	*<u>psa</u>ree*	fish (general)
θαλασσινά	*thalasee<u>na</u>*	seafood (general)
αντζούγιες	*ant<u>zoo</u>yes*	anchovies
μπακαλιάρος	*bakalee<u>a</u>ros*	cod
καβούρι	*ka<u>voo</u>ree*	crab
αστακός	*asta<u>kos</u>*	lobster
κέφαλος	*<u>ke</u>falos*	mullet
λιθρίνι	*lee<u>three</u>nee*	gray mullet
μύδια	*<u>mee</u>THya*	mussels
χταπόδι	*khtapo<u>THee</u>*	octopus
στρείδια	*<u>stree</u>THya*	oysters
γαρίδες	*gha<u>ree</u>THes*	shrimp
σαρδέλλα	*sar<u>THe</u>la*	sardine
καλαμάρι	*kala<u>ma</u>ree*	squid
τόννος	*<u>to</u>nos*	tuna

Vegetables

λαχανικά	*lakhaneeka*	vegetables (general)
αγκινάρες	*ageenares*	artichokes
μελιτζάνες	*meleetzanes*	eggplant
λάχανο	*lakhano*	cabbage
αγγούρι	*agooree*	cucumber
χωριάτικη σαλάτα	*khoryateekee salata*	Greek salad
καρότα	*karota*	carrots
σέλινο	*seleeno*	celery
κολοκύθι	*kolokeethee*	zucchini
μπάμιες	*bamee-es*	okra
κρεμμύδια	*kremeeтнya*	onions
αρακάς	*arakas*	peas
πατάτες	*patates*	potatoes
σαλάτα	*salata*	salad
σπανάκι	*spanakee*	spinach
ντομάτα	*domata*	tomato

Fruit

φρούτα	*froota*	fruit (general)
μήλο	*meelo*	apple
βερύκοκο	*vereekoko*	apricot
μπανάνα	*banana*	banana
χουρμάς	*khoormas*	date

σύκο	*seeko*	fig
σταφύλι	*stafeelee*	grape
γκρέιπφρουτ	*grapefruit*	grapefruit
λεμόνι	*lemonee*	lemon
πεπόνι	*peponee*	melon
πορτοκάλι	*portokalee*	orange
ροδάκινο	*roтнakeeno*	peach
αχλάδι	*akhlaтнee*	pear
ανανάς	*ananas*	pineapple
δαμάσκηνο	*тнamaskeeno*	plum
φράουλα	*fraoola*	strawberry

Staples, beans, and bread

ψωμί	*psomee*	bread
ρεβύθια	*reveetheea*	chickpeas
φακές	*fakes*	lentils
ζυμαρικά	*zeemareeka*	pasta
ρύζι	*reezee*	rice
ψωμάκι	*psomakee*	bread roll
ζάχαρη	*zakharee*	sugar
ταχινόσουπα	*takheenosoopa*	sesame seed soup
ψωμί φρυγανιά	*psomee freeghaneea*	toast
λαγάνα	*laghana*	unleavened bread

Classic dishes

μελιτζανοσαλάτα	*meleetzanosalata*	a dip of baked eggplant mashed with garlic, lemon, and olive oil
τζατζίκι	*tzatzeekee*	tzatziki; a dip of yogurt, garlic, cucumber, and olive oil
ταραμοσαλάτα	*taramosalata*	taramasalata, cod roe dip
κεφτεδάκια	*kefteTHakeea*	fried meat balls containing onions, bread crumbs, and herbs
σπανακόπιτα	*spanakopeeta*	pastry pies filled with spinach, feta, and eggs
μουσακάς	*moosakas*	moussaka; oven-baked layers of sliced eggplant and ground meat topped with bechamel sauce
ντολμαδάκια	*dolmaTHakeea*	vine leaves stuffed with rice and onions and flavored with herbs (sometimes containing ground meat)

Drinks

νερό	*nero*	water
μεταλλικό νερό	*metaleeko nero*	mineral water
τσάι	*tsaee*	tea
καφέ	*kafe*	coffee (instant)
Ελληνικό καφέ	*eleeneeko kafe*	Greek coffee

Μεταξά	*metaksa*	Metaxa, a Greek brandy
μπύρα	*beera*	beer
ούζο	*oozo*	ouzo
κρασί	*krasee*	wine
χυμό φρούτων	*kheemo frooton*	fruit juice
χυμό πορτοκάλι	*kheemo portokalee*	orange juice
χυμό λεμόνι	*kheemo lemonee*	lemon juice
λεμονάδα	*lemonaтна*	lemonade

Snacks

σάντουιτς	*sandwitch*	sandwich
ελιές (γεμιστές)	*elee-es (yemeestes)*	(stuffed) olives
μπιφτέκι	*beeftekee*	burger with breadcrumbs, onions, and herbs grilled over charcoal, sometimes topped with cheese or egg
τσιπς	*chips*	potato chips
πατάτες τηγανητές	*patates teeghaneetes*	french fries
λουκάνικα	*lookaneeka*	sausages
μπισκότα	*beeskota*	cookies
κέικ	*cake*	cake
τυροπιττάκια	*teeropeetakia*	baked triangular pastries containing feta and another hard cheese

Dairy products

αυγά	*avgha*	eggs
γιαούρτι	*yaoortee*	yogurt
κρέμα	*krema*	cream
βούτυρο	*vooteero*	butter
γάλα	*ghala*	milk
τυρί	*teeree*	cheese
φέτα	*feta*	feta; crumbly salted white cheese made from goat's milk
μυζήθρα	*meezeethra*	salted white soft cheese made from ewe's milk
μανούρι	*manooree*	similar to cottage cheese, a tasty dessert when mixed with honey

Herbs and spices

βασιλικός	*vaseeleekos*	basil
κανέλλα	*kanela*	cinnamon
γαρύφαλλο	*ghareefalo*	cloves
άνηθος	*aneethos*	dill
σκόρδο	*skorTHo*	garlic
δυόσμος	*THeeozmos*	mint
μουστάρδα	*moostarTHa*	mustard
ρίγανη	*reeghanee*	oregano
μαϊντανός	*maeeTHanos*	parsley
πιπέρι	*peeperee*	pepper

δεντρολίβανο	ᴛHendroleevano	rosemary
σαφράνη	safranee	saffron
αλάτι	alatee	salt
θυμάρι	theemaree	thyme

Desserts

τούρτα αμυγδάλου	toorta ameeghᴛHaloo	almond cake
ρεβανί	revanee	almond sponge cake with syrup
μπακλαβάς	baklavas	baklava; a flaky pastry with nut filling
κρέμα καραμελέ	krema karamele	caramel custard
δίπλες	ᴛHeeples	crispy fried dough sprinkled with nuts and sweetened with honey
φρουτοσαλάτα	frootosalata	fruit salad
χαλβάς	khalvas	halva; sesame seed paste and sugar, sometimes with pistachio nuts
μέλι	melee	honey
μαντολάτο	mandolato	nougat
παγωτό	paghoto	ice cream
ρυζόγαλο	reezoghalo	rice pudding
πάστα	pasta	cake
τάρτα	tarta	fruit tart

πίτα	*peeta*	pie
λουκουμάδες	*lookoomaтнes*	fritters; served with honey and cinnamon
μελομακάρονα	*melomakarona*	small Christmas cakes, containing walnuts and cinnamon
τσουρέκι	*tsoorekee*	similar to the Italian Panattone

ITALIAN

ESSENTIALS	
Hello.	**Ciao.** _chaao_
Good evening.	**Buonasera.** _bwona sayra_
A table for …	**Un tavolo per …** _oon tavolo pehr_
1/2/3/4.	**uno(-a)/due/tre/quattro.** _oono(-a)/doo-ay/tray/kwattro_
Thank you.	**Grazie.** _graatseeay_
The check, please.	**Il conto, per piacere.** _eel konto pehr peeachayray_
Good-bye.	**Arrivederci.** _arreevaydehrchee_

PLACES TO EAT

Most restaurants display a menu in the window. Many offer a tourist menu (**menù turistico**), a fixed-price three- or four-course meal with limited choice, or the specialty of the day (**piatto del giorno**). All restaurants must issue a formal bill (**la ricevuta fiscale**) with VAT, or sales tax (**I.V.A.**). A customer may actually be stopped outside the premises and fined if he or she cannot produce this receipt. The bill usually includes cover (**il coperto**) and service (**il servizio**) charges as well.

Autogrill _owtogreel_
A large restaurant on an expressway

Bar _bar_
Found on virtually every street corner; pay first and get a ticket from the cashier—then go to the counter and order

Caffè *kaffeh*
Coffee shop; generally food isn't served there except for breakfast; alcoholic beverages are also served

Gelateria *jaylatayreea*
Ice-cream parlor; Italian ice cream is very tasty, rich and creamy, often reminiscent of old-fashioned, homemade ice cream

Locanda *lokanda*
Simple restaurant serving local dishes

Osteria *ostayreea*
Inn; wine and simple food are served

Paninoteca *paneenotayka*
A sort of coffee shop where you can find sandwiches (**panini**), served hot or cold

Ristorante *reestorantay*
Classified by stars or forks and knives and endorsed by everyone including travel agencies and gastronomic guilds

Trattoria *trattoreea*
Simple food served; can be surprisingly good if you happen upon the right place

MEAL TIMES

La colazione *la kolatseeonay*
Breakfast: 7–10 a.m. Italians usually have a cappuccino and a brioche

Il pranzo *eel prandzo*
Lunch: 12:30–2 p.m.

La cena *la chayna*
Dinner: Begins at 8 p.m.

The names of meals can be confusing. Lunch is sometimes called **colazione** and dinner **pranzo**. If you are invited out, make sure of the time, so you don't turn up at the wrong meal.

ITALIAN CUISINE

Italian cuisine consists of a lot more than just pasta. You will be amazed at the rich variety available: tasty hors d'œuvres, long-simmered soups, traditional meat dishes, fresh fish and shellfish, high-quality poultry, an incredible number of cheeses, not to mention the magnificent cakes and ice cream.

Each of Italy's 18 regions has its own specialty, never lacking in flavor or originality, inspired by sun-drenched fruit and vegetables. Italian cooking is like the country itself: colorful, happy, generous, exuberant.

FINDING A PLACE TO EAT

Can you recommend a good restaurant?	**Può consigliare un buon ristorante?** *pwo konseelyaaray oon bwon reestorantay*
Is there a … near here?	**C'è … qui vicino?** *cheh … kwee veecheeno*
traditional local restaurant	**un ristorante con cucina tradizionale** *oon reestorantay kon koocheena tradeetseeonaalay*
inexpensive restaurant	**una trattoria** *oona trattoreea*
vegetarian restaurant	**un ristorante vegetariano** *oon reestorantay vayjaytareeaano*
Where can I find a/an …?	**Dove si trova …?** *dovay see trova*
café	**un bar** *oon bar*
fast-food restaurant	**una tavola calda (un self-service)** *oona tavola kalda (oon self-service)*
ice-cream parlor	**una gelateria** *oona jaylatayreea*
pizzeria	**una pizzeria** *oona peettsayreea*

RESERVATIONS

I'd like to reserve a table for 2.	**Vorrei prenotare un tavolo per due.** *vorrehee praynotaaray oon tavolo pehr dooay*
For this evening/ tomorrow at ...	**Per questa sera/domani alle ...** *pehr kwaysta sayra/domanee allay*
We'll come at 8:00.	**Arriveremo alle otto.** *arreevayraymo allay otto*
We have a reservation.	**Abbiamo una prenotazione.** *abbeeamo oona praynotatseeonay*

YOU MAY HEAR

A che nome, prego?	What's the name, please?
Mi dispiace.	I'm sorry.
Siamo al completo.	We're very busy/full.

Could we sit over there?	**Possiamo sederci là?** *posseeaamo saydayrchee la*
in a non-smoking area	**in una zona per non fumatori** *een oona dzona pehr non foomatoree*
by the window	**vicino alla finestra** *veecheeno alla feenaystra*

ORDERING

Excuse me!	**Scusi!** *scoosee*
May I see the wine list, please?	**Posso vedere la lista dei vini, per piacere?** *posso vedayray la leesta dehee veenee pehr peeachayray*

YOU MAY HEAR

E' pronto(-a) per ordinare?	Are you ready to order?
Che cosa prende/desidera?	What would you like?
Consiglio …	I recommend …
Non abbiamo …	We haven't got …
Vuole … con il Suo piatto?	Would you like … with your dish?

Do you have a set menu? **Avete un menù fisso?**
avaytay oon maynoo feesso

Can you recommend some typical local dishes? **Può consigliare dei piatti tipici della regione?** _pwo konseelyaarmee dehee peeattee teepeechee daylla rayjonay_

What is … ? **Cos'è …?** _kozay_

I'd like … **Vorrei …** _vorrehee_

a bottle/glass/ carafe of … **una bottiglia/un bicchiere/una caraffa di …** _oona botteelya/oon beekkeeehray/oona karaffa dee_

SPECIAL REQUESTS

I prefer … without the … **Preferisco … senza …** _prayfayreesko … sayntsa_

Could I have salad instead of vegetables, please? **Si può avere insalata al posto della verdura?** _see pwo avayray eensalaata al posto daylla verdoora_

Does the meal come with vegetables/ potatoes? **Il piatto include legumi/patate?** _eel peeatto eenklooday laygoomee/patatay_

Do you have any sauces? **Ha delle salse?** _ah dayllay salsay_

May I have some …?	**Mi può portare …?**
	mee pwo portaaray
bread	**del pane** *dayl panay*
butter	**del burro** *dayl boorro*
lemon	**del limone** *dayl leemonay*
mustard	**della senape** *daylla saynapay*
pepper	**del pepe** *dayl paypay*
salt	**del sale** *dayl salay*
seasoning (oil/vinegar)	**dei condimenti (olio/aceto)**
	dehee kondeemayntee (olyo/achayto)
sugar	**dello zucchero** *dayllo tsookkayro*
(artificial) sweetener	**del dolcificante** *dayl dolcheefeekantay*
Could you bring a child's seat, please?	**Può portare un seggiolone per bambini, per piacere?**
	pwo portaaray oon saydjolonay pehr bambeenee pehr peeachayray

GENERAL QUESTIONS

Could you bring a(n) (clean) …, please?	**Può portare … (pulito), per piacere?**
	pwo portaaray (pooleeto) pehr peeachayray
ashtray	**un portacenere**
	oon portachaynayray
cup/glass	**una tazza/un bicchiere**
	oona tattsa/oon beekkeeeehray
fork/knife	**una forchetta/un coltello**
	oona forkehtta/oon koltehllo
napkin	**un tovagliolo** *oon tovalyolo*

156

plate/spoon/little spoon	**un piatto/un cucchiaio/un cucchiaino** *oon peeatto/oon kookkeeaeeo/oon kookkeeaeeno*
I'd like …	**Vorrei …** *vorrehee*
a beer	**una birra** *oona beerra*
coffee	**un caffè** *oon kaffeh*
with milk	**con latte** *kon lattay*
tea	**un tè** *oon teh*
red/white wine	**del vino rosso/bianco** *dayl veeno rosso/beeanko*
Where are the restrooms?	**Dov'è la toilette?** *dovay la toylayttay*

SPECIAL REQUIREMENTS

I can't eat food containing …	**Non posso mangiare piatti che contengono …** *non posso manjaaray peeattee kay kontayngono*
salt/sugar	**sale/zucchero** *salay/tsookkayro*
Do you have meals/ drinks for diabetics?	**Avete piatti/bevande per diabetici?** *avaytay peeattee/bayvanday pehr deeabayteechee*
Do you have vegetarian dishes?	**Avete piatti vegetariani?** *avaytay peeattee vayjaytareeanee*

COMPLAINTS

There must be some mistake.	**Deve esserci un errore.** *dayvay ehssayrchee oon ehrroray*
That's not what I ordered.	**Non ho ordinato questo.** *non oh ordeenaato kwaysto*
I ordered …	**Ho ordinato …** *oh ordeenaato*

The meat is …	**La carne è …** la <u>kar</u>nay eh
overdone	**troppo cotta** <u>troppo</u> <u>kotta</u>
underdone	**non abbastanza cotta** non abba<u>stant</u>sa <u>kotta</u>
too tough	**troppo dura** <u>troppo</u> <u>doora</u>
This … is cold.	**Questo … è freddo.** kwaysto … eh <u>frehddo</u>
This isn't fresh.	**Questo non è fresco.** kwaysto non eh <u>fraysko</u>
How much longer will our food be?	**Quanto dobbiamo aspettare ancora?** <u>kwanto</u> dobbee<u>aa</u>mo aspay<u>tta</u>ray an<u>ko</u>ra
We can't wait any longer. We're leaving.	**Non possiamo più aspettare.** **Andiamo via.** non possee<u>aa</u>mo pee<u>oo</u> aspeht<u>taa</u>ray andee<u>aa</u>mo <u>vee</u>a

PAYING

Tipping: See page 332.

You may find **coperto** (cover charge), **supplemento** (surcharge) added to your bill.

The check, please.	**Il conto, per piacere.** eel <u>konto</u> pehr peea<u>chay</u>ray
We'd like to pay separately.	**Vorremmo pagare separatamente.** vor<u>rehm</u>mo pa<u>gaa</u>ray sayparata<u>mayn</u>tay
It's all together, please.	**Un conto unico, per piacere.** oon <u>konto</u> <u>oo</u>neeko pehr peea<u>chay</u>ray
I think there's a mistake.	**Penso ci sia un errore.** <u>payn</u>so chee <u>see</u>a oon ehr<u>ro</u>ray

158

What is this amount for?	**Per cosa è questa cifra?**
	pehr kosa eh kwaysta cheefra
I didn't order that.	**Non ho ordinato questo. Ho preso …**
I had …	*non oh ordeenaato kwaysto. oh prayzo*
I would like to pay with this credit card.	**Vorrei pagare con la carta di credito.**
	vorrehee pagaaray kon la karta dee kraydeeto
Could I have a receipt?	**Vorrei la ricevuta.**
	vorrehee la reechayvoota

COURSE BY COURSE
Breakfast Colazione

I'd like …	**Vorrei …** *vorrehee*
eggs	**delle uova** *dayllay wova*
fried/scrambled	**fritte/strapazzate**
	freettay/strapattsaatay
fruit juice	**un succo di frutta**
	oon sookko dee froota
grapefruit/orange	**un pompelmo/un'arancia**
	oon pompaylmo/oon arancheea
milk	**del latte** *dayl lattay*
jam	**della marmellata** *daylla marmayllaata*
marmalade	**della marmellata d'arance**
	daylla marmayllaata daranchay
honey	**del miele** *dayl mee-aylay*
rolls	**dei panini** *dehee paneenee*
toast	**del pane tostato**
	dayl paanay tostaato

Appetizers Antipasti

anchovies	**acciughe** _achoogay_	
assorted appetizer	**antipasto assortito** _anteepasto assorteeto_	
artichoke hearts in olive oil	**carciofini sott'olio** _karchofeenee sottolyo_	
cured pork shoulder	**coppa** _koppa_	
Bologna sausage	**mortadella** _mortadehlla_	
cured ham from Parma	**prosciutto crudo di Parma** _proshootto kroodo dee parma_	
pickled vegetables	**sottaceti** _sottachaytee_	

Bagna cauda _baanya kaooda_

Raw vegetables accompanied by a hot sauce made from anchovies, garlic, oil, butter, and sometimes truffles (northern Italy)

Pizza

Pizza (plural **pizze**) is one of Italy's best-known culinary exports. A **calzone** has basically the same ingredients, but the pastry forms a sealed sandwich, with the filling inside.

con i funghi	_kon ee foonggee_	with mushrooms
capricciosa	_kapreetchosa_	the cook's specialty
siciliana	_seecheeleeaana_	with black olives, capers, and cheese

Margherita _margayreeta_
Named after Italy's first queen, the pizza ingredients (tomato, cheese, and basil or oregano) reflect the national colors

Napoletana _napolaytaana_
The classic pizza with anchovies, tomatoes, and cheese

Quattro formaggi _kwattro formadjee_
Pizza with four types of cheese, including **gorgonzola** and **caciotta**

Quattro stagioni _kwattro stajonee_
"Four seasons", containing a variety of vegetables: tomatoes, artichokes, mushrooms, olives; plus cheese and ham

Soups Zuppe

brodo di manzo	_brodo dee manzo_	beef broth
busecca	_boozaykka_	thick tripe, vegetable, and bean soup
cacciucco	_kachookko_	spicy seafood chowder/stew
crema di legumi	_krehma dee laygoomee_	legumes cream soup
minestrone	_meenehstronay_	vegetable soup (some times with noodles) sprinkled with parmesan cheese
passato di verdura	_passaato dee vehrdoora_	mashed vegetable soup, generally with croutons
zuppa alla pavese	_tsooppa alla pavayzay_	consommé with egg, croutons, and cheese
zuppa di vongole	_tsooppa dee vonggolay_	clams and white wine soup

Pasta

Pasta (or **pastasciutta**) constitutes the traditional first course.
In addition to **spaghetti**, pasta comes in a variety of sizes and shapes, **penne** (quills), **tagliatelle** (flat noodles), and the following examples:

Cannelloni _kanaylonee_
Tubular dough stuffed with meat, cheese, or vegetables; covered with a white sauce and baked

Cappelletti _kapaylayttee_
Small ravioli filled with meat, ham, cheese, and eggs

Fettuccine *faytoocheenay*
Narrow flat noodles made with eggs

Lasagne *lazaanyay*
Thin layers of white or green (**lasagne verdi**) dough alternating with tomato sauce and ground meat, white sauce, and grated cheese; baked in the oven

Tortellini *tortehlleenee*
Rings of dough filled with ground meat in broth or with a sauce

Fish and seafood Pesci e frutti di mare

acciughe	*atchoogay*	anchovies
anguilla	*anggooeella*	eel
bianchetti	*beeangkayttee*	herring
gamberi	*gambayree*	shrimp
granchi	*grangkee*	crabs
merluzzo	*mayrloottso*	cod
polipo	*poleepo*	octopus
sogliola	*solyola*	sole

Fish specialties Specialità di pesce
Anguilla alla veneziana *anggooeella alla vaynaytseeaana*
Eel cooked in sauce made from tuna and lemon

Fritto misto *freetto meesto*
Fry of small fish and shellfish

Lumache alle milanese *loomaakay allay meelanaysay*
Snails with anchovy, fennel, and wine sauce

Stoccafisso *stokkafeesso*
Dried cod cooked with tomatoes, olives, and artichokes

Meat Carne
Small fowl considered gourmet dishes are lark (**allodola**) and ortolan (**ortolano**), grilled or roasted.

Vorrei …	*vorrehee*	I'd like some …
del manzo	*dayl mandzo*	beef
del pollo	*dayl pollo*	chicken
dell'anatra	*dayllaanatra*	duck
dell'oca	*daylloka*	goose
del prosciutto	*dayl proshootto*	ham
dell'agnello	*dayllanyehllo*	lamb
del maiale	*dayl maeeaalay*	pork
delle salsicce	*dayllay salseetchay*	sausages
del vitello	*dayl veetehllo*	veal

Meat dishes Piatti di carne

Bistecca alla fiorentina *beestaykka alla feeoraynteena*
Grilled steak flavored with pepper, lemon juice, and parsley

Cima alla genovese *cheema alla jaynovaysay*
Rolled veal stuffed with eggs, sausage, and mushrooms

Cotoletta alla milanese *kostolaytta alla meelanaysay*
Breaded veal cutlet

Fegato alla veneziana *faygato alla vaynaytseeaana*
Thin slices of calf's liver fried with onions

Filetto al pepe verde *feelaytto al paypay vehrday*
Filet steak in a creamy sauce with green peppercorns

Galletto amburghese *gallaytto amboorgaysay*
Young tender chicken, oven-roasted

Involtini *eenvolteenee*
Thin slices of meat rolled and stuffed with ham

Polenta e coniglio *polehnta ay koneelyo*
Rabbit stew with cornmeal mush

Pollo alla romana *pollo alla romaana*
Diced chicken with tomato sauce and sweet peppers

Saltimbocca alla romana *salteembokah alla romaana*
Veal cutlet braised in marsala wine with ham and sage

Vegetables/Salads Verdure/Insalate

You'll recognize: **asparagi**, **broccoli**, **carote**, **patate**, **spinaci**, **zucchini**.

cavolo	*kaavolo*	cabbage
cipolle	*cheepollay*	onions
funghi	*foonggee*	mushrooms
insalata mista	*eensalaata meesta*	mixed salad
lattuga	*lattooga*	lettuce
piselli	*peesehllee*	peas
pomodoro	*pomodoro*	tomato
ruchetta	*rookettah*	arugula/rocket
verdura mista	*vehrdoora meesta*	mixed vegetables

Carciofi alla giudea *karchofee alla jeeoodeea*
Deep-fried artichoke, originally a specialty of the old Jewish quarter in Rome

Carciofi alla romana *karchofee alla romaana*
Whole lightly stewed artichokes stuffed with garlic, salt, olive oil, wild mint (**mentuccia**), and parsley

Fagioli alla toscana *fajolee alla toskana*
Beans, seasoned with salt, black pepper, and olive oil

Fagioli in umido *fajolee een oomeedo*
All types of haricot beans cooked in tomato sauce and spices

Funghi porcini arrosto *foonggee porcheenee arrosto*
Boletus mushrooms with garlic, parsley, and chili peppers

Peperoni ripieni *paypayronee reepeeaynee*
Stuffed sweet peppers (usually containing ground meat); zucchini is also served this way (**zucchini ripieni**)

Sauces Salsa

al burro	*al boorro*	butter, grated parmesan
bolognese	*bolonyayzay*	tomatoes, ground meat, onions, herbs
carbonara	*karbonaara*	bacon, cheese, eggs, oil
pesto	*paysto*	basil leaves, garlic, cheese
al pomodoro	*al pommodoro*	tomatoes, garlic, basil

Cheese Formaggio

bel paese	smooth cheese with delicate taste
caciotta	firm, usually mild cheese
caciocavallo	firm, slightly sweet cheese from cow's or sheep's milk
gorgonzola	blue-veined cheese, rich with a tangy flavor
grana	a grained cheese similar to parmesan originating from Padova usually grated on pasta dishes
mascarpone	a thick, full-fat creamy cheese mostly used for desserts; similar to clotted cream
mozzarella	soft, unripened cheese, made from buffalo's milk in the south, elsewhere with cow's milk
parmigiano (-reggiano)	parmesan, a hard cheese generally grated for use in hot dishes and pasta but also eaten alone
pecorino	a hard cheese with a strong flavor made from sheep's milk usually grated on certain pasta dishes
provolone	a firm, tasty cheese
ricotta	soft cow's or sheep's milk cheese

Fruit Frutta

You'll recognize: **banane**, **dattero**, **limone**, **melone**, **pera**.

ciliege	*cheelee-ehjay*	cherries
uva	*oova*	grapes
arancia	*arancha*	orange
pesca	*pehska*	peach

prugna	_proonya_	plum
lamponi	_lamponee_	raspberries
fragole	_fraagolay_	strawberries
anguria	_angoorreea_	watermelon (northern Italy)
cocomero	_kokomayro_	watermelon (southern Italy)

Dessert Dolce

Cassata siciliana _kassaata seecheeleeaana_
Sponge cake with sweet cream cheese, chocolate, candied fruit

Tiramisù _teerameesoo_
Mascarpone, eggs, and sponge cake chocolate dessert

DRINKS

Aperitifs Aperitivi

americano _amayreekaano:_ vermouth with bitters, brandy, and lemon peel

aperol _apayrol:_ a non-alcoholic bitters

bitter analcolico _beettehr analkoleeko:_ a non-alcoholic aperitif

Campari _kampaaree:_ bitters with orange peel and herbs

Campari soda _kampaaree soda:_ Campari diluted with soda

Cynar _cheenaar:_ produced from artichoke

gingerino _jeenjehreeno:_ ginger-flavored aperitif

Martini _marhteenee:_ brand-name vermouth, sweet or dry

neat/straight	**liscio** _leesho_
on the rocks	**con ghiaccio** _kon geeacho_
with (seltzer) water	**con acqua (di seltz)** _kon akwa (dee sehltz)_

Beer Birra

Do you have … beer?	**Avete della birra …?**
	avayta daylla beerra
bottled/draft	**in bottiglia/alla spina**
	een botteelya/alla speena

Wine Vino

Some of the country's best come from northwestern Italy. Italy's best-known wines abroad are **Chianti classico** and **riserva** (superior quality); the best is produced between Florence and Siena.

Don't expect a trattoria to offer more than a few types of wine. In smaller places you may find **vino sfuso** (unbottled wine usually served as house wine) at a moderate price.

I'd like a bottle of white/red wine.	**Vorrei una bottiglia di vino bianco/rosso.** _vorrehee oona botteelya dee veeno beeanko/rosso_
I'd like the house wine, please.	**Desidero il vino della casa, per favore.** _dayzeedayro eel veeno dayllya kassa pehr favoray_
I'd like a corkscrew.	**Vorrei un cavatappi.** _vorrehee oon kavatappee_
Cheers!	**Salute!** _salooteh_

Reading the label

abboccato semi-dry	**leggero** light
amabile slightly sweet	**pieno** full-bodied
bianco white	**rosato/rosatello** rosé
DOC guarantee of origin	**rosso** red
DOCG highest quality wine	**secco** dry
dolce sweet	**spumante** sparkling
imbottigliato dal produttore bottled by producers	**vino del paese** local wine
	vino tipico basic table wine

Other drinks

You'll recognize: **brandy**, **cognac**, **gin e tonic**, **porto**, **rum**, **vodka**.

If you'd like something that approaches French cognac try _Vecchia Romagna etichetta nera_ or _Carpenet Malvolta Stravecchio_. Or, try an after-dinner drink (**un digestivo**):

Amaro *amaaro*

Bitter: *Amaro Averna*, *Amaro Lucano* or *Amaro Montenegro* (bittersweet), or *Fernet-Branca* (very bitter)

Liquore *leekworay*

Strega (sweet herb), *Sambuca* (aniseed-flavored), *Amaretto* (almond), *Millefiori* (herb and alpine flower), *Silvestro* (herb and nut)

Non-alcoholic drinks

I'd like (a) …	**Vorrei …** *vorrehee*
hot chocolate	**una cioccolata calda** *oona chokkolaata kalda*
lemonade	**una limonata** *oona leemonaata*
milk shake	**un frullato** *oon froollaato*
mineral water	**dell'acqua minerale** *dayllakwa meenayraalay*
carbonated/ non-carbonated	**gassata/naturale** *gassaata/natooraalay*
tonic water	**dell'acqua tonica** *dayllakwa toneeka*

Un caffè *oon kaffeh*

Try **un caffè** (espresso), strong and dark with a rich aroma, served in demi-tasses, or **un ristretto** (concentrated espresso); alternatively, ask for **un caffè lungo** (weaker coffee), which can be **con panna** (with cream), or **con latte** (with milk). **Un cappuccino** (coffee and hot milk, sometimes dusted with cocoa) is also a must; while in summer, **un caffè freddo** (iced coffee) is popular.

Un succo di frutta *oon sookko dee frootta*

Common juices include: **un succo di limone** (lemon), **di pompelmo** (grapefruit), **di pomodoro** (tomato), and **d'arancia** (orange); for a freshly squeezed fruit juice ask for **una spremuta**.

MENU READER

a puntino	*a poonteeno*	medium
affumicato(-a)	*affoomeekaato(-a)*	smoked
al forno	*al forno*	baked
al sangue	*al sanway*	rare/underdone
al vapore	*al vaporay*	steamed
alla griglia	*alla greelya*	grilled
arrosto(-a)	*arrosto(-a)*	roasted
ben cotto(-a)	*behn kotto (a)*	well-done
bollito(-a)	*bolleeto(-a)*	boiled
fritto(-a)	*freetto(-a)*	fried
impanato(-a)	*eempanaato(-a)*	breaded
in camicia	*een kameecha*	poached
in purè	*een pooreh*	creamed
in umido	*een oomeedo*	stewed
marinato(-a)	*mareenaato(-a)*	marinated
quasi crudo(-a)	*kwasee kroodo(-a)*	very rare
ripieno(-a)	*reepeeayno(-a)*	stuffed
saltato(-a)	*saltaato(-a)*	sautéed
speziato(-a)/piccante	*spaytsaato(-a)/peekkantay*	spicy
stufato(-a)	*stoofaato(-a)*	braised
tagliato(-a) a cubetti	*talyaato(-a) a koobayttee*	diced

A

a puntino medium
a scelta choice
abbacchio roast lamb; **~ al forno con patate** with potatoes; **~ alla cacciatora** "hunting style": diced and cooked with white wine, garlic, rosemary, anchovy paste and peppers
abbacchio alla scottadito tender grilled lamb cutlets

(all')abruzzese Abruzzi style; with red peppers and sometimes ham
acciughe anchovies
aceto vinegar
acetosella sorrel
acqua water; **~ calda** hot water; **~ minerale** mineral water; **~ tonica** tonic water
acquacotta soup of bread and vegetables, sometimes with egg and cheese

affettati cold cuts; **~ misti** mixed cuts of pork

affogato poached

aglio garlic; **~ olio, peperoncino** sauce of garlic, olive oil, sweet peppers, anchovies, and parmesan

agnello lamb; **~ abbacchio** very young lamb

agnolotti round-filled pasta

(all')agro dressing of lemon juice and oil

agrodolce sweet-sour dressing of caramelized sugar, vinegar, and flour

aguglie garfish

ai ferri grilled

ai funghi (pizza) with mushrooms

ai funghi porcini sauce of boletus mushrooms

al burro with butter and grated parmesan

al forno baked

al sangue rare/underdone

al sugo with tomato sauce and grated parmesan

al tartufo sauce of grated truffle

al, all', alla in the style of; with

ala wing

albicocca apricot

alfredo dairy sauce

alice anchovy

alici al limone baked anchovies with lemon juice

alla boscaiola with eggplant, mushrooms, and tomato sauce

alla carrettiera "cart driver style"; with hot peppers and pork

alla graticola barbequed

alla milanese with marrow, white wine, saffron, and parmesan

alla Norma with spices and tomato sauce (*Sicily*)

alla pescatora with tomatoes and seafood

alla rustica with garlic, anchovies, and oregano

alla spina draft (beer)

alle vongole sauce of clams, garlic, parsley, pepper, olive oil, sometimes tomatoes

allo spiedo broiled; spit-roasted

allodola lark

alloro bay leaf

amaro after-dinner drink/digestive

amatriciana sauce of tomatoes, pancetta, onions, garlic, and hot pepper

americano a vermouth

ananas pineapple

anelli small egg-pasta rings

anguilla eel; **~ alla veneziana** cooked in sauce made from tuna and lemon

anguria watermelon (*northern Italy*)

animelle di vitello calf's sweet-breads fried in butter and Marsala

anitra duck; **~ selvatica** wild duck

annegati slices of meat in white wine or Marsala

antipasti appetizers, hors d'oeuvres; **~ a scelta** of one's choice; **~ assortiti** assorted; **~ di mare** seafood

aperitivi aperitifs

Aperol a non-alcoholic bitters

arachidi peanuts

aragosta lobster

arancia orange

aranciata orangeade

arancini popular and tasty southern Italian rice snack specialties

aringa herring

arista loin of pork; ~ **alla fiorentina** roast with garlic, cloves, and rosemary

arrosto roast(ed)

arselle scallops

asparagi asparagus; ~ **alla Fiorentina** with fried eggs and cheese

assortito assorted

astice lobster

attesa: 15 minuti waiting time: 15 minutes

B

baccalà dried salt cod; ~ **alla romana** cooked with tomato sauce, garlic, and parsley; ~ **alla vicentina** cooked in milk

bagna cauda raw vegetables served with a hot sauce (*northern Italy*)

barbabietola beet

basilico basil

bavette type of flat spaghetti

beccaccia woodcock

beccaccino snipe

bel paese smooth cheese with delicate taste

bevande drinks; ~ **analcoliche** non-alcoholic drinks

bianchetti herring

bianco white (wine)

bibita soft drink

bicchiere glass

bieta swiss chard

bionda light (beer)

birra beer; ~ **rossa** stout (dark beer)

biscotti cookies/biscuits

bistecca steak; ~ **di cinghiale** wild boar in a sweet-sour sauce;

~ **alla fiorentina** grilled and flavored with pepper, lemon juice and parsley; ~ **di filetto** rib steak

bitter analcolico a non-alcoholic aperitif

bollito misto mixed boiled meats

bologna smooth, mild, slightly smoked sausage, usually of pork or beef, occasionally of veal or chicken

bolognese sauce of tomatoes, ground meat, onions, and herbs

bottiglia bottle

braciola chop or cutlet

branzino (sea) bass

brasato braised

briciolata olive oil, black pepper, and crisp breadcrumb sauce

broccoli broccoli; ~ **al burro e formaggio** with butter and cheese; ~ **alla romana** sauteed in olive oil and braised in wine

brodo bouillon, broth, soup

bruidda fish soup

bucatini thick spaghetti; ~ **con le sarde alla palermitana** with fresh sardines

budino pudding; ~ **di ricotta** souffle with ricotta cheese and candied fruits

burrida fish stew with dogfish and skate *(Sardinia)*

burro butter; ~ **e salvia** butter and sage sauce

busecca thick tripe, vegetable, and bean soup

C

cacciagione game

cacciucco spicy seafood chowder/stew

cachi persimmon

caciocavallo firm, slightly sweet cheese

caciotta firm, mild cheese

caffè coffee

caffè freddo iced coffee

calamaretti baby squid

calamari squid

caldo hot

camoscio chamois

Campari reddish-brown bitters, flavored with orange peel and herbs; has a quinine taste; **~ soda** *Campari* diluted with soda

canederli bread, ham, and salami dumplings

cannariculi fried honey biscuits

cannella cinnamon

cannelloni stuffed tubular pasta baked with a white sauce; **~ alla partenopea** with ricotta, mozzarella, and ham

cannoli sweetened ricotta cheese stuffed in deep-fried pastry shells

canoe di mele canoe-shaped pastry boats with rum pastry cream and glazed apples

canoe salate savory canoes

capellini thin type of spaghetti

caponata olives, eggplant, and anchovies *(Sicily)*

capone apparecchiate mahi mahi fish fried with tomatoes, capers, olives *(Sicily)*

cappelletti "little hats" filled pasta

capperi capers

cappone capon

capretto kid goat; **~ ripieno al forno** stuffed with herbs and oven-roasted

capricciosa the cook's specialty (pizza)

capriolo roebuck

carbonara sauce of bacon, pepper, pecorino, cheese, eggs, and olive oil

carciofi artichokes; **~ alla giudea** deep-fried; **~ alla romana** lightly stewed and stuffed

carciofini sott'olio artichoke hearts in olive oil

carne meat; **~ ai ferri** grilled

carota carrot; **~ rossa** beet

carpa carp

carrettiera sauce of tuna, mushrooms, tomato purée, freshly ground pepper

cassata ice cream with candied fruit (spumone); **~ siciliana** garnished sponge cake

castagna chestnut

castagnaccio chestnut cake with sultanas and pine nuts *(Tuscany)*

caviale caviar

cavolfiore cauliflower; **~ stracciato** boiled and fried in olive oil and garlic

cavolini di Bruxelles Brussels sprouts

cavolo cabbage

ceci chickpeas

cedro citron

cereali cereal

cervello brains

cervo deer

cetriolini pickles

cetriolo cucumber

chiodi di garofano cloves

cicoria chicory

ciliege cherries

cima alla genovese rolled veal stuffed with eggs, sausage, and mushrooms

cima genovese cold veal stuffed with onions, herbs, and calf's brains
cinghiale wild boar
cioccolata (calda) (hot) chocolate
cipolle onions
cipollina spring onion
clementino seedless mandarin orange
cocomero watermelon (*Rome, southern Italy*)
colazione breakfast
con with
con acqua (di seltz) with (seltzer or soda) water
con briciolata with toasted breadcrumbs
con i funghi with mushrooms
con ghiaccio on the rocks (with ice)
con il sugo di melanze e peperoni sauce with pepper and eggplant
con il latte with milk
con le lumache with snails and parsley
con il limone with lemon
con la panna with cream
con le polpettine with tiny meatballs
con la porchetta with tasty cold pork (sandwich)
con la salsa di noci with walnut sauce
conchiglie conch shell-shaped pasta
coniglio rabbit; **~ ai capperi** cooked with capers
contorno a scelta choice of vegetables
coppa cured pork shoulder
cosciotto leg
costata al prosciutto filled chop

costola rib
costolette di maiale al finocchio braised pork chops with white wine and fennel seed
cotechino con lenticchie sausage-like spicy pork mix
cotogna quince
cotoletta cutlet; **~ alla milanese** breaded veal cutlet
cotto cooked; **~ a vapore** steamed
cozze mussels
crema custard; **~ di legumi** legumes cream soup; **~ di pomodori** tomato cream soup
crespelle di farina dolce chestnut-flour crepes with ricotta and rum
crostacei shellfish
crostata pie; **~ di mele** apple pie; **~ di ricotta** cheesecake with raisins and Marsala
crudo di Parma cured ham from Parma
cumino cumin
cuscus couscous
Cynar aperitif produced from artichoke

D

d', di of
datteri dates
decaffeinato decaffeinated
dentice type of sea bream
digestivo after-dinner drink
ditali pasta thimbles
dolce cake; dessert; mild (cheese); sweet (wine)
doppio double (a double shot)

E

elicoidali short, twisted pasta tubes
eperlano smelt

F

fagiano pheasant; **~ al tartufo** stuffed with truffles

fagioli (haricot) beans; **~ all'uccelletto** cooked in tomatoes and black olives; **~ in umido** cooked in tomato sauce

fagioli alla toscana beans garnished with salt, black pepper, and olive oil

fagiolini green beans

faraona guinea fowl

farcito stuffed

farfalle butterfly-shaped pasta

farfallini small bow-shaped egg-pasta

favata beans and port stew *(Sardinia)*

fave broad beans

fazzoletti salati savory turnovers

fegato liver; **~ alla veneziana** thin slices fried with onions; **~ alla salvia** with tomatoes, garlic, and sage

fesa round cut from the rump

fetta di pizza slice of pizza

fettuccine egg-pasta ribbons; **~Alfredo** with parmesan and cream

fico fig

filetto filet; **~ al pepe verde** filet steak served in a creamy sauce with green peppercorns

finocchio fennel

focaccia savory flatbread; **~ alla salvia** sage bread; **~ alla salsiccia** sausage bread; **~ alle noci** walnut bread; **~ genovese** savory bread with sage and olive oil

focaccia al gorgonzola warm yeast flatbread topped with cheese

fonduta hot dip of Fontina cheese, egg yolks, and truffles

formaggio cheese

fragole strawberries

fragoline di bosco wild strawberries

freddo cold

frittata omelet; **~ campagnola** with onion, grated cheese, milk, and cream; **~ primaverile** with vegetables

fritte al buro nero brains with black butter

fritte alla fiorentina marinated, breaded, fried brains served with spinach

fritto fried

fritto misto a fry of various small fish and shellfish or meat and vegetables

frullato milk-shake

frustenga cornmeal fruit cake

frutta fruit

frutti di mare seafood

funghi mushrooms; **~ alla parmigiana** stuffed with breadcrumbs, Parmesan, garlic, herbs; **~ porcini arrosto** roasted or grilled with chili peppers

fusilli pasta twists

G

galletto amburghese young tender chicken, oven-roasted

gallina stewing fowl

gallo cedrone grouse

gamberetti shrimp

gamberi prawns

gassata carbonated (water)

gelato ice cream

gianduia cold chocolate pudding

gin e tonic gin and tonic
gingerino ginger-flavored aperitif
gnocchi alla genovese dumplings with pesto sauce
gnocchi di patate potato dumplings
gorgonzola blue-veined cheese
granchi crabs
granita coarse sorbet ice cream
gronghi conger eel

I

i nostri piatti di carne sono serviti con contorno our meat dishes are accompanied by vegetables
in bianco without tomato sauce
in bottiglia bottled (beer)
in casseruola in casserole
in umido stewed
indivia endive
insalata salad
insalata di frutti di mare shrimp and squid with lemon, pickles, and olives
insalata di pollo chicken salad with green salad, lemon, and cream
insalata mista mixed salad
insalata russa diced boiled vegetables in mayonnaise
involtini thin slices of meat (beef, veal, or pork) rolled and stuffed

L

lamponi raspberries
lamprede lampreys
lasagne thin layers of pasta lined with meat and tomato sauce with Bel Paese and Mozzarella cheeses; ~ **al forno** oven baked lasagna; ~ **con l'anitra** with duck; ~ **con le verdure** vegetable lasagna

lasagnette del lucchese lasagna with sauce of spinach, ricotta, chicken livers
lattaiolo cinnamon custard
latte milk
lattuga lettuce
lauro bay
leggero light (wine)
lenticchie lentils
lepre hare; ~ **in agrodolce** with pine kernels, sultanas, and chocolate; ~ **piemontese** cooked in Barbera wine, sprinkled with herbs and bitter chocolate
lesso boiled
limonata lemonade
limone lemon
lingua tongue
linguine type of flat spaghetti
liquore liqueur
liscio straight/neat
lo chef consiglia the chef recommends …
lombata/lombo loin
lombo di maiale al forno garlic-roasted pork loin
lombo di maiale al prosciutto grilled pork loin with prosciutto
luccio pike
luganeghe fresh pork sausages sold by the length
lumache snails; snail shell-shaped pasta
lumache alle milanese snails with anchovy, fennel, and wine sauce
lumache di mare sea snails
lunette half-moon-shaped stuffed pasta

M

maccheroni alla chitarra handmade pasta cut into strips
macchiato with milk (coffee)
maggiorana marjoram
maiale pork
malfatti thin pasta strips
mandarino tangerine
mandorle almonds
manzo beef
margherita tomato, cheese, and basil pizza
marinara sauce of tomatoes, olives, garlic, clams, and mussels
marinato marinated
marmellata jam; ~ **d'arance** marmalade
mascarpone a thick, full-fat creamy cheese mostly used for desserts, similar to clotted cream
Martini a brand-name vermouth, sweet or dry; not to be confused with a martini cocktail
medaglioni round filet
mela apple
melanzane eggplant
mele apples
melone melon
menta mint
menù a prezzo fisso set menu
merlano whiting
merluzzo cod
mezzo pollo arrosto half a roasted chicken
midollo marrow
miele honey
minestra soup; ~ **di funghi** cream of mushroom soup; ~ **di sedano e riso** celery and rice; ~ **in brodo** with noodles or rice

minestrone a thick vegetable soup (sometimes with noodles) sprinkled with parmesan cheese
mirtilli blueberries
misto mixed
molle soft (egg)
montone mutton
more blackberries
mortadella Bologna sausage
mostaccioli chocolate biscuits
mozzarella soft, unripened cheese; ~ **con i pomodori** with tomatoes

N

napoletana anchovies, tomatoes, cheese (pizza topping)
nasello coal-fish
naturale non-carbonated (water)
nero black (coffee)
nocciole hazelnuts
noce di cocco coconut
noce moscata nutmeg
noci walnuts
nodini veal chops

O

oca goose
odori herbs
olio (d'oliva) (olive) oil
olive olives
orata type of sea bream
orecchiette ear-shaped pasta
origano oregano
ortolano ortolan
osso buco braised veal knuckles and shins
ostriche oysters

P

palombacce allo spiedo wood pigeon, spit-roasted

pan di Spagna sponge cake
pancetta affumicata smoked bacon
pandorato alla crema di formaggio fried bread with cream cheese
pandoro large, Christmas sponge cake served with powdered vanilla
pane bread; **~ al latte** milk bread, **~ all'olio** olive oil white bread, **~ tostato** toast
pane, grissini e coperto bread, breadsticks (**grissini**), and table cover charge
panettone butter-enriched Christmas bread with candied fruit, sultanas, and raisins
panforte similar to **pangiallo**
pangiallo fairly hard nut and honey cake
panini rolls
panino imbottito sandwich
panna cotta delicious Italian adaptation of blancmange and creme brulé
panpepato very spicy nut cake
pansotti con salsa di noci alla ligure triangles stuffed with greens in walnut sauce
pappardelle fat ribbons of egg-pasta; **~ alla lepre** with hare sauce
papriot thick spinach soup
parmigiana breaded eggplant slices with tomato sauce and mozzarella
parmigiano (-reggiano) parmesan
passato di verdura mashed vegetable soup, generally with croutons
pasta pasta, noodles; **~ e ceci** with chickpeas; **~ e fagioli** with beans

pasta Maddalena plain génoise cake
pastasciutta pasta
pasticcini pastries
pasticcio macaroni, white sauce, meat, and tomato
pastiera ricotta cake with wheat berries
pastina small pasta pieces; **~ in brodo** in broth
patate potatoes
patatine fritte french fries
pecorino hard sheep's cheese
penne pasta quills
peperonata peppers sauteed with tomato and onion
peperoni peppers; **~ ripieni** stuffed
pera pear
pernice partridge
pesca peach
pescanoce nectarine
pesce all'acqua pazza fish cooked in seawater
pesce persico perch
pesce spada swordfish
pesche peaches
pesce fish; **~ al cartoccio** baked in a parchment envelope; **~ in carpione** boiled and cooked in vinegar, served cold with lemon
pestingolo rich fruit cake with figs and honey
pesto sauce of basil leaves, garlic, cheese, and sometimes pine kernels *(Liguria)* and marjoram
piatti di carne meat dishes
piatti freddi cold dishes
piatto del giorno dish of the day
piccante sharp (cheese)
piccata al marsala thin veal braised in marsala sauce

piccione pigeon
pieno full-bodied (wine)
pinoli pine nuts
piselli peas; **~ al prosciutto** cooked slowly with Parma ham and bacon
piviere plover
pizelle fried bread with tomato sauce
pizza pizza
polenta mush made from cornmeal; **~ alla piemontese** layered with meat; **~ e coniglio** with rabbit stew; **~ e uccelli** with roasted small birds *(northern Italy)*
pollame poultry
pollo chicken; **~ all'abruzzese** with sweet peppers; **~ alla romana** diced and served with tomato sauce and sweet peppers; **~ alla diavola** highly spiced and grilled chicken; **~ novello** spring chicken
polpette meat balls
polpettone meatloaf of seasoned beef or veal
polpo octopus
pomodori tomatoes
pomodori e capperi salad with capers
pompelmo grapefruit
porcellino da latte suckling pig
porcetto arrosto suckling spit-roasted pig *(Sardinia)*
porchetta roasted whole pig with fennels and sausages
porcini boletus mushrooms
porrata bacon and leeks in yeast dough crust
porro leek
porto port

prezzemolo parsley
primo piatto first course
prosciutto ham
prosciutto crudo con melone/con fichi sliced melon or figs with cured ham, from Parma
provolone firm cheese
prugna plum
prugna secca prune
puttanesca sauce of capers, black olives, parsley, garlic, olive oil, black pepper

Q

quaglia quail
quattro formaggi four types of cheese (pizza topping) or sauce
quattro stagioni vegetables, cheese, ham and bacon (pizza topping)

R

radicchio a kind of bitter red and white lettuce
ragù sauce like bolognese
ravanelli radishes
ravioli alla piemontese ravioli with beef and vegetable stuffing
razza ray
ribes red currants
ribes nero black currants
ricci sea urchins
ricciarelli delicate honey and almond biscuit *(Tuscany)*
ricotta soft cow's or sheep's milk cheese
rigatoni short, wide pasta tubes; **~ alla pagliata** with veal guts
risi e bisi rice with peas and bacon
riso rice
riso con le seppie rice cooked with the ink from squid

riso in bianco boiled rice with butter and grated parmesan

risotto rice casserole;
~ con fegatini with chicken livers;
~ con gamberetti in bianco with prawns and wine

rognoncini trifolatti kidneys sauteed with Marsala

rognoni kidneys

rombo turbot

rosato rosé (wine)

rosbif roast beef

rosmarino rosemary

rosso red (wine)

ruote wheel-shaped pasta

S

salame spicy sausages made with uncooked beef or pork, often flavored with pepper and garlic

salciccia small sausage, country-style pork mixture

sale salt

salmone salmon

salse sauces

saltimbocca veal cutlets with prosciutto ham; **~ alla romana** braised in marsala wine with sage

salumi assorted pork products

salvia sage

sardine sardines; **~ all'olio** in oil

sauersuppe sour tripe soup marinated in white wine vinegar

scalogno shallot

scaloppina veal cutlets; **~ alla valdostana** filled with cheese and ham; **~ al marsala** with Marsala wine

scampi shrimp

sciule pieuno onions stuffed with macaroons, breadcrumbs, cheese, spices, and sultanas

scorfano sea-scorpion, sculpin

scura dark (beer)

secco dry (wine)

secondo piatto second (main) course

sedano celery

selvaggina venison

semifreddo ice-cream cake

senape mustard

seppia cuttlefish

seppie con piselli baby squid and peas

sfogliatelle sweet Ricotta cheese turnovers

sgombri in umido stewed mackerel in white wine with green peas

sgombro mackerel

siciliana with black olives, capers, and cheese (pizza)

sodo hard (egg)

sogliola sole

sogliole alla mugnaia sole sautéed in butter, garnished with parsley and lemon

solubile instant (coffee)

sottaceti pickled vegetables

spaghetti all'amatriciana spaghetti with tomato, bacon, and Pecorino cheese sauce

spalla shoulder

specialità della casa specialties of the house

specialità di pesce fish specialties

specialità locali local specialties

spezie spices

spezzatino meat or poultry stew

spezzatino di cinghiale alla cacciatora diced wild boar stewed in white wine with garlic and bay leaves

spezzato di tacchino turkey casserole with olives *(Umbria)*

spiedino pieces of meat grilled or roasted on a skewer

spigola sea bass

spinaci spinach

spremuta di ... freshly squeezed (juice)

spumante sparkling (wine)

stecca di cioccolato chocolate bar

stelline small pasta stars

stoccafisso dried cod

storione sturgeon

stracciatella clear egg and cheese soup

stracotto meat stew with sausages, beef, and vegetables in white wine, slowly cooked for several hours *(Tuscany)*

strangola preti bread and spinach dumpling

straniera foreign (beer)

su ordinazione made to order

succo di frutta fruit juice

supplemento extra charge

supplì Italian rice croquettes with Mozzarella cheese and ground meat, breadcrumbed and fried

susina plum (yellow) or greengage

T

tacchino turkey

tagliatelle egg-pasta ribbons

tartufi truffles

tartufi di cioccolata chocolate truffles

timballo con le sarde macaroni, sardines, pine nuts, fennel, raisins

timo thyme

tiramisù sponge cake, mascarpone, eggs, and chocolate dessert

tisana herbal tea

tonno tuna

tonno alla livornese fried tuna in slices, stewed in garlic and tomato

tordo thrush

torrone delicious Italian nougat which can be found hard and crispy or soft, also chocolate flavored

torta cake; pie

torta di cioccolata chocolate cake

torta di frutta fruit cake

torta di mandorle almond pie

torta di mele apple pie

torta di ricotta delicious pie made with ricotta cheese (roughly similar to cheese cake)

torta manfreda liver pate with Marsala and Parmesan

torta margherita layered cake with meringue, fresh fruit, and whipped cream

tortelli di zucca big tortellini with pumpkin stuffing

tortellini stuffed egg-pasta rings; **~ alla panna con tartufi** with cream and truffles; **~ di picconcello** with pigeon stuffing

tortino di zucchine zucchini with white sauce

triglie red mullet; **~ alla livornese** baked; **~ alla siciliana** grilled with orange peel and white wine

trippa tripe; **~ alla fiorentina** and beef braised in a tomato sauce and served with cheese *(Tuscany)*; **~ verde** in green sauce

trota trout: **~ alla brace** grilled
tutto mare seafood sauce
tè tea; **~ freddo** iced tea

U

uova eggs
uova alla romana omelet with beans, onions, and herbs
uova e pancetta bacon and eggs
uova e prosciutto ham and eggs
uova fritte fried eggs
uova strapazzate scrambled eggs
uovo alla coque boiled egg
uva (bianca/nera) (white/black) grapes
uva passa raisins
uva spina gooseberries

V

vaniglia vanilla
veneziana sweet bread with whole almonds
verde with creamed green vegetables
verdura mista mixed vegetables
verdure vegetables; **~ di stagione** vegetables in season
vermicelli thin spaghetti
verza green cabbage
vincisgrassi cooked pasta with cream sauce and gravy
vino wine
vitello veal; **~ alla bolognese** cutlet cooked with Parma ham and cheese; **~ tonnato** cold with tuna fish sauce; **~ valdostana** stuffed with soft cheese
vongole clams

W

whisky (e soda/con seltz) whisky (and soda)
würstel frankfurters (*Tyrolia*)

Z

zabaglione egg yolks, sugar, and Marsala wine
zafferano saffron
zampone pig's foot filled with seasoned pork, boiled and served in slices
zenzero ginger
ziti long, solid eggless-pasta tubes
zucca pumpkin, gourd; **~ gialla al forno** baked and served with parmesan cheese (winter only)
zucchero sugar
zucchini ripieni stuffed zucchini (usually containing ground meat)
zuppa soup; **~ alla cacciatora** meat soup with mushrooms; **~ alla marinara** spicy fish chowder/stew; **~ alla pavese** consommé with poached egg, croutons and grated cheese; **~ alla senese** sausages with lentils; **~ alla veneta** vegetable soup with white wine and noodles; **~ di bue con spaghettini** spaghetti in beef soup; **~ di cipolle** onion soup with brandy; **~ di cozze** mussels soup; **~ di datteri di mare** sea dates (kind of mussel) soup; **~ di frutti di mare** seafood soup; **~ di pesce** spicy fish chowder/stew; **~ di vongole** clams and white wine soup
zuppa inglese sponge cake steeped in rum with custard or whipped cream

POLISH

ESSENTIALS

Hello.	**Dzien dobry.** *djyen' dobrri*
Good evening.	**Dobry wieczór.** *dobrri v-yechoorr*
A table for …, please.	**Proszę stolik na …** *prrosheh stoleek na*
1 (person)	**jedną osobę** *yed-nom osobeh*
2/3/4 (people)	**dwie/trzy/cztery osoby** *d-v-yeh/t-shi/ch-terri osobi*
Thank you.	**Dziękuję.** *djyen'kooyeh*
The check, please.	**Proszę rachunek.** *prrosheh rra-hoonek*
Good-bye.	**Do widzenia.** *do vee-dzen'ya*

PLACES TO EAT

Bar *barr*
A self-service cafeteria offering hot and cold food, sandwiches, desserts, and non-alcoholic drinks; some may serve beer

Bar Bistro *barr beestrro*
A small cafeteria or restaurant that serves hot/cold dishes and salads

Cocktail Bar *kok-tuyl barr*
Serves milkshakes, ice cream, cakes, and coffee—not cocktails

Bar Mleczny *barr mlechni*
A cafeteria that serves a variety of cheap dishes

Bufet *boofet*
A small restaurant, usually at a train station, which serves snacks and simple hot food, beer, and soft drinks

Kawiarnia *kavyarrn'ya*
A place to meet friends over a cup of coffee and cake or ice cream

Pub/Winiarnia *pub/veen'yarrn'ya*
Places that serve alcoholic drinks and sometimes light snacks

Restauracja *rrestahw-rrats-ya*
Apart from traditional Polish restaurants, there are many that
specialize in a particular international cuisine

Zajazd *zayazd*
A country inn close to a major road, offering good regional food

MEAL TIMES

Śniadanie *sh'n'yadan'ye*
Breakfast: 7–10 a.m.

Obiad/lunch *obyad/lunch*
Lunch: 2–5 p.m.

Kolacja *kolatsya*
The evening meal, served from 7 p.m. onwards; it can be either
a cold buffet or a hot meal

POLISH CUISINE

Heavy soups, meat with root and/or pickled vegetables, cabbage,
preserved fruit, and dry and pickled mushrooms are popular. So too
are dumplings, noodles, and fish on Friday. Modern Polish cuisine
offers imaginative derivatives of traditional dishes. More salads and
healthy snacks have been introduced, and vegetarian dishes are now
common in restaurants.

FINDING A PLACE TO EAT

Can you recommend
a good restaurant?

**Czy może pan polecić dobrą
restaurację?** *chi mozheh pan pole-
tch'eetch' dobrrom rrestahw-rrats-yeh*

Is there a(n) … restaurant near here?	**Czy jest tu niedaleko … restauracja?** *chi yest-too n'yedaleko … rrestahw-rrats-ya*
traditional Polish	**tradycyjna polska** *trradi-tsiy-na polska*
inexpensive	**niedroga** *n'ye-drroga*
traditional local	**tradycyjna regionalna** *trradi-tsiy-na rreg-yonalna*
vegetarian	**wegetariańska** *vegetarr-yan'ska*
Where can I find a(n) …?	**Gdzie mogę znaleźć…?** *g-djyeh mogeh z-nalesh'tch'*
café/restaurant	**kawiarnię/restaurację** *kav-yarrn'yeh/rrestahw-rrats-yeh*
ice-cream parlor	**lodziarnię** *lo-djyarr-n'yeh*
pizzeria	**pizzerię** *peet-tserr-yeh*

RESERVATIONS

I'd like to reserve a table …	**Chciał(a)bym zarezerwować stolik …** *h-tch'yahw(a)-bim za-rrezerr-vovatch' stoleek*
for this evening at …/ for tomorrow at …	**na dziś wieczór na …/na jutro o …** *na djeesh' v-yechoorr na/na yootrro o*
We'll come at 8:00.	**Przyjdziemy o ósmej.** *pshiy-djyemi o oosmey*
A table for two, please.	**Proszę stolik na dwie osoby.** *prrosheh stoleek na d-v-yeh osobi*
We have a reservation.	**Mamy rezerwację.** *mami rrezerr-vats-yeh*

YOU MAY HEAR

Na jakie nazwisko?	What's the name, please?
Przykro mi, nie mamy miejsc.	I'm sorry. We're very busy/full.
Dla palących czy nie palących?	Smoking or non-smoking?

Could we sit …?	**Czy możemy usiąść …?**
	chi mozhemi oo-sh'yon'sh'tch'
over there/outside	**tam/na zewnątrz** *tam/na zev-nonch*
in a non-smoking area	**w miejscu dla nie palących**
	v m-yeys-tsoo dla n'ye pa-lon-tsih
by the window	**przy oknie** *pshi okn'yeh*

ORDERING

Waiter!/Waitress!	**Proszę pana!/Proszę pani!**
	prrosheh pana/prrosheh pan'ee
May I see the wine list, please?	**Czy mogę zobaczyć listę win?**
	chi mogeh zoba-chitch' leesteh veen

YOU MAY HEAR

Czy chce pan już zamówić?	Are you ready to order?
Co chciałby pan zamówić?	What would you like?
Co chciałby pan do picia?	What would you like to drink?
Polecam …	I recommend …
Nie mamy …	We don't have …
Smacznego.	Enjoy your meal.

Do you have a set menu?	**Czy macie zestaw dnia?**
	chi match'yeh zestaf d-n'ya

Can you recommend some typical local dishes?	**Czy może pan polecić typowe dania regionalne?** *chi mozheh pan pole-tch'eetch' tipoveh dan'ya rreg-yonal-neh*
Could you tell me what … is?	**Czy może mi pan powiedzieć co to jest …?** *chi mozheh mee pan pov-ye-djyetch' tso to yest*
What's in it?	**Z czego to jest?** *s chego to yest*
I'd like …/I'll have …	**Chciał(a)bym …/Wezmę …** *h-tch'yahw(a)-bim/vez-meng'*
a bottle/glass/carafe of …	**butelkę/kieliszek/karafkę …** *bootel-keh/k-yelee-shek/karraf-keh*

SPECIAL REQUESTS

Could I have salad instead of vegetables, please?	**Czy mogę dostać sałatkę zamiast jarzyn?** *chi mogeh dostatch' sahwat-keh zam-yast yazhin*
Does the meal come with vegetables/potatoes?	**Czy to danie jest z jarzynami/kartoflami?** *chi to dan'yeh yest z yazhi-namee/karrtof-lamee*
May I have some …?	**Czy mogę prosić …?** *chi mogeh prro-sh'eetch'*
bread	**chleb** *h-lep*
butter	**masło** *maswo*
lemon	**cytrynę** *tsi-trri-neh*
mustard	**musztardę** *moosh-tarrdeh*
pepper	**pieprz** *p-yepsh*
salt	**sól** *sool*
oil and vinegar	**oliwę i ocet** *o-leeveh ee o-tset*

sugar	**cukier** _tsook-yerr_
artificial sweetener	**słodzik** _swodjeek_
vinaigrette	**winegret** _veene-grret_
Could you bring a child's seat, please?	**Czy może pan przynieść krzesełko dla dziecka?** _chi mozheh pan pshi-n'yesh'tch' k-shesehw-ko dla djyets-ka_
Where can I change the baby?	**Gdzie mogę przewinąć dziecko?** _g-djyeh mogeh p-shevee-non'tch' djyets-ko_

GENERAL QUESTIONS

Could I/we have a(n) …, please?	**Czy mógłbym/moglibyśmy dostać …?** _chi moog-bim/ moglee-bish'mi dostatch'_
(clean) ashtray	**(czystą) popielniczkę** _(chistom) pop-yeln'eech-keh_
(clean) cup/glass	**(czystą) filiżankę/szklankę** _(chistom) feelee-zhan-keh/sh-klan-keh_
(clean) fork/knife	**(czysty) widelec/nóż** _(chisti) veedelets/noosh_
(clean) plate/spoon	**(czysty) talerz/(czystą) łyżkę** _(chisti) talesh/(chistom) wishkeh_
(clean) napkin	**(czystą) serwetkę** _(chistom) serrvet-keh_
I'd like (a) …	**Chciał(a)bym …** _h-tch'yahw(a)-bim_
beer	**piwo** _peevo_
tea/coffee	**herbatę/kawę** _herr-bateh/kaveh_
black/with milk	**czarną/z mlekiem** _charr-nom/z-mlek-yem_

I'd like a ... of red/white wine.	**Chciał(a)bym ... czerwonego/ białego wina.** _h-tch'yahw(a)-bim cherr-vonego/b-yahwego veena_
glass/carafe/bottle	**kieliszek/karafkę/butelkę** _k-yelee-shek/karraf-keh/bootel-keh_
bottled/draft	**butelkę piwa/kufel piwa** _bootel-keh/koofel peeva_
That's all, thanks.	**To wszystko, dziękuję.** _to-f-shist-ko djyen'kooyeh_
Where are the restrooms?	**Gdzie są toalety?** _g-djyeh som to-a-leti_

SPECIAL REQUIREMENTS

I can't eat food containing ...	**Nie mogę jeść jedzenia zawierającego ...** _n'ye-mogeh yesh'tch'yedze-n'ya zav-yerrayon-tsego_
salt/sugar	**sól/cukier** _sool/tsook-yerr_
Do you have any dishes/ drinks for diabetics?	**Czy macie dania/napoje specjalne dla cukrzyków?** _chi match'yeh dan'ya/napoye spets-yalneh d-la tsook-shikoof_
Do you have vegetarian dishes?	**Czy macie dania wegetariańskie?** _chi match'yeh dan'ya vegetarr-yan'sk-yeh_

COMPLAINTS

That's not what I ordered.	**To nie to co zamówiłem.** _to n'yeh to tso zamoo-veewem_
I asked for ...	**Prosiłem o ...** _prro-sh'eehwem o_
I can't eat this.	**Nie mogę tego jeść.** _n'yeh mogeh tego yesh'tch'_

P
O
L
I
S
H

The meat is …	**Mięso jest …** _m-yenso yest_
overdone/underdone	**przesmażone/nie dosmażone**
	pshesma-zhoneh/n'ye dosma-zhoneh
too tough	**za twarde** _za t-farrde_
The food is cold.	**Jedzenie jest zimne.**
	yedze-n'yeh yest zh'eem-neh
This isn't fresh.	**To nie jest świeże.**
	to n'yeh yest sh'f-ye-zeh
How much longer will our food be?	**Jak długo jeszcze będziemy czekać na jedzenie?**
	yak d-woogo yesh'cheh ben-djyemi chekatch' na yedzen'yeh
We can't wait any longer. We're leaving.	**Nie możemy czekać dłużej. Wychodzimy.** _n'yeh mozhemi chekatch' d-woozhey. viho-djeemi_

PAYING

Tipping: See page 332.

The check, please.	**Proszę o rachunek.**
	prrosheh o rrahoonek
We'd like to pay separately.	**Chcemy zapłacić osobno.**
	h-tsemi zapwah-tch'eetch' osobno
It's all together.	**To wszystko razem.**
	to f-shist-ko rrazem
I think there's a mistake in this check.	**Chyba jest pomyłka w tym rachunku.** _hiba yest pomiwka f tim rrahoon-koo_
What is this amount for?	**Za co jest ta suma?**
	za tso yest ta sooma
I didn't have that. I had …	**Nie miałem tego. Miałem …**
	n'ye m-yahwem tego. m-yahwem

189

Can I pay with this credit card?	**Czy mogę zapłacić tą kartą kredytową?**
	chi mogeh zapwah-tch'eetch' tong kar-rtom krreditovom
That was a very good meal.	**To był bardzo dobry obiad.**
	to biw barrdzo dobrri ob-yat

COURSE BY COURSE
Breakfast Śniadanie

I'd like …	**Chciał(a)bym …** *h-tch'yahw(a)-bim*
eggs	**jajka** *yuyka*
boiled/fried	**gotowane/sadzone** *gotovaneh/sadzoneh*
scrambled eggs	**jajecznicę** *yuyech-n'ee-tseh*
juice	**sok** *sok*
grapefruit juice	**grejpfrutowy sok** *grreyp-frrootovi sok*
orange juice	**pomarańczowy sok** *pomarran'chovi sok*
honey/jam	**miód/dżem** *m-yoot/jem*
marmalade	**dżem pomarańczowy**
	jem pomarran'chovi
milk	**mleko** *m-leko*
rolls/toast	**bułeczki/tosty** *boo-wechkee/tosti*

Appetizers Zakąski

herring in sour cream	**śledź w śmietanie**
	sh'letch' f sh'm-ye-tan'yeh
herring in oil	**śledź w oliwie** *sh'letch' v oleev-yeh*
pike in aspic	**szczupak w galarecie**
	sh-choopak v galarre-tch'yeh
smoked eel	**węgorz wędzony** *ven'gosh vendzoni*
steak tartare	**befsztyk tatarski** *bef-shtik tatarr-skee*
paté in aspic	**pasztet w galarecie**
	pashtet v-galarre-tch'yeh

Naleśniki z kapustą i grzybami
nalesh'n'eekee s-kapoo-stom ee g-zhi-bamee
Pancakes stuffed with cabbage and mushrooms

Pieczarki w śmietanie *p-yecharr-kee f sh'm-ye-tan'yeh*
Mushrooms in a cream sauce

Bigos *beegos*
A dish of sweet and sour cabbage with a selection of meats,
mushrooms, and dried fruit

Soups Zupy

barszcz czerwony	*barsh-ch cherr-voni*	beet soup
bulion z pasztecikiem	*bool-yon s pashte-tch'eek-yem*	consommé with meat-filled pastries
rosół z kury (z makaronem)	*rosoow s koorri (z makarronem)*	chicken broth (with noodles)
kapuśniak	*kapoosh'n'yak*	sauerkraut or cabbage soup
ogórkowa	*ogoorrkova*	pickled cucumber soup
szczawiowa	*sh-chav-yova*	sorrel soup served with hard-boiled eggs
żurek	*zhoorrek*	sour rye grains and cream soup

Chłodnik *h-wod-n'eek*
A cold soup made with sour milk or yogurt, grated raw young
beets, and dill, served with hard-boiled eggs

Barszcz czerwony *barsh-ch cherr-voni*
A soup made from beef and vegetables (chiefly beets), and served
with sour cream (**ze śmietaną**) or without (**bez śmietany**)

Grochówka *g-rrohoofka*
A thick soup made from dried peas, often served with slices of
sausage

Pomidorowa *pomee-dorrova*
Tomato soup served either with sour cream and noodles (**ze śmietaną/z makaronem**) or without sour cream and noodles (**bez śmietany/bez makaronu**)

Egg dishes Potrawy z jaj

omlet z szynką	<u>omlet</u> s <u>shin</u>kom	omelet with ham
omlet z pieczarkami	omlet s p-yecharr-<u>ka</u>mee	omelet with mushrooms
omlet z dżemem	<u>omlet</u> z <u>je</u>mem	omelet with jam
jajka sadzone na boczku	<u>yay</u>ka sadz<u>o</u>neh na <u>boch</u>koo	eggs and bacon

Fish and seafood Ryby i owoce morza

dorsz	<u>dorr</u>sh	cod
flądra	<u>flon</u>drra	flounder
halibut	hal<u>ee</u>boot	halibut
homar	<u>ho</u>marr	lobster
karmazyn	karr<u>ma</u>zin	haddock
karp	<u>karr</u>p	carp
krab	<u>krr</u>ap	crab
krewetki	krre<u>vet</u>kee	shrimp
leszcz	<u>lesh</u>-ch	bream
lin	<u>leen</u>	tench
łosoś	<u>wo</u>sosh'	salmon
makrela	ma<u>krr</u>ela	mackerel
małże	<u>mawh</u>-zheh	mussels
ostrygi	ost<u>rri</u>gee	oysters
pstrąg	p-<u>strr</u>onk	trout
rak	<u>rr</u>ak	crayfish
sandacz	<u>san</u>dach	pike perch

szczupak	*sh-choopak*	pike
śledź	*sh'letch'*	herring
tuńczyk	*toon'chik*	tuna
węgorz	*ven'gosh*	eel

Sandacz po polsku *sandach po polskoo*
Pike perch (a fresh-water fish) Polish style—boiled in vegetable stock and served with chopped hard-boiled eggs and melted butter

Karp smażony *karrp smazhoni*
Carp in egg and bread crumbs, fried in butter, and served with fresh boiled vegetables and potatoes

Szczupak faszerowany *sh-choopak fasherrovani*
Stuffed pike served warm with lettuce, fresh tomatoes, boiled potatoes, and horseradish sauce

Karp po żydowsku *karrp po zhi-doskoo*
Carp Jewish style—seasoned with cloves, vinegar, salt, and pepper and cooked in beer with fried onions, raisins, and lemon peel

Meat and poultry Mięso i drób
bażant	*bazhant*	pheasant
boczek	*bochek*	bacon
cielęcina	*tch'yelen-tch'eena*	veal
gęś	*gensh'*	goose
golonka	*golonka*	shank (lower leg)
indyk	*eendik*	turkey
jagnię	*yag-n'yeh*	lamb
kaczka	*kachka*	duck
kiełbasy	*k-yehwbasi*	sausages
klopsy	*klopsi*	meat balls
kurczak	*koorrchak*	chicken
ozór	*ozoorr*	tongue

stek	*stek*	steak
szynka	*shinka*	ham
wieprzowina	*v-yepsho-veena*	pork
wołowina	*vowo-veena*	beef

Schab pieczony ze śliwkami *s-hap p-yechoni ze sh'leef-kamee*
Roast pork loin with prunes, served with roast potatoes and red cabbage

Kotlety wieprzowe panierowane z kapustą *kotleti v-yep-shoveh pan-yerro-vaneh s kapoos-tom*
Pork chops in bread crumbs, fried in butter and served with boiled potatoes, cabbage, and seasonal vegetables

Kaczka pieczona z jabłkami *kachka p-yechona s yapka-mee*
Roast duck with apples and toast, served with salad and red wine

Gołąbki *gowomp-kee*
Cabbage leaves stuffed with ground meat and rice

Zrazy zawijane z ogórkiem kiszonym
z-rrazi zavee-yaneh z ogoorr-k-yem kee-shonim
Filet of beef rolled with pickled cucumber and a piece of bacon, cooked in its own juices, served with mashed potatoes and vegetables

Gulasz wieprzowy *goolash v-yep-shovi*
Chopped pork cooked with butter, onions, pepper, garlic, and tomato purée, and served with potatoes or groats and a side salad

Baranina pieczona ze śmietaną
barran'eena p-yechona ze sh'm-ye-tanom
Roast marinated mutton seasoned with sour cream

Vegetables Jarzyny

bakłażan	*bakwah-zhan*	eggplant
brukiew	*brook-yef*	rutabaga
burak	*boorrak*	beet

cebule	*tseboola*	onions
cukinie	*tsookeen'yeh*	zucchini
czosnek	*chosnek*	garlic
fasolka szparagowa	*fasolka sh-parragova*	green beans
groszek	*grroshek*	peas
kalafior	*kalaf-yorr*	cauliflower
kapusta	*kapoosta*	cabbage
kartofle	*karrtofleh*	potatoes
marchew	*marr-hef*	carrots
młoda cebulka	*m-woda tseboolka*	shallots
ogórek	*ogoorrek*	cucumber
papryka	*paprika*	peppers
pieczarki/grzyby	*p-yecharr-kee/ g-zhibi*	mushrooms
pomidory	*pomee-dorri*	tomatoes
rzepy	*zhepa*	turnips
sałata	*sawahta*	lettuce
seler	*selerr*	celery root
seler łodygowy	*selerr wodigovi*	celery
szparagi	*sh-parragee*	asparagus

Salad Sałaty/Sałatki

Sałatka pomidorowa *sawaht-ka pomee-dorrova*
Tomato and onion salad

Sałatka kartoflana *sawaht-ka karrtoflana*
Potato salad

Zielona sałata *zh'yelona sawahta*
Green salad

Sałatka jarzynowa *sawaht-ka yazhi-nova*
A salad of cooked, mixed vegetables blended with cream and mayonnaise

Cheese Sery

biały ser	*b-yahwi serr*	white cheese (cow's milk)
brie	*brree*	Brie-type cheese
bryndza	*brindza*	ewe's milk
camembert	*kamamberr*	Camembert-type cheese
łagodne	*wagodneh*	mild
ostre	*ostrreh*	strong
pleśniowy	*plesh'n'yovi*	blue cheese
pół łagodny/ pół ostry	*poow-wagodni/ poow-ostrri*	medium
sery miękkie	*serri m-yen'k-k-yeh*	soft cheeses
sery topione	*serri top-yoneh*	processed cheeses
twarożek	*t-farro-zhek*	cottage cheese
żółte sery	*zhoow-teh serri*	hard cheeses

Classic dishes

Pierogi *p-yerrogee*
Stuffed dumplings with meat (**z mięsem**), mushrooms (**z grzybami**), cabbage (**z kapustą**), cheese (**z serem**), or fruit (**z owocami**), served warm with butter or sweet sauces

Leniwe pierogi *len'eeveh p-yerrogee*
Large dumplings made with flour, cooked potatoes, and white cheese, served warm with cream

Knedle ze śliwkami *k-nedleh ze sh'leef-kamee*
Dumplings stuffed with plums, served warm with cream or sugar

Kluski śląskie _klooskee sh'lons-k-yeh_
Dumplings made with flour and raw potatoes, served warm with fried bacon and onions

Placki kartoflane _plats-kee karrtoflaneh_
Potato pancakes made with grated raw potatoes and onions, fried and served with sour cream

Dessert Desery

krem owocowy	_krrem ovo-tsovi_	whipped cream with fruit
galaretka owocowa	_gala-rretka ovo-tsova_	fruit jelly
kompot owocowy	_kompot ovo-tsovi_	fruit compote
naleśniki	_nalesh'n'eekee_	pancakes
szarlotka	_sharr-lotka_	apple tart

Kisiel żurawinowy _keesh'yel zhoo-rravee-novi_
A soft jelly made with cranberries, served with milk or cream

Gruszki w syropie _grroosh-kee f sirrop-yeh_
Pears in thick syrup served with vanilla sauce

Racuszki z jabłkami _rratsoosh-kee z yapkamee_
Small pancakes made with sliced apples, fried and served with vanilla powdered sugar

Budyń orzechowy _boodin' ozhe-hovi_
A pudding made with eggs, sugar, walnuts, and bread crumbs, served with vanilla sauce

Fruit Owoce

arbuz	_arrboos_	watermelon
banany	_banani_	bananas
brzoskwinie	_bzhos-k-feen'yeh_	peaches

cytryny	*citrrini*	lemons
czereśnie	*che-rresh'n'yeh*	cherries
grejpfrut	*grreyp-frroot*	grapefruit
jabłka	*yapka*	apples
maliny	*maleeni*	raspberries
melon	*melon*	melon
morele	*morreleh*	apricots
pomarańcze	*poma-rran'cheh*	oranges
śliwki	*sh'leef-kee*	plums
truskawki	*trroos-kafkee*	strawberries
winogrona	*veeno-grrona*	grapes

DRINKS

Beer Piwo

The best Polish beers are **Żywiec**, **Okocim**, **EB**, **Heweliusz**, and **Brok**, but you can also find many international brands.

Do you have … beer?	**Czy macie piwo …?** *chi match'yeh peevo*
bottled/draft	**butelkowe/beczkowe** *bootel-koveh/bech-koveh*

Wine Wino

The cheapest wines come from Bulgaria, Hungary, Romania, and Georgia. Big supermarkets and liquor stores also stock other international wines.

Can you recommend a … wine?	**Czy może pan polecić … wino?** *chi mozheh pan poletch'eetch' … veeno*
red/white/blush [rosé]	**czerwone/białe/różowe** *cherr-voneh/b-yaweh/roozhove*
dry/sweet/sparkling	**wytrawne/słodkie/musujące** *vitrrav-neh/swot-k-yeh/moosooyontseh*

I'd like a corkscrew.	**Chciał(a)bym korkociąg.**	
	h-tch'yahw(a)-bim korrko-tch'yonk	
Cheers!	**Na zdrowie!** _nah zdrohviyeh_	

Spirits and liqueurs Wódki i likiery

Vodka, made from either potatoes or rye, is still the national drink. It is served cold and drunk neat from small glasses, either with a meal or on its own. You will find many flavored vodkas, as well as the regular "straight" type.

wódka	_vootka_	vodka
cytrynówka	_tsi-trri-noofka_	lemon-flavored vodka
jarzębiak	_yazhem-b-yak_	rowanberry vodka
myśliwska	_mish'leef-ska_	hunter's vodka
żubrówka	_zhoo-broofka_	Bison vodka
Goldwasser	_gold-vaserr_	"Goldwater" (with flakes of gold leaf)
miód pitny	_m-yoot peetni_	mead
winiak	_veen'yak_	Polish brandy
śliwowica	_sh'leevo-veetsa_	slivovitz (plum brandy)
czysta	_chista_	straight [neat]
z lodem	_z lodem_	on the rocks [with ice]
z wodą/tonikiem	_z vodom/ ton'eek-yem_	with water/tonic water

| I'd like a single/double … | **Chciał(a)bym pojedyńczą/ podwójną …** _h-tch'yahw(a)- bim poyedin'chom/pod-vooy-nom_ |
| brandy*/gin/whisky/vodka | **koniak/gin/whisky/wódkę** _kon'yak/djeen/weeski/vootkeh_ |

* "foreign brandy" as opposed to Polish brandy, **winiak**

Non-alcoholic drinks

Herbata *herr-bata*

Tea is usually drunk either black or with lemon. Traditionally, **esencja** (the essence) was brewed in a small ceramic teapot over a boiling kettle. The essence was poured into a glass or cup and boiling water added. Nowadays, tea bags are increasingly popular. Herbal teas (**herbaty ziołowe**) are popular too.

Kawa *kava*

Coffee is usually drunk strong without milk, espresso, or Turkish-style. Most cafés and bars serve capuccino as well.

I'd like …	**Chciał(a)bym …** *h-tch'yahw(a)-bim*
tea/coffee	**herbatę/kawę** *herr-bateh/kaveh*
black/with milk	**czarną/z mlekiem** *charr-nom/z-mlek-yem*
decaffeinated	**dekafinowaną** *deka-feeno-vanom*
espresso/Turkish coffee	**z ekspresu/po turecku** *zeks-prresoo/po-toorrets-koo*
(hot) chocolate	**gorącą czekoladę** *gorrontsom chekoladeh*
cola/lemonade	**colę/lemoniadę** *koleh/lemo-n'yadeh*
fruit juice	**sok owocowy** *sok ovo-tsovi*
orange/pineapple/tomato	**pomarańczowy/ananasowy/pomidorowy** *poma-rran'chovi/ananasovi/pomee-dorrovi*
milk shake	**napój mleczny** *napooy m-lechni*
mineral water	**wodę mineralną** *vodeh meene-rralnom*
carbonated/non-carbonated	**gazowaną/niegazowaną** *gazo-vanom/n'ye-gazo-vanom*

MENU READER

dobrze wysmażone	_dobzheh vismazhoneh_	well-done
duszone	_dooshoneh_	braised/stewed
gotowane	_gotovaneh_	boiled
mało wysmażone	_mahwo vismazhoneh_	rare
marynowane	_marinovaneh_	marinated
nadziewane/ faszerowane	_nadj'yevaneh/ fasherrovaneh_	stuffed
na parze	_na pazheh_	steamed
panierowane	_pan-yerrovaneh_	breaded
pieczone	_p-yechoneh_	baked/roasted
prawie surowe	_prav-yeh soorroveh_	very rare
smażone	_smazhoneh_	fried
średnio wysmażone	_sh'rredne-yo vismazhoneh_	medium
wędzone	_vedzoneh_	smoked
z frytury	_s frritoorri_	deep-fried
z przyprawami	_s pshiprravamee_	spicy
z rusztu	_z rrooshtoo_	grilled
z wody	_z vodi_	poached

A

agrest gooseberry
alkohole spirits/alcohol
ananas pineapple
anchois anchovies
anioł morski monkfish

arbuz watermelon

B

babeczka cake/pie
bakłażan eggplant
banan banana
baranina mutton

baranina pieczona ze śmietaną roast marinated mutton with sour cream

bardzo przyprawiony highly seasoned

bardzo wytrawne very dry (wine, etc.)

barszcz czerwony beet soup

bazylia basil

bażant pheasant

befsztyk tatarski steak tartare

bekas woodcock

bekon bacon

bez dodatków straight [neat]

beza meringue

bezkofeinowa decaffeinated

biała fasola butter beans

biała kapusta white cabbage

białko egg white

biały chleb white bread

bigos sweet and sour cabbage, a selection of meats, mushrooms, and dried fruit

biszkopt sponge cake

bita śmietana whipped cream

brokuły broccoli

brukselka Brussel sprouts

bryndza ewe's milk cheese

brzoskwinia peach

bulion clear soup

bułeczki rolls

bułka tarta bread crumbs

budyń blancmange

budyń orzechowy walnut and vanilla pudding

budyń z karmelem crème caramel

burak beet

C

cebula onions

chleb bread

chleb praśny (bez drożdży) unleavened bread

chłodnik cold yogurt, dill, and beet soup

chłodzone chilled

chrzan horseradish

ciasteczka cookies

ciasto wałkowane pastry

ciasto francuskie puff pastry

ciasto półkruche shortcrust pastry

ciasto cake

ciasto z bakaliami fruit cake

cielęcina veal

comber loin (usually game)

cukier sugar

cukinie zucchini

cykoria chicory/endive

cynamon cinnamon

cytryna lemon

cytrynówka lemon-flavored vodka

czarna black (coffee)

czarna porzeczka black currants

czarny chleb black bread

czekolada chocolate

czekolada pitna hot chocolate

czereśnie cherries

czerwona kapusta red cabbage

czerwone red (wine)

czerwone porzeczki red currants

czerwony cefal red mullet

czerwony pieprz chili pepper

czosnek garlic

Ć

ćwikła grated horseradish with beets

D

daktyle dates

danie dnia dish of the day

deser dessert

dojrzały ripe

domowy homemade
dorsz cod
drób poultry
dynia squash/pumpkin
dziczyzna game
dzik wild boar
dżem jam
dżem pomarańczowy marmalade

E

estragon tarragon

F

fasolka szparagowa green beans
fasola beans
fasola czerwona kidney beans
fasolka chińska bean sprouts
fasolka zielona sugarsnap peas
figi figs
figi suszone dried figs
figi świeże fresh figs
flaki tripe
flądra flounder
frytki french fries

G

galaretka jelly
galaretka z pigwy quince jelly
gałka muszkatołowa nutmeg
garnirowanie garnish, trimming
gazowana carbonated
gęsty rich (sauce)
gęś goose
gin z tonikiem gin and tonic
gin z wodą sodową i cytryną
gin fizz
głowizna pig's head
Goldwasser "Goldwater" (vodka
with gold leaf)
golonka shank (lower leg)
gołąb pigeon

gołąbki ground meat with rice
rolled in cabbage leaves
gorący hot (temperature)
gotowany na parze steamed
goździki cloves
granaty pomegranates
grejpfrut grapefruit
grillowane na węglu charcoal-
grilled
grochówka pea soup served with
slices of sausage
groch włoski chickpeas
groszek peas
gruszka pear
gruszka avocado avocado
gruszki w syropie pears in syrup
grzanka toast
grzyby wild mushrooms [ceps]
gulasz stew
gulasz z jagnięcia lamb stew

H

herbata tea (beverage)
herbatniki cookies
homar lobster

I

imbir ginger
indyk turkey

J

jabłko apple
jadłospis menu
jagnię lamb
jagody blueberries
jagody jałowca juniper berries
jaja eggs
jajecznica scrambled eggs
jajko na miękko soft-boiled egg
jajko na twardo hard-boiled egg
jarzębiak rowanberry vodka

jarzyny vegetables
jasny plain
jeżyny blackberries
jogurt yogurt

K

kabaczek marrow
kaczka duck
kaczka pieczona z jabłkami
roast duck with apples and toast
kalafior cauliflower
kałamarnica squid
kanapka sandwich
kapłon capon
kaparek caper
kapusta cabbage
kapusta kiszona sauerkraut
kapuśniak sauerkraut soup
karafka carafe
karczochy artichokes
karmazyn haddock
karp carp
karp po żydowsku carp with
spices cooked in beer
karp smażony carp in egg and
bread crumbs
kaszanka black sausage
kasztany jadalne chestnuts
(sweet)
kawa coffee
kawior caviar
kefir thin yogurt
kiełb gudgeon (freshwater fish)
kiełbaski sausages
kiełbaski wieprzowe pork
sausages
kisiel jelly
kisiel żurawinowy cranberry jelly
klops meatloaf
kluski noodles/dumplings
kluski śląskie flour and potato
dumplings with bacon and onions

kminek caraway
knedle ze śliwkami dumplings
stuffed with plums
kogut capon
koktail mleczny milkshake
kompot stewed fruit/compote
konserwowany cured (ham, etc.)
koper fennel
koperek dill
kopytka potato dumplings
korniszony gherkins
kość bone
kotlety chops
kotlety wieprzowe panierowane
pork chops in bread crumbs
koza goat
koźlę kid (goat)
krab crab
krakersy crackers
krewetki shrimp
krokiet croquette
królik rabbit
krupnik barley soup
kukurydza sweet corn
kurczak chicken
kurczak pieczony roast chicken
kurczak smażony fried chicken
kurczak z rusztu grilled chicken
kurki chanterelle mushrooms
kuropatwa partridge
kwaśny sour (taste)

L

langusta spiny lobster
lekki light (sauce, etc.)
lemoniada lemonade
leniwe pierogi flour, potato, and
curd cheese dumplings with cream
leszcz bream
likier liqueur
limona lime
lista win wine list

listek laurowy bay leaf
lód ice
lody ice cream
lukier icing

Ł

łagodny mild (flavor)
łopatka shoulder (cut of meat)
łosoś salmon
łosoś wędzony smoked salmon

M

majonez mayonnaise
majonez czosnkowy garlic mayonnaise
makaron pasta
makrela mackerel
maliny raspberries
małże mussels
mandarynka tangerine
marcepan marzipan
marchew carrots
marynata pickles
marynowany w occie marinated in vinegar
masło butter
maślanka buttermilk
mazurek kind of cake
mąka flour
mąka biała plain flour
mąka razowa whole-wheat flour
melasa molasses
miecznik swordfish
mielona wołowina ground beef
mieszane jarzyny mixed vegetables
mięso meat
mięso z rusztu grilled meat
mięta mint
migdały almonds
migdały w cukrze sugared almond

minóg morski lamprey
miód honey
miód pitny mead
mizeria cucumber salad with sour cream
mleko milk
młoda cebula shallots/spring onions
młoda kapusta spring cabbage
młody kurczak spring (baby) chicken
mocne full-bodied (wine)/strong (beer)
morele apricots
morwa mulberry
móżdżek brains
mrożony iced (drinks)
mus purée
musujący sparkling
musztarda mustard
myśliwska hunter's vodka

N

na szpikulcu skewered
nadziewane stuffed
naleśniki pancakes
naleśniki z kapustą i grzybami pancakes with cabbage and mushrooms
napój alkoholowy alcoholic drink
napój bezalkoholowy soft drink
napój owocowy fruit squash/cordial
napoje bezalkoholowe non-alcoholic drinks
nektarynka nectarine
nerki kidneys
nerkówka loin (cut of meat)
noga leg (cut of meat)
nóżki pigs' feet
nugat nougat

O

ogon oxtail
ogórek cucumber
ogórkowa pickled cucumber soup
okoń bass/perch
oliwki olives
oliwki nadziewane stuffed olives
omlet omelet
opieńki oyster mushrooms
oranżada orangeade
orzech kokosowy coconut
orzechy nuts
orzechy laskowe hazelnuts
orzechy mieszane assorted nuts
orzechy włoskie walnuts
orzeszki ziemne peanuts
orzeszki ziemne solone salted peanuts
ostre kiełbaski spicy sausage
ostry sharp/spicy (flavor)
ostrygi oysters
ośmiornica octopus
owoce fruit
owoce kandyzowane candied fruit
owoce morza seafood
owoce z puszki canned fruit
owoc kiwi kiwi fruit
owsianka porridge
ozór tongue

P

parówki frankfurters
paszteciki pastries filled with meat or fish
pasztet pâté
pasztet w galarecie paté in aspic
pączek donut
perliczka guinea fowl
pieczarki field mushrooms

pieczarki w śmietanie mushrooms in cream
pieczeń pot roast
pieczona wołowina roast beef
pieprz pepper (condiment)
pieprzny sos hot pepper sauce
piernik ginger cake
pierogi stuffed dumplings
pierogi z grzybami dumplings with mushrooms
pierogi z kapustą dumplings with cabbage
pierogi z mięsem dumplings with meat
pierogi z owocami dumplings with fruit
pierogi z serem dumplings with curd cheese
pierś breast
pierś kurczaka breast of chicken
pietruszka parsnips
pietruszka zielona parsley
pikle pickles
piwo beer
piwo jasne lager
placek tart/pie (sweet, savory)
placek migdałowy almond tart
placki kartoflane potato pancakes with sour cream
plaster/plasterek slice
płaszczka skate
płatki śniadaniowe cereal (breakfast)
płotka roach (carp-like fish)
podróbki giblets
podwójny double (a double shot)
polędwica tenderloin (cut of meat)
pół butelki half bottle
pomarańcza orange
pomidorowa tomato soup

pomidorowa z makaronem
tomato soup with noodles
pomidory tomatoes
poncz punch
porcja portion
portwine port
pory leeks
potrawa dish
potrawa zimna cold dish
potrawka casserole
prosiak suckling pig
prosty plain
przepiórka quail
przyprawiony seasoned
przyprawy seasoning/spices
pstrąg trout
pulpety meat balls
pyzy round dumplings

R

rabarbar rhubarb
racuszki small pancakes
racuszki z jabłkami apple
pancakes/fritters
raja ray
rak crayfish
razowy chleb rye bread
rodzynki raisins
rolmopsy pickled herring filet
rosół consommé/broth
rosół z kury chicken broth
rosół z mięsem i jarzynami meat
and vegetable broth
rostbef roast beef
rozmaryn rosemary
różowe blush [rosé]
rukiew wodna watercress
rumsztyk rumpsteak
ryba fish
ryba na parze steamed fish
ryba pieczona baked fish

ryba smażona fried fish
ryż rice
rzepa turnips
rzeżucha cress
rzeżucha wodna watercress
rzodkiewka radish

S

salceson pig's head/feet
sałatka salad
sałatka jarzynowa mixed cooked
vegetable salad
sałatka z kapusty coleslaw
sandacz pike perch
sandacz po polsku pike perch in
vegetable stock with hard-boiled
eggs
sardynki sardines
sarnina venison
schab loin of pork
schab pieczony ze śliwkami
roast pork sirloin with prunes
seler celery root
seler łodygowy celery
ser cheese
serce heart
ser miękki soft cheese
sernik cheese cake
ser owczy ewe's milk cheese
ser pleśniowy blue cheese
ser twardy hard cheese
ser z koziego mleka goat's milk
cheese
skarp turbot
słodka papryka sweet red peppers
słodki sweet
słodycze candy
słodzik sweetener
smażony fried
smażony na maśle fried in butter
soczewica lentils

sok juice
sok cytrynowy lemon juice
sok owocowy fruit juice
sok pomarańczowy orange juice
sok z limony lime juice
sól salt
sola sole
solony salted
sos sauce
sos budyniowy custard
sos czosnkowy garlic sauce
sos pomidorowy tomato sauce
sos słodko kwaśny sweet and sour sauce
sos z pieczeni gravy
specjalność domu specialty of the house
specjalność regionalna local specialty
specjalność zakładu specialty of the restaurant
stek steak
stek z polędwicy filet steak
strucla kind of rolled cake
suflet soufflé
surówka coleslaw
surowy raw
suszone daktyle dried dates
suszone śliwki prunes
syrop syrup
szafran saffron
szałwia sage
szarlotka apple pie
szaszłyk shashlik (lamb/mutton kebab)
szczaw sorrel
szczawiowa sorrel soup
szczupak pike
szczupak faszerowany stuffed pike with horseradish sauce
szczupak w galarecie pike in aspic

szczypiorek chives
szklanka glass
sznycel breaded pork or veal cutlet
szparagi asparagus
szpinak spinach
szprotki sprats (small herrings)
sztuka mięsa portion of cooked meat
szynka ham

Ś

śledź herring
śledź marynowany marinated herring
śledź w oliwie herring in oil
śledź w śmietanie herring in sour cream
śliwowica slivovitz (plum brandy)
ślimaki snails
śliwki plums
śmietana cream
śniadanie breakfast
świeże daktyle fresh dates
świeże owoce fresh fruit
świeży fresh

T

tarty grated
tłusty fatty
tonik tonic water
tort rich cake/gateau
trufle truffles
truskawki strawberries
trybulka chervil
tuńczyk tuna
twarożek fresh curd cheese
tymianek thyme

U

udziec leg (cut of meat)
utarty grated

W

wafle waffles
wanilia vanilla
wątłusz hake (similar to cod)
wątróbka liver
wątróbka z kurczaka chicken liver
w cieście in batter
w czosnku in garlic
wędliny charcuterie (shop specializing in meat products)
wędzony smoked
węgorz eel
węgorz wędzony smoked eel
wieprzowina pork
winegret vinaigrette
winiak Polish brandy
wino wine
wino deserowe dessert wine
winogrona grapes
winogrona czerwone black grapes
winogrona zielone white grapes
wino musujące sparkling wine
wino stołowe table wine
wiśnie cherries
witlinek whiting
woda water
woda gorąca hot water
woda mineralna mineral water
woda sodowa soda water
woda z lodem iced water
wódka vodka
wódki spirits
w oliwie in oil
wół ox
wołowina beef
w plasterkach sliced
wytrawny dry

Z

zając hare
zakąski appetizers/snacks
zapiekany gratin/au gratin
z bąbelkami carbonated (drinks)
zboże corn
z cukrem with sugar
z cytryną with lemon
z frytury deep-fried
zielona fasolka green beans
zielony pieprz green peppers
zielona sałata green salad
ziemniaki potato
ziemniaki gotowane boiled potatoes
ziemniaki pieczone roast potatoes
ziemniaki tłuczone mashed/creamed potatoes
zimna zupa cold soup
zimne napoje cold drinks
zioła herbs
zioła mieszane mixed herbs
z kością on the bone
z lodem on the rocks [with ice]
z lodu chilled (wine, etc.)
z mlekiem with milk/white (coffee)
z przyprawami hot (spicy)
zrazy rolled meat stuffed with pickled cucumber and bacon
zrazy zawijane z ogórkiem kiszonym filet of beef with pickled cucumber and bacon
zupa soup
zupa krem cream soup
zupa jarzynowa vegetable soup

Ż

żeberka spare ribs
żółtko egg yolk
żółty ser hard cheese
żubrówka Bison vodka
żurek sour rye soup

PORTUGUESE

ESSENTIALS

Hello.	**Olá.** _ollah_
Good evening.	**Boa tarde.** _boaer tard_
A table for …	**Uma mesa para …** _oomer mayzer per-rer_
1/2/3/4	**um(a)/dois/três/quatro** _oom(er)/doysh/traysh/kwatroo_
Thank you.	**Obrigado(-a).** _obrigadoo(-er)_
I'd like to pay.	**Queria pagar.** _ker-reeer per-gar_
Good-bye.	**Adeus.** _er-deoosh_

PLACES TO EAT

Most distinctive are the **pousadas** and **casas de fados** or **adegas típicas**, the little restaurants where you eat or drink to the sound of the **fado**, the national folk song.

Adega típica _er-deger teepyker_
Small restaurant you may be treated to **fado** singing

Café _ker-feh_
Coffee shop and bar; you should be able to get a snack there

Casa de fados _kazer der fadoosh_
A typical Portuguese restaurant where you can hear **fado**

Cervejaria _server-zher-reeer_
A beerhouse where you can drink beer and eat seafood snacks

Comida a quilo/Buffet _koomeeder er keeloo/boofeh_
Restaurant open only at lunchtime, serving a buffet of salads, meat, vegetables, and fruits; you pay by the weight of your plate

Confeitaria *konfayter-reeer*
A pastry shop, also serving coffee, tea, and other drinks

Estalagem *ishter-lazhaym*
Privately owned inn, serving regional specialties

Marisqueira *mer-reeshkayrer*
Restaurant specializing in seafood

Pousada *pohzader*
State-owned inn, specializing in local dishes; near places of interest

Restaurante *rishtowrawnt*
According to the cuisine and standard of service: **de luxo** (luxury), **de primeira**, **de segunda**, or **de terceira classe** (first, second, or third class)

MEAL TIMES

O pequeno almoço *oo perkaynoo ahlmoassoo*
Breakfast: 7–10 a.m. It consists of coffee, rolls, butter, and jam

O almoço *oo ahlmoassoo*
Lunch: the main meal served from12:30–2:30 p.m, consists of soup, fish or meat, and a dessert

O jantar *oo zhahntahr*
Dinner: 7:30–9:30 p.m., except in a **casa de fado**, where the show starts around 10 p.m.

PORTUGUESE CUISINE

There is no shortage of freshly picked vegetables and fruit, and fish and seafood straight from the sea. **Bacalhau**, dried cod, served with boiled potatoes, remains the favorite national dish, followed by custards and all kinds of pastries. Pork comes in many guises, as do chicken and veal.
Most restaurants display a menu (**ementa** or **cardápio**). A **prato do dia** (dish of the day) usually offers a good meal at a fair price.

FINDING A PLACE TO EAT

Can you recommend a restaurant?	**Pode recomendar-me um restaurante?** *pod rer-koomayn-darmer oom rishtowrawnt*
Is there a(n) … near here?	**Há … perto daqui?** *ah … pehrtoo der-kee*
traditional local restaurant	**um restaurante com especialidades regionais** *oom rishtowrawnt kawm ishper-syalidadish rer-zhyoonighsh*
inexpensive restaurant	**um restaurante barato** *oom rishtowrawnt ber-ratoo*
vegetarian restaurant	**um restaurante vegetariano** *oom rishtowrawnt ver-zher-ter-ryanoo*
Where can I find a(n) …?	**Onde posso encontrar …?** *ond possoo aynkontrar*
café	**um café** *oom ker-feh*
fast-food restaurant	**um restaurante de comidas rápidas** *oom rishtowrawnt der koomeedush rapidush*
ice-cream parlor	**uma gelataria/casa de gelados** *oomer zher-ler-ter-reeer/ kazer der ger-ladoosh*
pizzeria	**uma pizzaria** *oomer peezzer-reeer*

RESERVATIONS

I'd like to reserve a table …	**Queria reservar uma mesa …** *ker-reeer rer-zervar oomer mayzer*
for today at …	**para hoje às …** *per-rer oazh ash*
for two	**para dois** *per-rer doysh*

| We'll come at 8:00. | **Vamos às oito.** *vamooz ash <u>oy</u>too* |
| We have a reservation. | **Fizemos uma reserva.** *fee<u>ze</u>moosh <u>oo</u>mer rer-<u>zehr</u>ver* |

YOU MAY HEAR

| **Em que nome?** | What's the name, please? |
| **Desculpe, mas estamos cheios.** | I'm sorry. We're very busy/full. |

Could we sit …?	**Podemos sentar-nos …?** *po<u>day</u>moosh sayn<u>tar</u>noosh*
over there/outside	**ali/lá fora** *er-<u>lee</u>/lah <u>for</u>er*
in the non-smoking area	**na área para não-fumadores** *ner <u>ar</u>yer <u>per</u>-rer nawm foomer-<u>doa</u>rish*
by the window	**(junto) à janela** *(<u>zhoon</u>too) ah zher-<u>ne</u>ler*

ORDERING

| Waiter!/Waitress! | **Se faz favor!** *ser fash fer-<u>voar</u>* |
| May I see the wine list, please? | **A carta dos vinhos, se faz favor.** *er <u>kar</u>ter doosh <u>vee</u>nyoosh ser fash fer-<u>voar</u>* |

YOU MAY HEAR

Deseja(m) encomendar?	Are you ready to order?
O que deseja(m)?	What would you like?
Recomendo …/ Não temos …	I recommend …/ We don't have …
Bom apetite!	Enjoy your meal.

Do you have a set menu?	**Tem ementa [cardápio] a preço fixo?** *taym eemaynter [karda-pyoo] er praysoo feeksoo*
Can you recommend some typical local dishes?	**Pode recomendar-me alguns pratos regionais?** *pod rer-koomayndarmer algoonsh pratoosh rer-zhyoonighsh*
Could you tell me what … is?	**Pode dizer-me o que é …?** *pod deezairmer oo kee eh*
What's in it?	**Tem/Leva o quê?** *taym/lever oo kay*
What kind of … do you have?	**Que variedade de … tem?** *ker ver-ryedad der … taym*
I'd like …	**Queria …** *ker-reeer*
a bottle/glass/carafe of …	**uma garrafa/um copo/jarro de …** *oomer ger-rrafer/oom koppoo/jarroo der*

SPECIAL REQUESTS

Does the meal come with vegetables/potatoes?	**Vem com legumes/batatas?** *vaym kawm ler-goomish/ ber-tatush*
Do you have any sauces?	**Que molhos tem?** *ker mollyoosh taym*
May I have some …?	**Pode trazer-me …?** *pod trer-zairmer*
bread	**pão** *pawm*
butter	**manteiga** *mawntayger*
lemon	**limão** *leemawm*
mustard	**mostarda** *mooshtarder*
olive oil	**azeite** *er-zayter*

pepper	**pimenta** _peemaynter_
salt	**sal** _sal_
seasoning	**tempero** _taympayroo_
sugar	**açúcar** _er-sookar_
(artificial) sweetener	**adoçante (artificial)** _er-doosawnt (urteefeesyal)_
vinegar	**vinagre** _veenagrer_
Could we have a child's seat, please?	**Pode trazer uma cadeirinha de criança?** _pod trer-zair oomer ker-dayreenyer der kryawnser_
Where can I feed/change the baby?	**Onde posso alimentar/mudar o bebé?** _ond possoo er-leemayntar/moodar oo bebeh_

GENERAL QUESTIONS

Could I have a (clean) …, please?	**Pode trazer-me … (limpo/-a)?** _pod trer-zairmer … (leempoo/-er)_
ashtray	**um cinzeiro** _oom seenzayroo_
cup/glass	**uma chávena/um copo** _oomer shav-ner/oom koppoo_
fork/knife	**um garfo/uma faca** _oom garfoo/oomer faker_
spoon/plate	**uma colher/um prato** _oomer koolyehr/oom pratoo_
napkin	**um guardanapo** _oom gwerder-napoo_
I'd like …	**Queria …** _ker-reeer_
beer	**uma cerveja** _oomer servayzher_

coffee/tea/chocolate	**um café/um chá/um chocolate** *oom ker-feh/oom shah/oom shookoolat*
black/with milk	**uma bica/um garoto** *oomer beeker/oom ger-roatoo*
cola/lemonade	**uma cola/uma limonada** *oomer koler/oomer leemoonader*
fruit juice	**um sumo de frutas** *oom soomoo der frootush*
mineral water	**uma água mineral** *oomer agwer meeneral*
(a glass of) red/white wine	**(um copo de) vinho tinto/branco** *(oom koppoo der) veenyoo teentoo/brawnkoo*
Nothing more, thanks.	**Mais nada, obrigado(-a).** *mighsh nader obrigadoo(-er)*
Where are the restrooms?	**Onde são as casas de banho?** *ond sawm ush kazush der banyoo*

SPECIAL REQUIREMENTS

I can't eat food containing …	**Não posso comer alimentos que contenham …** *nawm possoo koomair er-leemayntoosh ker kontaynyawm*
salt/sugar	**sal/açúcar** *sal/er-sookar*
Do you have meals/drinks for diabetics?	**Tem pratos/bebidas para diabéticos?** *taym pratoosh/ber-beedush per-rer dyer-bettikoosh*
Do you have vegetarian meals?	**Tem pratos vegetarianos?** *taym pratoosh ver-zher-ter-ryanoosh*

COMPLAINTS

That's not what I ordered.	**Não encomendei isso.** *nawm aynkoomaynday eesoo*
I asked for …	**Pedi …** *per-dee*
I can't eat this.	**Não posso comer isto.** *nawm possoo koomair eeshtoo*
The meat is …	**A carne …** *er karn*
overdone	**está cozida demais** *ishtah koozeeder der-mighsh*
rare	**está mal cozida** *ishtah mal koozeeder*
too tough	**é muito dura** *eh mweentoo doorer*
The food is cold.	**A comida está fria.** *er koomeeder ishtah freeer*
This isn't fresh.	**Isto não é fresco.** *eeshtoo nawm eh frayshkoo*
How much longer will our food be?	**Ainda demora muito?** *er-eender der-morer mweentoo*
We can't wait any longer. We're leaving.	**Não podemos esperar mais. Vamo-nos embora.** *nawm poodaymoosh ishper-rar mighsh. vamoonoosh aymborer*

PAYING

Tipping: See page 332.

I'd like to pay.	**Queria pagar.** *ker-reeer per-gar*
We'd like to pay separately.	**Queríamos contas separadas.** *ker-reeermoosh kontush ser-per-radush*
It's all together.	**É tudo junto.** *eh toodoo zhoontoo*

I think there's a mistake in this bill.	**Creio que há um engano na conta.** _krayoo ker ah oom aynganoo ner konter_
What is this amount for? '	**Isto é de quê?** _eeshtoo eh der kay_
I didn't have that. I had …	**Não escolhi isso. Eu escolhi …** _nawm ishkolyee eesoo. eoo ishkolyee_
Can I pay with this credit card?	**Posso pagar com este cartão de crédito?** _possoo per-gar kawm aysht kertawm der kreditoo_
Could I have a receipt?	**Queria uma factura.** _ker-reeer oomer fatoorer_
That was a very good meal.	**Foi uma refeição excelente.** _foy oomer rer-faysawm ayshser-laynt_

COURSE BY COURSE

Breakfast Pequeno almoço

I'd like …	**Queria …** _ker-reeer_
eggs	**ovos** _ovoosh_
fried eggs	**ovos estrelados** _ovooz ishtrer-ladoosh_
scrambled eggs	**ovos mexidos** _ovoosh mer-sheedoosh_
fruit juice	**sumo de fruta** _soomoo der frooter_
jam	**doce de fruta** _doass der frooter_
(cold/hot) milk	**leite (frio/quente)** _layt (freeoo/kaynt)_
rolls	**papo-secos** _papoo saykoosh_
toast	**torradas** _toorradush_

Appetizers Acepipes

Choose carefully, for Portuguese appetizers can be filling.
Appetizers/starters may also be listed on the menu under **Petiscos**.

assorted cold cuts	**carnes frias** _karnersh freeersh_	
squid Milanese	**lula à milanesa** _looler ah meelernehsa_	
smoked pork filet	**paio** _pighoo_	
spicy chicken stew	**pipis** _pippeesh_	

Chouriço _shohreesoo_
Smoked pork sausage flavored with paprika and garlic

Pimentos assados _peemayntoosh er-sadoosh_
Sweet peppers, roasted and served cold with olive oil and vinegar

Santola recheada _sawntoller rer-shyader_
Spider-crab stuffed with its own meat

Soups Sopas

sopa ...	_soaper_	
açorda à Alentejana	_erssoarder ah erlaynterzherner_	bread soup with garlic and herbs
à pescador	_ah pishker-doar_	fish soup
canja	_kanzher_	chicken soup with rice
de agriões	_der gryoynsh_	potato and watercress soup
de cozido	_der koozeedoo_	meat broth with vegetables and macaroni
de feijão	_der fayzhawm_	red kidney bean and cabbage soup
de feijão verde	_der fayzhawm vaird_	potato and green bean soup
de grelos	_der grayloosh_	turnip sprout soup
transmontana	_trawnshmontarner_	vegetable soup with bacon and bread

Caldo verde _kaldoo vaird_
Thick potato and kale soup with smoked sausage

Gaspacho _gushpashoo_
Chilled soup with diced tomatoes, sweet peppers, onions, cucumber, and croutons

Migas de bacalhau _meegush der ber-ker-lyow_
Dried cod soup flavored with garlic and thickened with bread

Sopa seca _soaper sayker_
Thick soup with beef, chicken, ham, smoked sausage, cabbage, and bread

Salads Saladas

salada	_ser-lader_	salad
de alface	_dalfass_	green salad
de atum	_der ertoong_	tuna and potato
mista	_meeshter_	tomato and lettuce
russa	_rooser_	boiled potatoes and carrots with mayonnaise

Salada completa _ser-lader komplehter_
Green leaves, tomato, palm hearts, boiled eggs, onions, and carrots

Fish and seafood Peixes mariscos

atum	_ertoong_	tuna
camarões grandes	_kermerrawms grawndis_	shrimp
espadarte	_ishper-darter_	swordfish
lagosta	_lergoashter_	lobster
linguado	_leengwadoo_	sole
lulas	_loolersh_	squid
pargo	_pargoo_	bream
polvo	_poalvoo_	octopus

Amêijoas à Bulhão Pato *er-mayzhooush ah boolyawm patoo*
Clams with coriander, garlic, and onion

Amêijoas à Portuguesa *er-mayzhooush ah poortoogayzer*
Clams cooked with garlic, parsley, and olive oil

Arroz de atum *er-rroash der-toom*
Tuna with rice, egg, tomato, and mayonnaise

Cabeça de pescada cozida *ker-bayser der pishkader koozeeder*
Fish stew, made from fish heads, especially hake

Bacalhau à Brás *ber-ker-lyow ah brash*
Dried cod fried with onions and potatoes, cooked in beaten egg

Bacalhau à Gomes de Sá *ber-ker-lyow ah goamish der sah*
Dried cod with olives, garlic, onions, parsley, and hard-boiled eggs

Bacalhau podre *ber-ker-lyow poadrer*
Baked layers of cod and fried potatoes

Caldeirada *kaldayrader*
Several kinds of fish with onions, tomatoes, potatoes, and olive oil

Lulas recheadas *loolush rer-shyadush*
Squid stuffed with egg yolk, minced ham, onion, and tomato

Meat and poultry Carnes e aves

Bife is the word for steak, even if it is veal, pork, or fish.

carne de vaca	*karn der vakker*	beef
galinha/frango	*ger-leenyer/frawngoo*	chicken
costeleta	*kooshter-layter*	chop/cutlet
presunto	*prer-soontoo*	cured ham
borrego	*boorraygoo*	lamb
carne de porco	*karn der poarkoo*	pork
coelho	*kwaylyoo*	rabbit

bife	*beef*	steak
medalhão	*mer-der-<u>lyawm</u>*	tenderloin steak
vitela	*vee<u>te</u>ler*	veal

Arroz de frango *er-<u>rroash</u> der <u>frawn</u>goo*
Fried chicken with white wine, ham, and rice in a casserole

Bife na frigideira *beef ner freezhee<u>day</u>rer*
Beef steak fried in butter, white wine, and garlic; served with ham and fried bread

Coelho assado *kw<u>ay</u>lyoo er-<u>sa</u>doo*
Roast rabbit with onions, cooked with white wine

Cozido à Portuguesa *koo<u>zee</u>doo ah poor<u>too</u>gayzer*
Boiled beef, bacon, smoked sausage, and vegetables; served with rice

Ensopado de cabrito *ayn<u>soo</u>padoo der ker-<u>bree</u>too*
Stew of kid (goat) and vegetables, served on slices of bread

Frango na púcara *<u>frawn</u>goo ner <u>poo</u>kerer*
Chicken stewed in port and cognac, then fried with almonds

Rojões à moda do Minho *roo<u>zhoynsh</u> ah <u>mod</u>der doo <u>mee</u>nyoo*
Chopped pork, marinated in white wine, onions, and herbs, and then fried

Tripas à moda do Porto *<u>tree</u>push ah <u>mod</u>der doo <u>poar</u>too*
Tripe cooked with pork products, beans, and chicken, served with rice

Vegetables Legumes

You'll recognize **brócolos**, **espargos**, **lentilhas**, **tomates**.

alface	*al<u>fass</u>*	lettuce
cebolas	*ser<u>boa</u>lush*	onions
cogumelos	*koogoo<u>me</u>loosh*	mushrooms
ervilhas	*eer<u>vee</u>lyush*	peas

favas	*favush*	broad beans
feijão	*fayzhawm*	kidney beans
feijão verde	*fayzhawm vaird*	green beans
pimentos	*peemayntoosh*	sweet peppers

Arroz *erroash*

Rice, which may be served **~ de alhos** (with garlic), **~ de cozido** (cooked in meat stock), **~ de feijão** (with red or white beans), **~ de frango** (with fried chicken in a casserole)

Batatas *bertatush*

Potatoes, these may be **~ cozidas** (boiled), **~ cozidas com pele** (boiled in their skins), **~ fritas** (fries), **~ palha** (matchsticks), **puré de ~** (mashed)

Fruit Frutas

You'll recognize **banana**, **coco**, **lima**, **limão**, **melão**, **pêra**, **tangerina**.

abacate	*er-ber-kat*	avocado
abacaxi	*er-bakashee*	pineapple
ameixas	*er-mayshush*	plums
cerejas	*ser-rayzhush*	cherries
laranja	*ler-rawnzher*	orange
maçã	*mer-sah*	apple
morangos	*moorawngoosh*	strawberries
pêssego	*paiser-goo*	peach

Cheese Queijo

Cheeses are usually a mixture of sheep's and goat's milk, or cow's and goat's milk.

creamy   **Queijo da Serra, Azeitão, Évora, Castelo Branco** (blue), **Serpa**

| goat's milk cheese | **Cabreiro** (must be eaten fresh), **Cardiga** |
| cow's milk cheese | **São João**, **São Jorge**, **Bola** (hard cheese), **Ilha** (from the Azores Islands); **Queijo do Sertão** (Brazilian) |

Desserts/Pastries Sobremesas/Pastelaria

Cakes, custards and sweets—usually made of egg yolks—are part of every meal. You may find them a bit too sweet.

arrufada de Coimbra	*er-rroofader der kooeembrer*	cinnamon dough cake
bolo podre	*boaloo poadrer*	honey and cinnamon cake
broas castelares	*broaersh kershterlahrish*	sweet-potato biscuits
leite-creme	*layt krem*	custard, often with caramel topping
marmelada	*murmer-lader*	thick quince paste
mousse de maracujá	*mooss der marakoozhah*	passion fruit mousse
ovos moles de Aveiro	*ovoosh mollish davayroo*	beaten egg yolks cooked in syrup
pudim flan	*poodeem flan*	caramel custard
quindim	*keendeen*	coconut and egg yolk pudding

Babá-de-moça *babah dzhee moaser*
Dessert made of egg yolk, coconut milk, and syrup

Canjica *kawnzheeker*
Dessert made with dried white sweet corn and milk

Pastel de Tentúgal *pushtell der tayntoogal*
Very thin flaky pastry filled with beaten egg yolks cooked in syrup

Pudim Molotov _poodeem mollotof_
Fluffy egg-white mousse immersed in caramel sauce

DRINKS

Aperitifs Aperitivos

The Portuguese like to sip an aperitif before dinner; some drink vermouth while others prefer a dry port or madeira, or a **Moscatel de Setúbal** served chilled.

Please bring me a vermouth.
Por favor, traga-me um vermute.
por fervoar trager mer oom vehrmooter

Beer Cerveja

Beer is a popular drink, always served cold. Try local brews, such as **Sagres**. Beer is often served with **tremoços** (salted lupin seeds) or **amendoins** (peanuts).

I'd like …	**Queria…** _ker-reeer_
a dark beer	**uma cerveja preta** _oomer servayzher prayter_
a draft beer	**uma imperial [um chope]** _oomer eenperryal [oom shoppi]_
a lager	**uma cerveja (branca)** _oomer servayzher (branker)_
a bottle/glass/mug	**uma garrafa/um copo/uma caneca** _oomer ger-rafer/oom koppoo/oomer ker-nehker_

Wines Vinhos

Portugal may be best known for its blush [rosé] and fortified wines, but you'll find a variety of excellent red and white wines as well.

I'd like a (half) bottle of … wine.	**Queria uma (meia-)garrafa de vinho …** *ker-reeer oomer (mayer) ger-rafer der veenyoo*
red/white/blush [rosé]	**tinto/branco/rosé** *teentoo/brawnkoo/rozeh*
a carafe/half liter/glass	**um jarro/meio-litro/copo** *oom zharoo/mayoo leetroo/ koppoo*
I'd like a corkscrew.	**Queria um saca-rolhas.** *ker-reeer oom saker roalyush*
Cheers!	**Saúde!** *sahood*

Um (vinho da) Madeira *oom (veenyoo der) merdayrer*
Excellent red and white aperitif and dessert wines from Madeira

Um (vinho do) Porto *oom (veenyoo doo) poartoo*
Port, there are two types: the younger ruby variety (**tinto aloirado**) is full-colored and full-bodied, while the tawny (**aloirado**) is less sweet, amber-colored, and delicate

Um vinho verde *oom veenyoo vaird*
"Green wine," produced in the Minho area in northwest Portugal, made from unripened grapes; faintly sparkling and acid in taste, very refreshing and with low alcohol content

Reading the label

adega	vineyard/winery	**ligeiro**	light
branco	white	**palacio**	vineyard
casta	grape	**quinta**	vineyard
colheita	vintage	**rosé**	blush [rosé]
DOC	highest quality wines	**seco**	dry
doce	sweet	**solar**	vineyard
encorpado	full-bodied	**tinto**	red
engarrafado na Origem		**vinho**	wine
wine bottled at estate		**vinho de mesa**	table wine
espumante	sparkling	**vinho regional**	regional wine
extra-seco	very dry	**VQPRD**	quality wines from
IPR	quality wines	smaller defined regions	

Other drinks

You'll recognize **gim tónico, rum, porto** (port wine)**, vermute, vodka, whisky com soda.** You may also like to try a Portuguese brandy, like **Antiqua, Borges,** or **Constantino.**

aguardente …	*agwahdent*	… spirit
de figo	*der <u>fee</u>goo*	fig spirit
de medronho	*der mer-<u>droan</u>yoo*	arbutus berry* spirit
velha	<u>*vehl*</u>*ya*	brandy
batida …	*bat<u>shee</u>der*	cachaça cane spirit with fruit juice, sugar, ice
de caju	*dzhee ka<u>zhoo</u>*	batida, with cashew nut
de coco	*der <u>koa</u>koo*	batida with coconut
de maracujá	*der mer-rer-koo<u>zhah</u>*	batida with passion fruit

* small strawberry-like fruit

caipirinha	*kighpeereenyah*	cachaça, crushed lime, sugar, and ice
caipirinha de vodka	*kighpeereenyah dzhee vodka*	caipirinha made with vodka
Cuba livre	*koober leebrer*	rum and cola
ginjinha	*zhenzheenyer*	spirit distilled from morello cherries

Non-alcoholic drinks

Look for the bars advertising **sucos** (juices) with lots of fresh fruit on display.

I'd like some …	**Queria …** *ker-reeer*
fruit juice	**um sumo** *oom soomoo*
orange juice	**um sumo de laranja natural** *oom soomoo der ler-rawnzher ner-tooral*
mineral water	**uma água mineral** *oomer agwer meener-ral*
carbonated/non-carbonated	**com gás/sem gás** *kawm gash/saym gash*
tea/coffee	**um chá/um café** *oom shah/oom ker-feh*
with milk/lemon	**com leite/limão** *kawm layt/lymawm*

MENU READER

alourado(-a) **no forno**	*er-lohradoo(-er)* *noo foarnoo*	oven-browned
aos cubos	*owsh kooboosh*	diced
assado(-a)	*er-sadoo(-er)*	roasted
com natas	*kawm natush*	creamed
cozido(-a)	*koozeedoo(-er)*	boiled
cozido(-a) a vapor	*koozeedoo(-er)* *er ver-poar*	steamed
escalfado(-a)	*ishkalfadoo(-er)*	poached
estufado(-a)	*ishtoofadoo(-er)*	braised
frito(-a)	*freetoo(-er)*	fried
[de]fumado(-a)	*[day]foomadoo(-er)*	smoked
grelhado(-a)	*gre-lyadoo(-er)*	grilled
guisado(-a)	*geezadoo(-er)*	stewed
marinado(-a)	*mer-reenadoo(-er)*	marinated
no forno	*noo foarnoo(-er)*	baked
panado(-a)	*per-nadoo(-er)*	breaded
mal passado(-a)	*mal per-sadoo(-er)*	rare/underdone
meio passado(-a)	*mayoo per-sadoo(-er)*	medium
bem passado(-a)	*baym per-sadoo(-er)*	well-done
picante	*peekawnt*	spicy
recheado(-a)	*rer-shyadoo(-er)*	stuffed
salteado(-a)	*saltyadoo(-er)*	sautéed

A

à .../à moda de ... ... style
à escolha of your choice
à la carte/lista a la carte
abacate avocado

abacaxi pineapple
abóbora pumpkin
açafrão saffron
acarajé fried beans

acepipes (variados) (assorted) appetizers

açorda thick soup with bread; **~ alentejana** with poached eggs; **~ à moda de Sesimbra** with fish

açorda à Alentejana bread soup with garlic and herbs

açúcar sugar

adocicado slightly sweet

agrião, agriões watercress

água water

água de coco coconut juice

água mineral mineral water; **~ com gás** carbonated; **sem gás** non-carbonated

água-pé weak wine

aguardente spirit; **~ bagaceira** distilled from grape husks; **~ de figo** fig spirit; **~ de medronho** arbutus berry spirit; **~ velha** well-aged brandy

aipo celery

alcachofra artichoke

alcaparras capers

aletria sweet noodle pudding

alface lettuce

Algarvia almond layer cake

alheira garlic sausage of breadcrumbs and ground meat; **~ à transmontana** served with fried eggs, fried potatoes, and cabbage

alho garlic

alho porro leek

almoço lunch

almôndegas fish or meat balls

alperces apricots

amargo bitter

amêijoas baby clams; **~ à Bulhão Pato** fried in olive oil with garlic

and coriander; **~ à espanhola** baked with onions, tomatoes, and peppers; **~ ao natural** steamed with herbs; **~ na cataplana** steamed with smoked ham

ameixas plums; **~ secas** prunes

amêndoa amarga almond liqueur

amêndoas almonds

amendoins peanuts

amoras blackberries

ananás pineapple

anchovas anchovies

anis anise liqueur

Antiqua aged Portuguese grape brandy

ao ... in the style of ...

aperitivos aperitifs

arenque herring

arroz rice; **~ à grega** with diced vegetables; **~ de alhos** with garlic; **~ de Cabidela** with chicken blood; **~ de cenoura** with carrots; **~ de coco** with coconut milk; **~ de cozido** cooked in a meat stock; **~ de feijão** with red or white beans; **~ de frango** with fried chicken casserole; **~ de grelos** with turnip sprouts; **~ de manteiga** with butter; **~ de pato no forno** baked with duck, cooked with bacon and chouriço; **~ de tomate** with tomato

arroz doce rice pudding

arrufada de Coimbra raised dough cake flavored with cinnamon

atum tuna; **bife de ~** tuna steak marinated and fried

aveia oats

avelãs hazelnuts

aves poultry

azeda sorrel

azedo sour

azeite olive oil

azeitonas (pretas/de Elvas/recheadas) olives (black/green/stuffed)

B

babá-de-moça egg yolk dessert

bacalhau cod; ~ **à Brás** fried with onions and potatoes; ~ **à Gomes de Sá** dried cod with olives and eggs; ~ **à provinciana** poached, with potatoes and broccoli; ~ **à transmontana** braised with cured pork or chouriço; ~ **cozido com todos** poached, with boiled cabbage, onions, and potatoes; ~ **de caldeirada** braised, with onions and tomatoes; ~ **e ovos** salted, with potatoes and black olives

bagaço spirit made from grape husks

banana banana

barriga-de-freira dessert made of egg yolk, bread, and syrup

batatas potatoes

batatas cozidas (com pele) boiled potatoes (in their skins)

batatas doces sweet potatoes

batatas fritas fries

batatas palha potato matchsticks

batida mixed drink of cachaça, fruit juice, sugar, ice; ~ **de caju** with cashew nut; ~ **de coco** with coconut; ~ **de maracujá** with passion fruit

batido milk shake

baunilha vanilla

bebida drink; ~ **sem álcool/não alcoólica** soft drink; ~ **espirituosa** spirits

bebidas incluídas drinks included

berbigão type of cockle

beringela eggplant

besugo bream (fish)

beterraba beet

bica espresso

bife steak/cutlet

bife na frigideira fried beef steak

bife à milanesa breaded veal cutlet

bifinhos de vitela slices of veal filet served with Madeira wine sauce

bola de Berlim donut

bolachas cookies

bolachas de água e sal crackers

bolinhos de amêndoa almond biscuits

bolinhos de bacalhau fried dried cod balls

bolinhos de canela cinnamon biscuits

bolo cake, pastry; ~ **de arroz** rice cake; ~ **de chila do Algarve** pumpkin jam cake (*Algarve*); ~ **inglês** cake with candied fruit; ~ **podre** cake flavored with honey and cinnamon; ~ **rei** Christmas cake

Borges aged Portuguese grape brandy

borracho squab

borrego lamb

(na) brasa charcoal-grilled

broas castelares sweet-potato cookies

broas de mel corn flour and honey cookies

brócolos broccoli

C

C/ with
cabrito kid
caça game
cacau cocoa
cachorro quente hot dog
cafezinho strong black coffee
café coffee; **~ sem cafeína** caffeine-free; **~ duplo** large cup; **~ frio** iced; **~ com leite** with milk; **~ instantâneo** instant
caipirinha cachaça (sugar cane spirit), crushed lime, sugar, and ice; **~ de vodka** caipirinha made with vodka, rather than cachaça
(em) calda (in) syrup
caldeirada fish simmered with tomatoes and potatoes ; **~ à fragateira** fish, shellfish, and mussels simmered in a fish stock with tomatoes and herbs, served on toast; **~ à moda da Póvoa** hake, skate, sea-bass, and eel simmered with tomatoes in olive oil
caldo consommé
caldo de cana sugar-cane juice
caldo verde potato and kale soup
camarões shrimp; **~ à baiana** in spicy tomato sauce with boiled rice; **~ fritos** fried; **~ grandes** large shrimp
canapé small open sandwich
caneca pint-size beer mug
canela cinnamon
canja chicken soup with rice .
capão capon
caracol snail; spiral bun with currants

caracóis à Algarvia snails flavored with oregano (*Algarve*)
caranguejo crab
carapau mackerel; **~ de escabeche** fried and dipped in vinegar and olive-oil sauce
cardápio menu
caril curry powder
carioca small weak coffee
carne de porco pork; **~ à alentejana** chopped pork cooked with clams, tomatoes, and onions (*Alentejo*)
carne de sol sun-dried meat, jerky
carne de vaca beef
carne picada chopped meat
carneiro mutton; **~ guisado [ensopado]** stewed with tomatoes, garlic, bay leaves, and parsley
carnes meat; **~ frias** assorted cold cuts
caseiro homemade
castanhas chestnuts; **~ de caju** cashew nuts
(água de) Castelo carbonated mineral water
(na) cataplana steamed in a copper pan
cavacas glazed cookies
cavala mackerel
cebolas onions
cenouras carrots
cerejas cherries
cerveja beer; **~ branca** lager; **~ em garrafa** bottled; **~ imperial** draft; **~ preta** stout
cherne black grouper
chicória chicory

chispalhada pig's feet stewed with white beans, cabbage, bacon, and blood sausage

chispe pig's foot

chocolate quente hot chocolate

chocos cuttlefish; **~ com tinta** cooked in their own ink

chouriço smoked pork sausage

churrasco misto mixed barbecue (beef, sausage, and pork)

chá tea; **~ com leite** with milk; **~ com limão** with lemon; **~ de limão** made from lemon peel infusion; **~ maté** infusion from maté-tree leaf ·

cobrança de suplemento para grupos de … ou mais service charge for parties of … or more

coco coconut

codorniz quail

coelho rabbit; **~ assado** roast

coentro coriander

cogumelos (button) mushrooms

colorau paprika

com leite with milk

comida caseira homemade

cominhos cumin

compota compote, stewed fruit

condimentos seasoning

congro conger eel

conhaque cognac

Constantino aged Portuguese brandy

conta bill

copo glass

coração heart

cordeiro lamb

corvina croaker (fish)

costeleta chop/cutlet

couve cabbage

couve lombarda savoy cabbage

couve portuguesa kale

couve roxa red cabbage

couve-de-Bruxelas brussels sprouts

couve-flor cauliflower

coxinha de galinha pastry filled with chicken

cozido à portuguesa beef and pork boiled with chouriço (*northern Port.*)

cozinha cooking/cuisine

cravinhos cloves

creme cream; **~ leite** custard

crepe pancake

criação poultry

cru raw

crustáceos shellfish

Cuba livre rum and cola

curau mashed sweet corn cooked in coconut milk with sugar and cinnamon

D

da época in season

da estação subject to availability

dendê palm oil

doce sweet; **meio-~** medium-sweet; **~ de fruta** jam; **~ de laranja** marmalade

doce de abóbora pumpkin dessert

doces desserts; **~ de ovos e amêndoa** marzipan

dose portion

E

eiró eel

ementa menu/set menu; **~ turística** tourist menu

empada de galinha chicken pie
empadinha roasted pastry
empadão large type of pie;
~ de batata shepherd's pie
enchidos assorted pork products made into sausages
enguia eel
ensopado de cabrito kid stew
entrada starter/appetizer
entrecosto spare rib
erva-doce aniseed
ervilhas peas
espadarte swordfish
espargos asparagus
esparguete spaghetti
esparregado purée of assorted greens in cream
especialidades specialties;
~ da casa of the house;
~ regionais/da região local specialties
espetada cooked on a skewer
(no) espeto spit-roasted
espinafres spinach
espumante sparkling (wine)
esturjão sturgeon

F

faisão pheasant
farinha flour
farofel manioc (cassava) flour
farófias beaten egg white poached in milk, topped with cinnamon and egg custard
fatias slices; **~ da China** cold, baked egg yolks topped with syrup flavored with lemon and cinnamon;
~ douradas French toast
favas broad beans

febras de porco à alentejana pieces of pork filet grilled with onions, chouriço, and bacon
feijão bean; **~ branco** navy;
~ catarino pink; **~ encarnado** red;
~ frade black-eyed; **~ guisado [ensopado]** stewed with bacon in a tomato sauce; **~ preto** black;
~ verde green beans
feito a pedido made to order
fiambre boiled ham
fígado liver; **~ de aves** chicken
figos figs
filete filet of fish
filhó fritter; **~ de abóbora** of pumpkin purée
fios de ovos fine golden strands of egg yolk cooked in syrup
folhado sweet puff-pastry delicacy
(no) forno baked
framboesas raspberries
frango chicken; **~ assado** roast chicken; **~ na púcara** chicken stewed in Port wine (*northern Port.*)
fresco fresh, chilled
(na) frigideira sautéed
frio cold
fritada de peixe deep-fried fish
fruta fruit; **~ em calda** in syrup;
~ do conde custard apple
frutos do mar seafood

G

galantina pressed meat in gelatin
geleia de fruta jam
geleia de laranja marmalade
galinha stewing chicken

galinhola woodcock
galão weak milky coffee served in a glass
gambas shrimp
ganso goose
garoto (white) coffee served in a small cup
garoupa large grouper (fish)
garrafa bottle; **meia-~** half bottle
gasosa lemonade
gaspacho chilled soup
gelado ice cream; chilled/iced
gelatina jelly
gelo ice, ice cubes; **com ~** with ice; **sem ~** without ice
genebra Dutch gin
gengibre ginger
gim gin
ginjinha spirit distilled from morello cherries
girafa draft beer in fluted glass
gratinado oven-browned
grelos turnip sprouts
groselha red currant
grão chickpeas; **~ com bacalhau** stew of chickpeas, potatoes, and dried cod filets
guaraná a tropical fruit drink

H

hortaliça fresh vegetables
hortelã mint

I

incluído no preço included in price
imperial draft beer
inhame yam
iogurte yogurt

iscas sliced liver; **~ à portuguesa** marinated in white wine with garlic and herbs, then fried
iva incluído sales tax [VAT] included

J

jantar dinner
jardineira mixed vegetables
jarro carafe
javali wild boar

K

kibe meat and bulgur (cracked wheat) croquette

L

lagosta lobster; **~ americana** fried with onions and garlic, flambéed in brandy, served in Madeira wine sauce; **~ suada** with onions, garlic, and tomatoes
lagostim crayfish; **~-do-rio** fresh-water crayfish
lampreia lamprey; **~ à moda do Minho** marinated, then poached and served with rice
lanche snack
laranja orange
laranjada orangeade
lavagante lobster
lebre hare
legumes vegetables
leite milk; **~ com chocolate** chocolate drink
leite de coco coconut milk
leite-creme custard, often with caramel topping

leitão suckling pig; **~ à Bairrada** coated with spicy lard and spit-roasted; **~ recheado** stuffed with spicy minced bacon, chouriço, and giblets, then roasted

lentilhas lentils

licor liqueur

lima lime

limonada type of lemon drink

limão lemon

língua tongue

linguado sole; **~ à meunière** sautéed in butter, served with parsley and lemon juice; **~ com recheio de camarão** filled with shrimp in a white sauce

linguiça very thin chouriço

lista dos vinhos wine list

lombo loin

louro bay leaf

lulas squid; **~ de caldeirada** simmered with white wine, onions, and parsley; **~ recheadas** braised and stuffed

M

maçã apple

maçapão marzipan

macarrão macaroni

Madeira Madeira wine

maduro mature

maionese mayonnaise

malagueta hot pepper

mamão papaya

manga mango

manjericão basil

manteiga butter

mãozinhas de vitela guisadas calves' feet braised with onions, parsley, and vinegar

(à) marinheira with white wine, onions, and parsley

mariscos seafood

marmelada thick quince paste

massa pasta; dough, pastry

massapão marzipan

massapães almond macaroons

mate ice-cold Paraguay tea

mazagrã chilled black coffee served on the rocks with sugar and lemon slice

medalhão tenderloin steak

medronho arbutus berry (small strawberry-like fruit)

meia desfeita poached pieces of dried cod fried with chickpeas, onions, and vinegar, topped with hard-boiled eggs and chopped garlic

meia dose half portion

meio-frango assado half a roast chicken

mel honey

melancia watermelon

melão melon; **~ com presunto** with ham

mero red grouper (fish)

mexilhões mussels

migas de bacalhau dried cod soup

mil-folhas millefeuille/puff pastry with jam and cream

milho sweet corn

mioleira brains

miolos brains; **~ mexidos com ovos** lamb brains fried and served with scrambled eggs

moelas spicy stew of chicken stomach

morangos strawberries; **~ silvestre** wild

morcela blood sausage

mortadela mortadella (Bologna sausage)

mostarda mustard

mousse de chocolate chocolate mousse

mousse de maracujá passion fruit mousse

muito mal passado rare (meat, etc.)

N

nabiças turnip greens

nabos turnips

nata(s) fresh cream; **~ batida(s)** whipped

(ao) natural plain, without dressing, sauce, etc.

nêsperas loquat (fruit)

noz nut; **~ moscada** nutmeg

O

óleo oil; **~ de amendoim** peanut oil

omelete omelet; **~ de camarão** shrimp; **~ de chouriço** smoked sausage; **~ de espargos** asparagus

orégão oregano

osso bone

ostras oysters; **~ do Algarve** oysters baked in butter and dry wine (*Algarve*); **~ recheadas** oyster shells stuffed with oysters, onions, garlic, breadcrumbs, egg yolk, lemon juice, then oven-browned

ou servido com … the same served with …

ovos eggs; **~ Portuguesa** baked in a tomato shell with spices and breadcrumbs; **~ cozidos** boiled; **~ escalfados** poached; **~ estrelados/fritos** fried; **~ mexidos** scrambled; **~ moles de Aveiro** beaten yolks cooked in syrup (*Aveiro*); **~ quentes** soft-boiled eggs; **~ verdes** eggs stuffed with boiled yolks, onions, and parsley, and fried

P

paio smoked, rolled pork filet; **~ com ervilhas** simmered with peas and chopped onions

panqueca pancake

pão (escuro/integral) bread (brown/wholewheat); **~ de centeio** rye bread

pão de queijo pastry made with cheese and manioc flour

pão-de-ló coffee cake

pãozinho bread roll

papo-seco roll

papos-de-anjo egg yolk macaroons

para dois for two

pargo bream (fish)

passas (de uvas) raisins

pastel small pie

pastel de coco coconut pastry

pastel de feijão bean pastry

pastel de massa tenra soft crust pastry pie filled with ground meat

pastel de nata/de Belém small cream tart

pastel de Santa Clara tartlet with almond-paste filling

pastel de Tentúgal flaky pastry filled with beaten egg yolks

pato duck; **~ estufado** braised in white wine with onions, parsley, and bay leaf

peito de galinha chicken breast

peixe fish; **~-agulha** garfish; **~-espada** cutlass fish

pepino cucumber

pepinos de conserva pickles

pequeno almoço breakfast

pêra pear

perca perch

perdiz partridge; **~ à caçador(a)** simmered with carrots, onions, white wine, and herbs; **~ com molho de vilão** poached and served with cold sauce of olive oil, vinegar, and onions

perna de galinha chicken leg

pernil ham

pêro variety of eating apple

peru turkey

pés de porco pig's feet

pescada whiting; **~ cozida com todos** poached and served with boiled potatoes and green beans

pescadinhas de rabo na boca fried whole whiting

pêssego peach

petiscos appetizers

pevide pip (seed); salted pumpkin seed

pikles pickled vegetables

pimenta pepper

pimentos sweet peppers; **~ assados** roasted

pinhoada pine nut brittle

pinhão pine nut

pipis spicy giblet stew

piri-piri seasoning of hot chili pepper and olive oil

polvo octopus

pombo pigeon; **~ estufado** braised with bacon, onions, and white wine, served with fried bread

porco pork

(vinho do) Porto port

posta slice of fish or meat

prato do dia dish of the day

prato feito set meal

prato principal main course

pratos combinados set dishes

pratos frios cold dishes

pré-pagamento payment in advance

preço suplementar extra charge/supplement

prego small steak, often served in a roll

presunto cured ham; **~ cru** dried ham

preço price

primeiro prato first course

pudim de bacalhau dried-cod loaf, served with tomato sauce

pudim flan caramel custard

pudim Molotov mousse in caramel sauce

pudim à portuguesa custard flavored with brandy and raisins

puré de batatas mashed potatoes with milk and butter

puro straight/neat

Q

queijada small cottage-cheese tart; **~ de Sintra** flavored with cinnamon

queijinhos do céu marzipan balls rolled in sugar

queijo cheese

quente hot; **~ e frio** hot fudge sundae

quiabo okra

quindim pudding made with coconut and egg yolks

R

rabanada french toast

rabanetes radishes

raia skate (fish)

rainha-cláudia greengage plum

recheio stuffing, forcemeat

refeição meal; **~ completa** set menu; **~ ligeira** snack

refogado onions fried in olive oil

refrescos soft drinks

repolho cabbage

rins kidneys

rissóis de camarão deep-fried pastry envelopes filled with shrimp

robalo sea bass

rodela round slice

rojões à alentejana pork cubes fried with baby clams, diced potatoes, and onions

rojões à moda do Minho fried chopped meat

rolo de carne picada meatloaf

rolos de couve lombarda savoy cabbage leaves stuffed with ground meat

romã pomegranate

rosca ring-shaped white bread

rosmaninho rosemary

ruivo red gurnard (fish)

S

sal salt

salada salad; **~ completa** with tomato, palm hearts, boiled eggs; **~ de alface/escarola** green salad; **~ de agrião** watercress; **~ de atum** tuna and potato; **~ de feijão frade** black-eyed bean; **~ de pimentos assados** made with grilled sweet peppers; **~ de tomate** tomato; **~ mista** tomato and lettuce; **~ russa** diced boiled potatoes and carrots with mayonnaise

salgado salty/salted

salmonete red mullet; **~ grelhado com molho de manteiga** grilled and served with melted butter, chopped parsley, and lemon; **~ setúbalense** grilled red mullet

salmão salmon

salsa parsley

salsicha sausage

salva sage

sandes/sanduíche sandwich

santola spider-crab; **~ recheada** stuffed with its own meat

sarapatel pork or mutton stew, thickened with blood

sarda mackerel

sardinhas sardines

sável shad (herring-like fish)

seco dry; **meio-~** medium-dry

sêmola semolina

sericá alentejano cinnamon soufflé

serviço incluído service included
sidra cider
só por encomenda made to order
sobremesas dessert
solha flounder
sonho type of doughnut
sopa soup; **~ à pescador** fish soup
sopa de ~ type of soup; **~ abóbora** pumpkin; **~ agriões** potato and watercress; **~ camarão** shrimp; **~ cenoura** carrot; **~ coentros** with coriander, bread, and poached eggs; **~ cozido** meat broth with vegetables and macaroni; **~ ervilhas** green pea; **~ favas** broad bean; **~ feijão frade** black-eyed bean; **~ grelos** turnip sprout; **~ grão** chickpea; **~ hortaliça** vegetable; **~ rabo de boi** oxtail; **~ tomate** tomato with poached eggs and bread
sopa do dia soup of the day
sopa juliana soup with shredded vegetables
sopa seca thick beef and chicken soup
sopa transmontana vegetable soup with bacon and bread
sumo fruit juice **~ de abacaxi** pineapple; **~ de laranja** orange; **~ de toranja** grapefruit
sugestão do chefe the chef recommends
suspiro meringue

T

taça long-stemmed glass, cup
tainha gray mullet (fish)
tâmaras dates
tangerinas tangerines
tarte de amêndoa almond tart
tempero seasoning
tenro tender
tigelada dessert of eggs beaten with milk and cinnamon
tinto red (wine)
todos os pratos servidos com ... all meals served with ...
tomates tomatoes
tomilho thyme
toranja grapefruit
tornedó round cut of prime beef
torrada toast
torrão de ovos marzipan candy
torta swiss roll; **~ de laranja** with orange juice; **~ de Viana** filled with lemon curd
tosta toasted sandwich; **~ mista** with ham-and-cheese
toucinho bacon; **~ do céu** kind of marzipan pudding
tremoço salted lupin seed
tripas à moda do Porto tripe cooked with pork, served with rice
trouxa de vitela veal olive
trouxas de ovos egg yolks poached in sweetened water and topped with syrup
trufa truffle
truta trout
túberas truffles
tutano marrow

U

uvas grapes
uísque whisky

V

vaca, carne de beef
vagens green beans
variado assorted
veado venison
vegetais variados choice of
vegetables
vieira scallop
vinagre vinegar
vinho wine; **~ da casa** house
wine; **~ da Madeira** Madeira
wine; **~ do Porto** port; **~ da
região** local wine; **~ generoso**
well-aged and fortified; **~ licoroso**
naturally sweet; **~ verde** "green
wine"
vitela veal

X

xinxim de galinha chicken in
shrimp sauce

RUSSIAN

PLACES TO EAT

Бар *bar*
Bar found in hotels

Блинная *bleenaya*
Blini bar; serves Блины (**bleeni**), Russian pancakes, with various toppings, sweet and savory

Буфет *boofyet*
Snack bar; good for light meals

Закусочная *zakoosachnaya*
A kind of snack bar

Кафе *kafye*
Café; despite its name, a Russian "café" is the equivalent of a Western restaurant; many close by 9 p.m., 11 p.m. at the latest

Кафе-кондитерская *kafye-kandeetyerskaya*
These cafés serve coffee and cakes

Кафе-мороженое *kafye-marozhenaya*
Ice-cream parlor serving ice cream, drinks, and cocktails

Кафетерий *kafeetyereey*
Cafeteria; usually with no seats, serving small dishes, snacks, and salads

Пельменная *peelmyenaya*
Small restaurant serving mainly пельмени (**peelmyenee**), a kind of meat dumpling

Пивной бар *peevnoy bar*
Beer bar; serves beer and appetizers, often crowded

Пирожковая *peerashkovaya*
Snack bar; sells пирожки (**peerashkee**), savory pastries with various fillings (meat, cabbage, rice, jam)

Ресторан *reestaran*
Restaurant; often a place where you go for a meal and a whole evening's entertainment, with music and dancing; reserve a table in advance; try restaurants where they serve Georgian, Armenian, Azerbaijani, or Uzbek specialities

Столовая *stalovaya*
Cafeteria; self-service, low prices, no alcohol

Чайная *chaynaya*
Tearoom or small café

Шашлычная *shashlichnaya*
An establishment serving шашлык (**shashlik**), pieces of lamb grilled on skewers, as well as other typical dishes from the Caucasus and Central Asia

MEAL TIMES

Breakfast (завтрак **zaftrak**): 7 a.m.–10 a.m.

Lunch (обед **abyet**): 11 a.m.–4 p.m.

Dinner (ужин **oozhin**): 6 p.m.–10 or 10:30 p.m.

RUSSIAN CUISINE

The country's geographical, climatic, and ethnic variety is reflected in a rich and varied cuisine. The Russians have a "sweet tooth" and are very fond of desserts and pastries, as well as their excellent ice cream. Eating plays an important part in Russian social life, and it is while dining that you'll find Russians at their most hospitable. Don't forget to wish your table companions a hearty appetite—Приятного аппетита! (*preeyatnava apeeteeta*).

FINDING A PLACE TO EAT

Can you recommend a good restaurant?	Какой ресторан Вы рекомендуете? *kakoy reestaran vi reekameendooeetye*
Is there a(n) … near here?	Здесь есть … поблизости? *zdyes' yest' pableezastee*
traditional local restaurant	национальный ресторан *natsianal'niy reestaran*
Russian/Georgian restaurant	русский/грузинский ресторан *roosskeey/groozeenskeey reestaran*
inexpensive restaurant	недорогой ресторан *needaragoy reestaran*
vegetarian restaurant	вегетарианский ресторан *veegeetaryanskiy reestaran*
Where can I find a(n) …?	Где находится …? *gdye nakhodeetsa*
café	кафе *kafe*
ice-cream parlor	кафе-мороженое *kafe marozheenaye*
pizzeria	пиццерия *peetseereeya*

RESERVATIONS

I'd like to reserve a table for two.	Я хотел(а) бы заказать столик на 2. *ya khatyel(a) bi zakazat' stoleek na dvaeekh*
For this evening/ tomorrow at …	на сегодня вечером/завтра на … *na seevodnya vyecheeram/ zaftra na*
We'll come at 8:00.	Мы будем в 8 часов. *mi boodem v voseem' chyasof*
We have a reservation.	У нас заказ. *oo nas zakas*
Could we sit …?	Можно нам сесть …? *mozhna nam syest'*
over there/outside	вон там/на улице *von tam/na ooleetse*
in a non-smoking area	где не курят *gdye nyee kooryat*
by the window	у окна *oo akna*
Smoking or non-smoking?	Курящий или некурящий? *kooryashchyeey eelee neekooryashchyeey*

ORDERING

Always check prices carefully before ordering, to avoid an unpleasant surprise.

Waiter!/Waitress!	Официант!/Официантка! *ofeetsiant/ofeetsiantka*
May I see the wine list, please?	Можно посмотреть карту вин? *mozhna pasmatryet' kartoo veen*
Do you have a set menu?	У Вас есть меню? *oo vas yest' meenyoo*

Can you recommend some typical local dishes?	Что Вы рекомендуете типично местное? *shto vi reekameen-dooeetye teepeechna meestnaye*
Could you tell me what … is?	Скажите, что такое ...? *skazhitye shto takoye*
What's in it?	Что туда входит? *shto tooda fkhodeet*
I'll have …	Я возьму ... *ya vaz'moo*
a bottle/glass/carafe of …	бутылку/стакан/графин ... *booteelkoo/stakan/grafeen*

SPECIAL REQUESTS

Could I have salad instead of vegetables, please?	Можно мне салат вместо овощей? *mozhna mnye salat vmyesta avashchyey*
Does the meal come with vegetables/potatoes?	Это блюдо с овощами/ с картошкой? *eta blyooda s avashchyamee/s kartoshkoy*
May I have some …?	Можно мне ...? *mozhna mnye*
bread	хлеба *khlyeba*
butter	масла *masla*
lemon	лимон *leemon*
mustard	горчицу *garchyeetsa*
pepper	перец *pyereets*
salt	соль *sol'*
seasoning	приправы *preepavi*
sugar	сахар *sakhar*
artificial sweetener	сахарин *sakhareen*
blue cheese dressing	сырная заправка *sirnaya zaprafka*

vinaigrette	уксусная заправка *ooksoosnaya zaprafka*
Could we have a child's seat, please?	Можно детский стульчик, пожалуйста. *mozhna dyetskeey stool'chyeek pazhalsta*
Where can I change the baby?	Где можно перепеленать ребёнка? *gdye mozhna peereepeeleenat' reebyonka*

GENERAL QUESTIONS

Could I/we have a(n) (clean) …, please?	Можно (чистый) … , пожалуйста? *mozhna (chyeestiy) pazhalsta*
ashtray	пепельницу *pyepeel'neetsoo*
cup/glass	чашку/стакан *chyashkoo/stakan*
fork/knife/spoon	вилку/нож/ложку *veelkoo/nosh/loshkoo*
napkin	салфетку *salfyetkoo*
plate/spoon	тарелку *taryelkoo*
I'd like …	Я хотел(а) бы … *ya khatyel(a) bi*
beer	пиво *peeva*
(hot) chocolate	(горячий) шоколад *(garyacheey) shakalat*
tea/coffee	чай/кофе *chyay/kofye*
black/with milk	чёрный/с молоком *chyorniy/s malakom*
fruit juice	сок *sok*
mineral water	минеральную воду *meeneeral'nooyoo vodoo*

| red/white wine | красное/белое вино |
| | *krasnaye/byelaye veeno* |

| Nothing more, thanks. | Ничего больше, спасибо. |
| | *neechyeevo bol'she spaseeba* |

| Where are the restrooms? | Где туалет? *gdye tooalyet* |

SPECIAL REQUIREMENTS

| I can't eat food containing … | Мне нельзя есть … |
| | *mnye neel'zya yest'* |

| flour/fat | мучное/жирное |
| | *moochnoye/zheernaya* |

| salt/sugar | солёное/сладкое |
| | *salyonaye/slatkaye* |

| Do you have meals/drinks for diabetics? | Есть что-нибудь для диабетиков? *yest' shtoneebood' dlya deeabyeteekaf* |

| Do you have vegetarian dishes? | Есть что-нибудь для вегетарианцев? |
| | *yest' shtoneebood' dlya veegeetareeantsef* |

COMPLAINTS

| There must be some mistake. | Вы должно быть ошиблись. |
| | *vi dalzhno bit' ashiblees'* |

| That's not what I ordered. | Это не то, что я заказывал(а). |
| | *eta nee to shto ya zakazival(a)* |

| I asked for … | Я просил(а)... *ya praseel(a)* |

| I can't eat this. | Это невозможно есть. |
| | *eta neevazmozhna yest'* |

| The meat is … | Мясо ... *myasa* |

| overdone | пережарено *peereezhareena* |

underdone	недожарено *needazhareena*
too tough	очень жёсткое *ochyeen' zhostkaye*
The food is cold.	Это холодное. *eta khalodnaye*
This isn't fresh.	Это несвежее. *eta neesvyezheeye*
How much longer will our food be?	Сколько ещё ждать? *skol'ka eeshchyo zhdat'*
We can't wait any longer. We're leaving.	Мы не можем больше ждать. Мы уходим. *mi nee mozhem bol'she zhdat' mi ookhodeem*

PAYING

Tipping: See page 332.

The check, please.	Можно счёт, пожалуйста? *mozhna shchyot pazhalsta*
We'd like to pay separately.	Мы будем платить отдельно. *mi boodeem plateet' addyel'na*
It's all together, please.	Всё вместе, пожалуйста. *fsyo vmyestye pazhalsta*
What is this amount for?	А это за что? *a eta za shto*
I didn't have that. I had …	Я это не заказывал(а). У меня было … *ya eta nee zakazival(a) oo meenya bila*
Can I pay with this credit card?	Можно платить кредитной карточкой? *mozhna plateet' kreedeetnigh kartachkoy*
Could I have a receipt, please?	Можно отдельный чек? *mozhna addyel'niy chyek*
That was a very good meal.	Всё было очень вкусно. *fsyo bila ochyeen' fkoosna*

COURSE BY COURSE

Breakfast Завтрак

A Russian breakfast can be quite hearty. If you are feeling hungry, try hot cereals, ham, eggs, sausages, and cheese.

I'd like …	Я бы хотел(а) … *ya bi khatyel(a)*
a boiled egg	вареное яйцо *varyonaya yaytso*
fried eggs	яичницу *yaychneetsoo*
scrambled eggs	яичницу-болтунью *yaychneetsoo-baltoonyoo*
ham and eggs	яичницу с ветчиной *yaeechneetsoo c veechyeenoy*
oatmeal porridge/yogurt	овсянку/йогурт *avsyankoo/yagoort*
fruit juice	фруктовый сок *frooktoviy sok*
orange/grapefruit juice	апельсиновый/ грейпфрутовый сок *apeel'seenoviy/greypfrootaviy sok*
jam/honey	джем/мёд *dzhem/myot*
bread/toast	хлеб/тост *khlyep/tost*

Appetizers Закуски

These are often offered as full meals. When ordering an appetizer, just say На закуску … (**na za*koo*skoo**) and the name of the dish(es).

ассорти мясное/ рыбное	*asartee* *myasnoye/ribnaye*	assorted meats/fish
икра	*eekra*	caviar
ветчина	*veetchyeena*	ham
грибы	*greebi*	mushrooms

кильки	_keel'kee_	spiced herring (sprats)
колбаса	_kalbasa_	sausage (mortadella)
креветки	_kreevyetkee_	shrimp
осетрина	_asyertreena_	sturgeon
паштет	_pashtyet_	paté (mostly liver)
селёдка, сельдь	_seelyotka, syel'd'_	herring

Soups Супы

бульон _boolyon_	broth/consommé
суп из курицы _soop eez kooreetsi_	chicken soup
уха _ookha_	fish soup
грибной суп _greebnoy soop_	mushroom soup
гороховый суп _garokhaviy soop_	pea soup
картофельный суп _kartofeel'niy soop_	potato soup
… с лапшой/пирожками/гренками _s lapshoy/peerozhkamee/gryenkamee_	… with noodles/savory pastries/croutons

Борщ _borshch_
Borscht—made from beef, vegetables (chiefly beets), and sour cream; regional varieties include: московский **maskofskee** (Moscow, with extra bacon), украинский **ookrayeenskee** (Ukrainian, with garlic), and холодный **khalodniy** (cold borscht)

Окрошка _akroshka_
A cold summer soup made from kvass (a Russian soft drink), cucumber, egg, onion, and sour cream

Солянка _salyanka_
A soup made with salted cucumbers and olives, with either meat or fish

Харчо _kharcho_
A spicy Georgian soup made with mutton and rice

Шурпа *shoorpa*
Uzbek mutton soup with bacon and tomatoes

Щи *shchyee*
A thick soup made with cabbage or sauerkraut; regional varieties include: зелёные с яйцом **zeelyonye s yeetsom** (flavored with sorrel and thickened with beaten egg), кислые **keesliye** (made with sauerkraut), свежие **svyezhiye** (made with fresh cabbage)

Salads Салаты

зелёный салат	*zeelyoniy salat*	green salad
картофельный салат	*kartofeelniy salat*	potato salad
салат из крабов	*salat eez krabaf*	crabmeat salad
салат из редиски	*salat eez reedeeskee*	radish salad
салат из свежей капусты	*salat eez svyezhey kapoostee*	raw cabbage salad
салат с сельдью	*salat s syel'dyoo*	herring salad

Fish and seafood Рыба и дары моря

треска	*treeska*	cod
карп	*karp*	carp
краб	*krap*	crab
палтус	*paltoos*	halibut
сельдь, селёдка	*syel'd', seelyotka*	herring
омар	*amar*	lobster
макрель	*makryel'*	mackerel
устрицы	*oostreetsi*	oysters
креветки	*kreevyetkee*	shrimp
сёмга	*syomga*	salmon

лососина	*lasaseena*	salmon
шпроты	*shproti*	sprats (herring)
форель	*faryel'*	trout
тунец	*toonyets*	tuna

Осетрина под белым соусом *aseetreena pad byelim sooosam*
Sturgeon served with a white sauce

Осетрина паровая *aseetreena paravaya*
Steamed sturgeon served with a light sauce

Осетрина по-русски *aseetreena parooskee*
Poached sturgeon served with a tomato sauce and vegetables

Судак жареный в тесте *soodak zharyeniy v tyestee*
Pike perch fried in batter

Судак отварной соус яичный *atvarnoy sooos yaeechnyi*
Pike perch poached and served with an egg sauce

Meat/Poultry Мясо/Птица

говядина	*gavyadeena*	beef
молодая баранина	*maladaya baraneena*	lamb
печёнка	*peechyonka*	liver
свинина	*sveeneena*	pork
телятина	*teelyateena*	veal
кура	*koora*	chicken
утка	*ootka*	duck
гусь	*goos'*	goose
кролик	*kroleek*	rabbit
индейка	*eendyeyka*	turkey

Азу *azoo*
Chopped meat in a savory sauce

Бефстроганов *beefstroganaf*
Beef Stroganoff; strips of steak cooked in cream and brandy sauce

Говядина тушёная *gavyadeena tooshonaya*
Braised beef with aromatic vegetables

Голубцы *galloopsi*
Cabbage stuffed with meat and rice

Шашлык *shashlik*
Pieces of lamb grilled on skewers

Утка тушеная с яблоками *ootka tooshyonaya s yablakamee*
Duck roasted with apples

Котлеты по-киевски *katlyeti pa keeyefskee*
Chicken Kiev—breast of chicken stuffed with butter and garlic

Чахохбили из кур *chakhakhbeelee ees koor*
Chicken casserole, served with tomatoes and lots of onions

Meat cuts Сорта мяса

грудинка/	*groodeenka/*	breast/leg/
нога/крыло	*naga/krilo*	wing
антрекот/	*antreekot/*	entrecote/
ромштекс/филе	*ramshteks/feele*	rump/filet
биточки	*beetochbki*	rissoles
котлета	*katlyeta*	cutlet/chop
ростбиф	*rostbeef*	roast beef

Vegetables Овощи

| фасоль | *fasol'* | beans |
| свёкла | *svyokla* | beet |

капуста	*ka<u>poo</u>sta*	cabbage
морковь	*mar<u>kof'</u>*	carrots
цветная капуста	*tsvyeet<u>na</u>ya ka<u>poo</u>sta*	cauliflower
огурец	*agoo<u>ryets</u>*	cucumber
баклажан	*bakla<u>zh</u>an*	eggplant
грибы	*<u>gree</u>bi*	mushrooms
лук	*look*	onions
горох	*ga<u>rokh</u>*	peas
перец	*<u>pye</u>reets*	pepper
картофель	*kar<u>to</u>feel'*	potato
сладкая кукуруза	*<u>slat</u>kaya kookoo<u>roo</u>za*	sweetcorn
помидоры	*pomee<u>do</u>ri*	tomatoes
молодые кабачки	*mala<u>di</u>ye kabach<u>kee</u>*	zucchini

Fruit Фрукты

яблоки	*<u>ya</u>blaki*	apples
абрикосы	*abree<u>ko</u>si*	apricots
бананы	*ba<u>na</u>ni*	bananas
черешня	*chyee<u>rye</u>shnya*	cherries
виноград	*veena<u>grad</u>*	grapes
лимоны	*lee<u>mo</u>ni*	lemons
дыня	*<u>di</u>nya*	melon
апельсины	*apeel'<u>see</u>ni*	oranges
персики	*<u>pyer</u>seeki*	peaches
груши	*<u>groo</u>shi*	pears
ананас	*ana<u>nas</u>*	pineapple

сливы	*sleevi*	plums
клубника	*kloobneeka*	strawberries
арбуз	*arboos*	watermelon

Cheese and dairy products
Сыр и молочные продукты

брынза	*brinza*	ewe's milk cheese (salty)
кефир	*keefeer*	kefir (buttermilk)
ряженка	*ryazhinka*	baked sour milk, often served chilled
сливки	*sleefkee*	cream

сметана *smeetana*
Sour cream, an integral part of Russian cuisine, used in soups, salads, vegetable, and meat dishes as well as in desserts

Cheeses come in many regional varieties:

сыр ...	*sir*	... cheese
латвийский	*latveeskeey*	Latvian
пошехонский	*pashyekhonskeey*	Poshekhonsky
российский	*rasseeyskee*	Russian

сырок *sirok*
Fresh white cheese (or spread)

творог *tvarok*
White unsalted cheese similar to cottage cheese

топлёное молоко *taplyonoye malako*
Baked milk, served chilled

ватрушка *vatrooshka*
Cheese pastry often served as a savory with soups or as a sweet with tea, milk, etc.

Pies and dumplings Пирожки и пельмени

| пельмени | *peel'myenee* | stuffed dumplings |
| пирог/пирожки | *peerok/peerozhkee* | large pie/small pie |

пирог *peerok*
Large pie filled with meat, cabbage, mushroom, fish, and topped with pastry

пирожки *peerashkee*
Small pies with various fillings: meat, cabbage, mushrooms, onions, jam

хачапури *khachyapooree*
Georgian speciality: a kind of hot pancake filled with cheese

вареники *varyeneekee*
Ukrainian dumplings filled with white cheese

сырники со сметаной *sirneekee sa smeetanay*
White cheese fritters served with sour cream

Dessert Сладкое

ватрушка	*vatrooshka*	cottage cheese pastry
кисель	*keesyel'*	fruit jelly
компот	*kampot*	fruit compote
оладьи с яблоками	*aladee c yablakamee*	small apple pancakes
рисовый пудинг	*reesaviy poodeeng*	rice pudding
ромовая баба	*romavaya baba*	rum baba
рулет	*roolyet*	sponge roll
яблоко в тесте	*yablaka v tyestye*	apple baked in pastry
взбитые сливки	*vzbeetiye sleefkee*	whipped cream

блинчики с вареньем _bleenchyeekee s varyeneeyam_
Small pancakes served with jam

мороженое _marozhyenaye_
Ice cream; available in many flavors, including vanilla
(ванильное **vaneel'naye**), fruit (фруктовое **frooktovaye**),
chocolate (шоколадное **shakalatnaye**)

пирог _peerok_
Pies or tarts served with a variety of fruit or cheese fillings,
including lemon (с лимоном **s leemonam**), cottage cheese
(творогом **tvaragom**), and fruit (фруктами _frooktamee_)

Pancakes Блины

Russian pancakes are made with yeast and different fillings.
Smaller and thicker than Western pancakes, they are usually
served with sour cream (сметана) and/or butter.

блины с икрой	_bleeni s eekroy_	pancakes with caviar
блины с сёмгой	_bleeni s syomgoy_	pancakes with salmon
блины со сметаной	_bleeni so smetanay_	pancakes with sour cream
блины с вареньем	_bleeni s varyenyem_	pancakes with jam
блины с брынзой	_bleeni s brinzoy_	pancakes with ewe's milk cheese

DRINKS
Wine Вино

Wines from many countries are available throughout Russia. And
it is sometimes easier to find French, California, and Italian wines
than to find old favorites from Georgia such as **Tsinandali** (a dry,
white wine), **Mukuzani** (a red table wine), and **Kindzmaraooli**
(red, a little sweet). Russian champagne or sparkling wine is a
popular drink.

I'd like a bottle of…	Я хотел(а) бы бутылку... *ya khatyel(a) bi bootilkoo*
red wine	красного вина *krasnava veena*
white wine	белого вина *byelava veena*
champagne	шампанского *shampanskava*
blush [rosé] wine	розового вина *rozavava veena*
dry/sweet/sparkling wine	сухое/сладкое/шипучее вино *sookhoye/slatkaye/ sheepoochyeeye veeno*
I'd like a corkscrew.	Мне нужен(а) штопор. *mnye noozhen (noozhna) shtopar*

Beer Пиво

Many Russian beers taste weak to the Western palate, but it is worthwhile trying some while you are in Russia. **Zhigulyovskoye** and **Stolichnoye** are well-known brands.

Russian beer	жигулёвское *zheegoolyevskaye*
Riga beer	рижское *rishskaye*
Moscow beer	московское *maskofskaye*
Please bring me a bottle of beer.	Принесите мне, пожалуйста, бутылку пива. *preeneeseetye mnye pazhalsta bootilkoo peeva*
Lager, please.	Светлого пива, пожалуйста. *svyetlava peeva pazhalsta*

Vodka Водка

Vodka is served chilled and always neat in small glasses. The etiquette of vodka drinking is as follows: drain the glass in one gulp, then chase it down with a morsel of food (usually a piece of black bread or salted cucumber). It is common to propose a toast when raising your glass.

The smallest measure of vodka you can order is 50 grams (1.7 oz.), the next measure being 100 grams.

Please give me 50 grams of vodka.	Дайте мне, пожалуйста, 50 грамм водки. *daytye mnye pazhalsta peedeesyat' gram votkee*	
I would like …	Я хотел(а) бы... *ya khatyel(a) bi*	
brandy (cognac)/sherry	коньяк/херес *kanyak/khyeres*	
whisky/gin/rum	виски/джин/ром *veeskee/dzhin/rom*	
liqueur	ликёр *leekyor*	
Cheers!	За ваше здоровье! *za vashe zdarov'ye*	

Non-alcoholic drinks

A drink called "cocktail" (коктейль **kakteyl'**), offered in ice-cream parlors, is a non-alcohol soft drink made from fruit juice or lemonade, to which ice cream and sometimes whipped cream is added. Elsewhere this drink is called a "milk cocktail" (молочный коктейль **malochniy kakteyl'**).

Kvass (квас) is a popular soft drink and a good thirst quencher in the summer, made from black bread and yeast.

Coffee Кофе

Coffee is not a traditional Russian drink. If you want strong coffee, ask for "eastern-style coffee" (кофе по-восточному **kofee pa vastochynamoo**), similar to Turkish coffee. If you order coffee with milk, you'll often get a glass of very sweet coffee with condensed milk.

кофе	*kofye*	coffee
чёрный/с молоком	*chyorniy/s malakom*	black/with milk
без кафеина	*bees kafeyna*	decaffeinated

Tea Чай

Tea is the most popular Russian beverage. During your stay you will probably see one of the traditional Russian samovars (самовар **samovar**) used to heat the water for tea making. Tea is usually served in glasses, and it is often sweetened with honey or jam.

чай	*chyay*	tea
чёрный/с молоком	*chyorniy/ s malakom*	black/with milk
с лимоном	*s leemonam*	with lemon
чай со льдом	*chyay so l'dom*	iced tea

MENU READER

This Menu Reader gives listings of common food types and dishes.
The Russian words are shown in large type to help you identify the
basic ingredients making up a dish from a menu that has no English.

варёный	_varyoniy_	boiled
жареный	_zhareeniy_	fried
жареный на гриле	_zhareeniy na greelee_	grilled
жаркое	_zharkoye_	roasted
копчёный	_kapchyoniy_	smoked
паровой	_paravoy_	steamed
отварной	_atavarnoy_	poached
тушёный	_tooshoniy_	stewed
соте	_sate_	sautéed
фарширо-ванный	_farsheerovaniy_	stuffed
маринованный	_mareenovaniy_	marinated

Meat, fish, and poultry

мясо	_myasa_	meat
говядина	_gavyadeena_	beef
свинина	_sveeneena_	pork
телятина	_talyateena_	veal
молодая баранина	_maladaya baraneena_	lamb
кура	_koora_	chicken

утка	*ootka*	duck
рыба	*riba*	fish
дары моря	*dari morya*	seafood
икра	*eekra*	caviar
яйца	*yaytsa*	eggs

Vegetables

овощи	*ovashchee*	vegetable(s)
бобы/фасоль	*babi/fasol'*	beans
шпинат	*shpeenat*	spinach
картофель	*kartofeel'*	pototoes
помидоры	*pameedori*	tomatoes
салат	*salat*	lettuce
огурец	*agooryets*	cucumber
морковь	*markof'*	carrots
лук	*look*	onions
брокколи	*brakolee*	broccoli
капуста	*kapoosta*	cabbage
свёкла	*svyokla*	beet

Fruit

фрукты	*frookti*	fruit
яблоко	*yablako*	apple
апельсин	*apeel'seen*	orange

банан	*banan*	banana
дыня	*dinya*	melon
арбуз	*arboos*	watermelon
груша	*groosha*	pear
слива	*sleeva*	plum
клубника	*kloobneeka*	strawberries
киви	*keevee*	kiwi fruit
ананас	*ananas*	pineapple

Staples: bread, rice, pasta, etc.

хлеб	*khlyep*	bread
рис	*rees*	rice
лапша	*lapsha*	noodles
каша	*kasha*	porridge
макароны	*makaroni*	pasta
спагетти	*spagyetee*	spaghetti
бобовые	*baboviye*	beans

Basics

соль	*sol'*	salt
перец	*pyereets*	pepper
горчица	*garcheetsa*	mustard
сахар	*sakhar*	sugar
уксусная заправка	*ooksoosnaya zaprafka*	vinaigrette

Classic dishes

азу	*azoo*	chopped meat in a savory sauce
бефстроганов	*beefstroganaf*	Beef Stroganoff, strips of beef filet cooked with shallots in cream and brandy
говядина тушёная с кореньями	*gavyadeena toshonaya s karyenyami*	braised beef with aromatic vegetables
жаркое из свинины с черносливом	*zharkoyl ees sveeneeni cheernasleevam*	roast pork with plums
утка тушёная с яблоками	*ootka tooshonaya s yablakamee*	roast duck with apples
котлеты по-киевски	*katlyeti pa keeyefskee*	Chicken Kiev, breast of chicken stuffed with butter and garlic
чахохбили из кур	*chakhakhbeelee ees koor*	chicken casserole, served with tomatoes and onions
голубцы	*galooptsi*	cabbage stuffed with rice and meat
пельмени	*peel'myenee*	stuffed dumplings
шашлык	*shashlik*	pieces of lamb grilled on skewers
осетрина под белым соусом	*aseetreena pat byelim sooosam*	steamed sturgeon in white sauce
осетрина по-русски	*aseetreena pa rooskee*	poached sturgeon served with tomato sauce and vegetables

судак жареный в тесте	*soodak zhareeniy f tyestye*	battered pike perch deep fried in batter
судак отварной соус яичный	*soodak atvarnoy sooos yaeechniy*	poached pike perch in an egg sauce

Drinks

вода	*vada*	water
молоко	*malako*	milk
чай	*chay*	tea
кофе	*kofye*	coffee
(горячий) шоколад	*(garya cheey) shakalat*	(hot) chocolate
водка	*votka*	vodka
виски	*veeskee*	whisky
джин	*dzheen*	gin
пиво	*peeva*	beer
вино	*veeno*	wine
шампанское	*shampanskaya*	champagne
фруктовый сок	*frooktoviy sok*	(fruit) juice
апельсиновый сок	*apeel'seenavay sok*	orange juice
сок из грейпфрута	*sek ees greypfroota*	grapefruit juice
лимонад	*leemanat*	lemonade

кока-кола	*kola*	cola
содовая вода	*sodavaya vada*	soda water
тоник	*toneek*	tonic water
молочный коктейль	*malochniy kakteyl'*	milk shake
минеральная вода	*meeneeral'naya vada*	mineral water
квас	*kvas*	soft drink

Snacks

жареный картофель	*zhareeniy kartofeel'*	french fries
гамбургер	*gamboorgeer*	hamburger
колбаса	*kalbasa*	sausage
омлет	*amlyet*	omelet
бутерброд	*bootirbrot*	sandwich
чипсы	*cheepsi*	potato chips
мороженое	*marozheenaya*	ice cream
блины	*bleeni*	pancakes
печенье	*peechyenye*	cookie
пирожное	*peerozhnaya*	cake (small)
торт	*tort*	cake (large)

Soups/soup-based dishes

борщ	borshch	borscht, a substantial soup made with beef and beets, served with sour cream
щи	shchee	shchee, cabbage soup with many regional varieties
бульон	boolyon	broth or consommé made from a variety of ingredients
бульон из куры	boolyon ees koori	chicken soup
окрошка	akroshka	summer soup, cold soup made with cucumber, egg, onion, and sour cream
суп	soop	thick soup, usually made with either peas, mush-rooms, or potatoes
уха	ookha	fish soup
харчо	kharcho	spicy Georgian soup made with mutton and rice
шурпа	shoorpa	an Uzbek soup made with mutton, bacon, and tomato

Dairy/soy products

сыр	sir	cheese
йогурт	yogoort	yogurt
сливки	sleeftee	cream
масло	masla	butter
молоко	malako	milk

соевый творог	*soyeviy tvarok*	tofu
кефир	*keefeer*	kefir, sour milk, similar to thinner types of plain yogurt
топлёное молоко	*taplyonaye malako*	baked milk served chilled
сырок	*sirok*	fresh white cheese

Desserts

ватрушка	*vatrooshka*	cottage cheese tart
кисель	*keesyel'*	fruit jelly topped with sugar, milk, or cream
компот	*kampot*	fruit compote
оладьи с яблоками	*aladyee s yablakamee*	small apple pancakes
рисовый пудинг	*reesavay poodeeng*	rice pudding
ромовая баба	*romavaya baba*	rum baba
рулет	*roolyet*	sponge roll
яблоко в тесте	*yablaka b tyestye*	apple baked in pastry
блинчики с вареньем	*bleencheekee s varyenyem*	pancakes with jam
пирог	*peerok*	pie or tart served with a variety of fillings

SPANISH

PLACES TO EAT

Bar _bar_
Bar; drinks and tapas served, sometimes hot beverages

Café _kafeh_
Found on virtually every street corner, the café is where people get together over a coffee, soft drink, or glass of wine

Cafetería _kafetereeya_
Coffee shop; there's counter service or—for a small amount more— you can choose a table

Casa de comidas _kassa deh komeedass_
Simple inn serving cheap meals

Heladería _eladereeya_
Ice-cream parlor

Merendero *merendero*
Cheap open-air bar; you can usually eat outdoors

Parador *parador*
Government-supervised and located in an historic castle, palace, or former monastery usually noted for excellent regional dishes

Pastelería/Confitería *pastelereeya/konfeetereeya*
Pastry shop; some serve coffee, tea, and drinks

Posada *possada*
A simple inn; the food is usually good

Refugio *refookhyo*
Mountain lodge serving simple meals

Restaurante *restowranteh*
Restaurant; classified more by the decor than the quality of cooking

Salón de té *salon deh teh*
Tea room; an upmarket cafeteria

Taberna *taberna*
Similar to an English pub; always a variety of tapas and snacks

Tasca *taska*
Similar to a bar; drinks/tapas are served at the counter; standing only

Venta *benta*
Restaurant; often specializing in regional cooking

MEAL TIMES

El desayuno *el dessayoono*
Breakfast: 7–10 a.m, traditionally toast/roll and coffee

La comida *la komeedah*
Lunch: served from around 2 or 3 p.m.; the Spaniards linger over a meal, so service may seem on the leisurely side

La merienda *la maryendah*
Light meal between 5–6 p.m.

La cena *la theyna*
Dinner: 8:30 p.m. (10 p.m. in Madrid) to 11 p.m.

SPANISH CUISINE

The variety of Spanish cuisine comes from Celtic, Roman, Arab, and New World influences, together with the profusion of Atlantic and Mediterranean seafood.

Most restaurants will offer a good value daily special (**menú del día**)—usually a three-course meal with house wine at a set price. Service and taxes are included in the price.

FINDING A PLACE TO EAT

Can you recommend a good restaurant?	**¿Puede recomendarme un buen restaurante?** *pwedeh rekomendarmeh oon bwen restawranteh*
Is there (a/an) … near here?	**¿Hay … cerca de aquí?** *eye … therka deh akee*
inexpensive restaurant	**un restaurante barato** *oon restawranteh barato*
traditional local restaurant	**un restaurante típico** *oon restawranteh teepeeko*
vegetarian restaurant	**un restaurante vegetariano** *oon restawranteh bekhetareeyano*
Where can I find a(n) …?	**¿Dónde puedo encontrar …?** *dondeh pwedo enkontrar*
café/restaurant	**una cafetería/un restaurante** *oona kafetereeya/oon restawranteh*
fast food restaurant	**un restaurante de comida rápida** *oon restawranteh deh komeeda rapeeda*

ice-cream parlor	**una heladería** _oona eladereeya_
pizzeria	**una pizzería** _oona peethereeya_
steak house	**una churrasquería** _oona choorraskereeya_

RESERVATIONS

I'd like to reserve a table …	**Quiero reservar una mesa …** _keeyero reserbar oona mesa_
for 2.	**para dos.** _para dos_
for this evening/ tomorrow at …	**para esta noche/mañana a las …** _para esta nocheh/manyana a las_
We'll come at 8:00.	**Llegaremos a las 8:00.** _l-yegaremos a las ocho_
We have a reservation.	**Tenemos una reserva.** _tenemos oona reserba_

YOU MAY HEAR

| **Lo siento. Tenemos mucha gente/está completo.** | I'm sorry. We're very busy/full. |

Could we sit …?	**¿Podríamos sentarnos …?** _podreeyamos sentarnos_
over there/outside	**allí/fuera** _al-yee/fwera_
in a non-smoking area	**en una zona de no fumadores** _en oona thona deh no foomadores_
by the window	**al lado de la ventana** _al lado deh la bentana_

ORDERING

| Waiter/Waitress! | **¡Camarero/Camarera!** _kamarero/kamarera_ |

May I see the wine list?	**¿Puedo ver la carta de vinos?** _pwedo behr la karta deh beenos_

Do you have a set menu?	**¿Tienen un menú del día?** _teeyenen oon menoo del deeya_
Can you recommend some typical local dishes?	**¿Puede recomendarme algunos platos típicos de la zona?** _pwede rekomendarmeh algoonos platos teepeekos deh la thona_
Could you tell me what … is?	**¿Podría decirme lo que … es?** _podreeya detheermeh lo keh … es_
What's in it?	**¿Qué lleva?** _keh l-yeba_
I'll have …	**Tomaré …** _tomareh_
a bottle/glass/ carafe of …	**una botella/un vaso/una garrafa de …** _oona botel-ya/oon baso/oona garrafa deh_

SPECIAL REQUESTS

Could I have salad instead of vegetables, please?	**¿Podría tomar ensalada en lugar de verduras, por favor?** _podreeya tomar ensalada en loogar de berdooras por fabor_
Does the meal come with vegetables/ potatoes?	**¿Viene la comida con verduras/ patatas?** _beeyeneh la komeeda kon berdooras/patatas_

274

Do you have any bread/mayonnaise?	**¿Tienen pan/mayonesa?** *tee<u>ye</u>nen pan/mayo<u>ne</u>sa*
May I have some …?	**¿Me puede traer …?** *me <u>pwe</u>deh tra<u>yer</u>*
butter	**mantequilla** *mante<u>kee</u>l-ya*
lemon	**limón** *lee<u>mon</u>*
mustard	**mostaza** *mos<u>ta</u>tha*
pepper	**pimienta** *peemee<u>ye</u>nta*
salt	**sal** *sal*
seasoning	**aderezo** *ade<u>re</u>tho*
sugar	**azúcar** *a<u>thoo</u>kar*
artificial sweetener	**edulcorante artificial** *edoolko<u>ran</u>te arteefee<u>thee</u>yal*
vinaigrette	**vinagreta** *beena<u>gre</u>ta*
Could we have a child's seat, please?	**¿Podrían ponernos una silla para niños?** *po<u>dree</u>yan po<u>ner</u>nos <u>oo</u>na <u>seel</u>-ya <u>pa</u>ra <u>nee</u>ños*
Where can I feed/ change the baby?	**¿Dónde puedo darle de comer/cambiar al niño?** <u>don</u>deh <u>pwe</u>do <u>dar</u>leh deh ko<u>mer</u>/kambee<u>yar</u> al <u>nee</u>ño*

GENERAL QUESTIONS

Could I have a(n) (clean) …, please?	**¿Podría traerme … (limpio/a), por favor?** *po<u>dree</u>ya tra<u>yer</u>me … (<u>leem</u> peeyo/a) por fa<u>bor</u>*
cup/glass	**una taza/un vaso** *<u>oo</u>na <u>ta</u>tha/oon <u>ba</u>so*
fork/knife	**un tenedor/cuchillo** *oon tene<u>dor</u>/koo<u>cheel</u>-yo*
napkin	**una servilleta** *<u>oo</u>na serbeel-<u>ye</u>ta*

plate/spoon	**un plato/una cuchara**
	oon plato/oona koochara
I'd like (a) …	**Quiero …** *keeyero*
beer	**una cerveza** *oona therbetha*
tea/coffee/chocolate	**un té/un café/un chocolate**
	oon teh/oon kafeh/oon chokolateh
black/with milk	**solo/con leche** *solo/kon lecheh*
fruit juice/mineral water	**un zumo de fruta/un agua mineral**
	oon thoomo deh froota/oon agwa meeneral
red/white wine	**un vino tinto/blanco**
	oon beeno teento/blanko
Nothing more, thanks.	**Nada más, gracias.**
	nada mas gratheeyas
Where are the restrooms?	**¿Dónde están los servicios?**
	dondeh estan los serbeetheeyos

SPECIAL REQUIREMENTS

I mustn't eat food containing …	**No debo comer comida que tenga …**
	no debo komer komeeda keh tenga
salt/sugar	**sal/azúcar** *sal/athookar*
Do you have meals/drinks for diabetics?	**¿Tienen comidas/bebidas para diabéticos?** *teeyenen komeedas/bebeedas para deeyabeteekos*
Do you have vegetarian meals?	**¿Tienen comidas vegetarianas?** *teeyenen komeedas bekhetareeyanas*

COMPLAINTS

That's not what I ordered.	**Eso no es lo que pedí.**
	eso no es lo keh pedee
I asked for …	**Pedí …** *pedee*

276

I can't eat this.	**No puedo comerme esto.**
	no pwedo komermeh esto
The meat is …	**La carne está …** *la karneh esta*
overdone	**demasiado hecha** *demaseeyado echa*
underdone	**cruda** *krooda*
too tough	**demasiado dura** *demaseeyado doora*
The food is cold.	**La comida está fría.**
	la komeeda esta freeya
This isn't fresh.	**Esto no está fresco.** *esto no esta fresko*
How much longer will our food be?	**¿Cuánto más tardará la comida?**
	kwanto mas tardara la komeeda
We can't wait any longer. We're leaving.	**No podemos esperar más. Nos vamos.**
	no podemos esperar mas. nos bamos

PAYING

Tipping: See page 332.

The check, please.	**La cuenta, por favor.**
	la kwenta por fabor
We'd like to pay separately.	**Queremos pagar por separado.**
	keremos pagar por separado
It's all together, please.	**Póngalo todo junto, por favor.**
	pongalo todo khoonto por fabor
I think there's a mistake in this check.	**Creo que hay un error en esta cuenta.**
	kreyo keh eye oon error en esta kwenta
What is this amount for?	**¿De qué es esta cantidad?**
	deh keh es esta kanteedath
I didn't have that. I had …	**Yo no tomé eso. Yo tomé …**
	yo no tomeh eso. yo tomeh
Can I pay with this credit card?	**¿Puedo pagar con esta tarjeta de crédito?** *pwedo pagar kon esta tarkheta deh kredeeto*

Could I have a receipt?	**¿Podría darme un recibo?**
	podreeya darmeh oon retheebo
That was a very good meal.	**La comida estuvo muy buena.**
	la komeeda estoobo mwee bwena

COURSE BY COURSE

Breakfast Desayuno

I'd like …	**Quiero …** _keeyero_
fried eggs	**huevos fritos** _weboss freetoss_
scrambled eggs	**huevos revueltos** _weboss rebweltoss_
fruit juice	**un zumo de fruta**
	oon thoomo deh froota
jam	**mermelada** _mermelada_
milk	**leche** _lecheh_
a roll	**panecillo** _penetheel-yo_

Appetizers Entremeses

Croquetas _kroketass_
Croquettes made with ham, fish, egg, etc.

Ensaladilla rusa _ensaladeel-ya rroossa_
Potatoes with peas, tuna, boiled eggs, and olives with mayonnaise

Champiñones al ajillo _champeenyones ahl akheel-yo_
Mushrooms fried in olive oil with garlic

Tapas _tapass_
A huge variety of snacks served in some cafés and bars, ranging from meat balls, cheese, smoked ham, mushrooms, fried fish plus sauces and exotic-looking specialties of the house; **una tapa** is a mouthful, **una ración** half a plateful, and **una porción** a generous amount

aceitunas (rellenas)	*athetoonass (rel-yenass)*	(stuffed) olives
albóndigas	*albondee-ass*	spiced meat balls
almejas	*almekhass*	clams
calamares	*kalamaress*	squid
callos	*kal-yoss*	tripe (in hot sauce)
caracoles	*karakoless*	snails
chorizo	*choreetho*	spicy sausage
gambas	*gambass*	shrimp
jamón	*khamon*	ham
mejillones	*mekheel-yoness*	mussels
pimientos	*peemyentoss*	peppers
pinchos	*peenchoss*	grilled skewered meat

Soups Sopas

caldo gallego	*kaldo gal-yego*	meat and vegetable broth
consomé al jerez	*konsomeh al khereth*	chicken broth with sherry
sopa de ajo	*sopa deh akho*	garlic soup
sopa de fideos	*sopa deh feedeyoss*	noodle soup
sopa de mariscos	*sopa deh mareeskoss*	seafood soup
sopa de verduras	*sopa deh berdoorass*	vegetable soup

Ajo blanco *akho blanko*
Cold garlic and almond soup garnished with grapes (*Andalucia*)

Gazpacho *gathpacho*
Cold tomato soup with cucumber, green pepper, bread, onion, and garlic

Sopa castellana *sopa kasteel-yana*
Baked garlic soup with chunks of ham and a poached egg

Sopa de cocido _sopa deh kotheedo_
Broth, with beef, ham, sausage, chickpeas, cabbage, turnip, onion, and potatoes

Egg dishes Huevos

Huevos a la flamenca _weboss a la flamenka_
Eggs baked with tomato, onion, and diced ham

Huevos al nido _weboss al needo_
"Eggs in the nest"—egg yolks set in soft rolls, fried and covered in egg white

Huevos rellenos _weboss rrel-yenos_
Boiled eggs filled with tuna fish and dressed with mayonnaise

Tortilla _torteel-ya_
Round Spanish omelet; popular varieties include: **~ de patatas** (potato with onions), **~ de jamón** (ham), **~ paisana** (potatoes, peas, shrimp, or ham), **~ de queso** (cheese), **~ de setas** (mushroom)

Fish and seafood Pescado y mariscos

atún	_atoon_	tuna
bacalao	_bakalao_	cod
boquerones	_bokeroness_	herring
caballa	_kabal-ya_	mackerel
chipirones	_cheepeeroness_	baby squid
langosta	_langosta_	lobster
mero	_mero_	sea bass
pez espada	_peth espada_	swordfish
pulpo	_poolpo_	octopus
trucha	_troocha_	trout

Bacalao a la catalana _bakalao a la katalana_
Salt cod in ratatouille sauce, with onions, eggplant, zucchini, tomatoes, and pepper

Calamares a la romana *kalamaress al la rromana*
Squid rings deep-fried in batter

Pulpo a la gallega *poolpo a la gal-yega*
Octopus dressed with olive oil and paprika

Lenguado a la vasca *lengwado a la baska*
Baked sole with sliced potatoes in a mushroom, red pepper, and tomato sauce

Trucha a la navarra *troocha a la nabarra*
Grilled trout stuffed with ham

Paella

Basically, paella is made of saffron rice garnished with meat, fish, seafood, and/or vegetables. Here are four popular styles:

Paella de verduras *pa-el-ya de berdoorass*
Artichokes, peas, broad beans, cauliflower, garlic, peppers, tomato

Paella de marisco *pa-el-ya de mareesko*
Fish and seafood only

Paella valenciana *pa-el-ya balenthyana*
Chicken, seafood, peas, tomato, chili pepper, garlic

Paella zamorana *pa-el-ya thamorana*
Ham, pork loin, pig's feet, chili pepper

Meat Carne

carne de buey	*karneh deh bwehee*	beef
carne de cerdo	*karneh deh therdo*	pork
carne de cordero	*karneh deh kordero*	lamb
carne de ternera	*karneh deh ternera*	veal
chuletas	*chooletass*	chops
conejo	*konekho*	rabbit
filete	*feeleteh*	steak
hígado	*eegado*	liver

jamón	*khamon*	ham
pato	*pato*	duck
pavo	*pavo*	turkey
pollo	*pol-yo*	chicken
riñones	*reenyoness*	kidneys
salchichas	*salcheechass*	sausages
tocino	*totheeno*	bacon

Specialties Especialidades

Asado de cordero *assado deh kordero*
Roast lamb with garlic and wine

Cochinillo asado *kocheeneel-yo assado*
Crispy roasted suckling pig

Cocido madrileño *kotheedo madreelenyo*
Hotpot, stew

Empanada gallega *empanada gal-yega*
Pork and onion pie

Estofado de ternera *estofado deh ternera*
Veal stew with wine, carrots, onions, and potatoes

Lomo de cerdo al jerez *lomo deh therdo al khereth*
Roast loin of pork with sherry

Pollo en pepitoria *pol-yo en pepeetoreeya*
Chicken in egg and almond sauce

Riñones al jerez *reenyoness al khereth*
Lamb kidneys in an onion and sherry sauce

Vegetables Verduras

berenjena	*berekhena*	eggplant
cebolla	*thebol-ya*	onion

champiñones	*champee<u>nyo</u>ness*	button mushrooms
guisantes	*gee<u>ssa</u>ntes*	peas
judías verdes	*khoo<u>dee</u>eass <u>verd</u>ess*	green beans
lechuga	*le<u>choo</u>ga*	lettuce
patatas	*pat<u>a</u>tas*	potatoes
pimientos	*peem<u>yen</u>toss*	sweet red
morrones	*mor<u>ron</u>ess*	peppers
repollo	*repol-yo*	cabbage
setas	*<u>se</u>tass*	mushrooms
zanahorias	*thana-<u>ory</u>ass*	carrots

Ensalada *ensa<u>la</u>da*
Salad; typical varieties to look out for: **~ de atún** (tuna), **~ de
lechuga** (green); **~ de pepino** (cucumber), **~ del tiempo** (seasonal),
~ valenciana (with green peppers, lettuce, and oranges)

Lentejas estofadas *len<u>te</u>khass esto<u>fa</u>dass*
Green lentils with onions, tomatoes, carrots, and garlic

Pisto *<u>pee</u>sto*
A stew of green peppers, onions, tomatoes, and zucchini; also
referred to as **frito de verduras**

Fruit Fruta

cerezas	*the<u>re</u>thass*	cherries
ciruelas	*theer<u>we</u>lass*	plums
frambuesas	*fram<u>bwe</u>sass*	raspberries
fresas	*<u>fre</u>sass*	strawberries
manzana	*man<u>tha</u>na*	apple
melocotón	*meloko<u>ton</u>*	peach
naranja	*na<u>ran</u>kha*	orange
plátano	*<u>pla</u>tano*	banana
pomelo	*po<u>me</u>lo*	grapefruit
uvas	*<u>oo</u>vass*	grapes

Cheese Queso

Burgos _boorgos_
A soft, creamy cheese

Cabrales _kabrales_
A tangy, veined goat cheese

Manchego _manchego_
Hard cheese of ewe's milk from La Mancha

Perilla _pereel-ya_
A firm, bland cheese made from cow's milk; sometimes known
as **teta**

Roncal _rronkal_
A sharp ewe's milk cheese from northern Spain; hand-pressed,
salted, and smoked with leathery rind

tipo roquefort	_teepo rokefort_	blue
suave	_swabeh_	mild
cremoso	_kremosso_	cream
curado	_kurado_	ripe
duro	_dooro_	hard
blando	_blando_	soft
fuerte	_fwerteh_	strong

Dessert Postre

bizcocho	_beethkocho_	sponge cake
brazo de gitano	_bratho deh geetano_	rum cream roll
canutillos	_kanooteel-yos_	custard horns with cinnamon
crema catalana	_krema katalana_	caramel pudding
flan	_flan_	crème caramel
fritos	_freetos_	fritters
galletas	_gal-yetas_	cookies

mantecado	*mantekado*	almond ice cream
pastel de queso	*pastel deh keso*	cheesecake
tarta de manzana	*tarta deh manthana*	apple tart
tortitas	*torteetas*	waffles

Helado *elado*

Ice cream; popular flavors include: **~ de chocolate** (chocolate),
~ de fresa (strawberry), **~ de limón** (lemon), **~ de moka** (mocha),
~ de vainilla (vanilla)

DRINKS

Aperitifs Aperitivos

Sherry (**jerez** *khereth*) is Spain's most renowned drink:

Fino *feeno*

Pale, dry sherries that make good aperitifs; Spaniards themselves
are especially fond of **amontillado** and **manzanilla**

Oloroso *olorosso*

Sweet, heavier, darker sherries; they're fine after-dinner drinks—
one exception is **amoroso,** which is medium dry

Beer Cerveza

Spanish beer, generally served cool, is good and relatively inexpensive.

A beer, please.	**Una cerveza, por favor.**
	oona therbetha por fabor
light beer	**cerveza rubia** *therbetha roobya*
dark beer	**cerveza negra** *therbetha negra*
foreign beer	**cerveza extranjera**
	therbetha ekstrankhera
small/large beer	**cerveza pequeña/grande**
	therbetha pekenya/grandeh

Wine Vino

Spain has the largest area under vine in the world. The best wine comes from **Rioja**. Wine makers there add **garantía de origen** to wine they feel is of above average quality. The **Penedés** region is a source of the world's best-selling white sparkling wine, **cava**. Ask for the patron's own wine "**el vino de la casa.**"

I want a bottle of white/red wine.	**Quiero una botella de vino blanco/tinto.** *keeyero oona botel-ya deh beeno blanko/teento*
a carafe	**una garrafa** *oona garrafa*
a half bottle	**media botella** *medya botel-ya*
a glass	**un vaso** *oon basso*
a small glass	**un chato** *oon chato*
a liter	**un litro** *oon leetro*
a pitcher	**una jarra** *oona kharra*
I'd like a corkscrew.	**Quiero un sacacorchos.** *keeyero oon sakakorchos*

Reading the label

añejo mature
blanco white
bodegas cellar
cava white, sparkling wine
de cuerpo full-bodied
DO (Denominación de Origen) regulated quality
DOCa superior Rioja
dulce sweet
embotellado en bottled in
espumoso sparkling
gran reserva aged 3 years in a barrel then 3 years in the bottle (exceptional years only)

joven young
liviano light
moscatel sweet dessert wine
muy seco very dry
reserva aged over 3 years
rosado rosé
seco dry
tinto red
vino de calidad quality wine
vino de cosecha vintage wine
vino de crianza aged in oak barrels for minimum of 6 months

Spirits and liqueurs Licores

You'll recognize: **ginebra** (gin), **ron** (rum), **oporto** (port wine), **vermut**, **vodka**, and **whisky**.

doble	_dobleh_	double (a double shot)
solo	_solo_	straight/neat
con hielo	kon _yelo_	on the rocks
con soda/tónica	kon _soda_/ _toneeka_	with soda/tonic

Sangría sangreea

Wine punch made with red wine, fruit juice, brandy, slices of fruit; diluted with soda and ice

Cheers! | **¡Salud!** sah_lood_

Non-alcoholic drinks

I'd like a cup of coffee.	**Quiero una taza de café.** _keeyero oona tatha deh kafeh_
(hot) chocolate	**un chocolate (caliente)** oon choko_lateh (kaliyenteh)_
iced fruit juice	**un granizado** oon graneethado
lemonade	**una limonada** _oona leemonada_
milk	**leche** _lecheh_
milk shake	**un batido** oon bateedo
orangeade	**una naranjada** _oona narankhada_
(iced/mineral) water	**agua (helada/mineral)** agwa (elada/meeneral)

MENU READER

a la brasa	*a la brasa*	braised
adobado(-a)	*adobado(-a)*	marinated
ahumado(-a)	*ahoomado*	smoked
al grill	*al greel*	grilled
al horno	*al orno*	baked
al vapor	*al bapor*	steamed
asado(-a)	*asado*	roasted
bien hecho(-a)	*beeyen echo*	well-done
con especias	*kon espetheeyas*	spicy
con nata	*kon nata*	creamed
cortado en taquitos	*kortado en takeetos*	diced
dorado(-a) al horno	*dorado(-a) al orno*	oven-browned
empanado(-a)	*empanado(-a)*	breaded
escaldado(-a)	*eskaldado(-a)*	poached
frito(-a)	*freeto(-a)*	fried
guisado(-a)	*geesado(-a)*	stewed
hervido(-a)	*erbeedo*	boiled
medio hecho(-a)	*medeeyo echo*	medium
muy hecho(-a)	*mwee echo*	well-done
muy poco hecho(-a)	*mwee poko echo(-a)*	rare
poco hecho(-a)	*poko echo*	medium rare
refrito(-a)	*refreeto(-a)*	sautéed
relleno(-a)	*rel-yeno(-a)*	stuffed

A

a la parrilla grilled/broiled
a la romana deep-fried
a punto medium (done)
abocado sherry made from sweet and dry wine
acedera sorrel

aceitunas (rellenas) (stuffed) olives
achicoria chicory
agua water; **~ caliente** hot water; **~ helada** iced water; **~ mineral** mineral water
aguacate avocado
aguardiente spirits (eau-de-vie)

ajo garlic; **~ blanco** garlic soup
ajoaceite garlic mayonnaise
al adobo marinated
al ajillo in garlic and oil
albahaca basil
albaricoques apricots
albóndigas spiced meat balls
alcachofas artichokes
alcaparra caper
alioli garlic mayonnaise
aliñado seasoned
almejas clams; **~ a la marinera**
cooked in hot, pimento sauce
almendra almond;
~ garrapiñada sugared
almuerzo lunch
almíbar syrup
alubia bean
amontillado medium-dry sherry
with nutty taste
anchoas anchovies
añejo mature
anguila ahumada smoked eel
angula baby eel
Angélica Basque herb liqueur
anisado aniseed-based soft drink
anticucho beef heart grilled on
skewer with green peppers
anís anisette
aperitivos aperitifs
apio celery
arándanos blueberries
arenque (ahumado) (smoked)
herring
arepa pancake made of corn
arroz rice; **~ a la cubana** boiled
rice served with tomato sauce and a
fried egg; **~ a la valenciana** with
vegetables, chicken, shellfish;

~ blanco boiled, steamed; **~ negro**
with seafood and squid ink;
~ primavera with spring vegetables; **~ con costra** with pork meat
balls; **~ con leche** rice pudding
asado roast
asturias (queso de ...) strong,
fermented cheese
atún tuna
avellanas hazelnuts
aves poultry
azafrán saffron
azúcar sugar

B

bacalao cod
banderillas pickles, chili
peppers, and olives on a skewer
batata sweet potato, yam
batido milk shake
bebidas drinks
bebidas sin alcohol
non-alcoholic drinks
becada woodcock
berberecho cockle
berenjena eggplant
berraza parsnip
berro cress
berza cabbage
besugo (sea) bream
bien hecho well-done
biftec beef steak
bizcocho sponge cake; **~ borracho**
steeped in rum and syrup
bizcotela glazed cookie
blanco white
blando soft; medium
Bobadilla Gran Reserva
wine-distilled brandy

bocadillo sandwich
bocadillo de jamón ham sandwich
bollos cake
bonito tuna
boquerones kind of anchovy
botella bottle
brevas blue figs
(en) brocheta (on a) skewer
budín blancmange, custard
buey ox
burgos (queso de ...) soft, creamy cheese
buñuelitos small fritters

C

caballa mackerel
cabra goat
cabrales (queso de ...) tangy goat cheese
cabrito kid
cacahuetes peanuts
café coffee
calabacín zucchini
calabaza pumpkin
calamares squid; **~ a la romana** fried in batter
caldereta de cabrito kid stew
caldillo de congrio conger-eel soup with tomatoes and potatoes
caldo consommé
caldo gallego meat and vegetable broth
caliente hot
Calisay quinine-flavored liqueur
callos tripe; **~ a la madrileña** tripe in piquant sauce with spicy pork sausage and tomatoes
camarón shrimp

canela cinnamon
cangrejo (de mar/de río) crab/crayfish
cantarela chanterelle mushroom
capón capon
caracoles snails
caramelos candy
Carlos I wine-distilled brandy
carne meat
carne a la parrilla charcoal-grilled steak
carne de buey beef
carne de cangrejo crabmeat
carne de cerdo pork
carne de cordero lamb
carne de ternera veal
carne molida ground beef
carne picada ground meat
carnero mutton
carta menu; **a la ~** a la carte
casero homemade
castanola sea perch
castañas chestnuts
catalana spicy pork sausages
caza game
(a la) cazadora with mushrooms, spring onions, herbs in wine
Cazalla aniseed liqueur
cazuela de cordero lamb stew with vegetables
cebollas onions
cebolleta spring onion
cebollinos chives
cebrero (queso de ...) blue-veined cheese
cena dinner, supper
centolla spider-crab, served cold
cerdo pork

cereales cereal
cerezas cherries
cerveza beer
chalote shallot
champiñones button mushrooms
chancho adobado pork braised with sweet potatoes, orange, and lemon juice
chanfaina goat's liver and kidney stew, served in a thick sauce
chanquete herring
chato a small glass
chile chili pepper
chilindrón sauce of tomatoes, peppers, garlic, ham, and wine *(Pyr.)*
chimichurri hot parsley sauce
Chinchón aniseed liqueur
chipirones baby squid
chirivías parsnips
chocolate (caliente) (hot) chocolate
chopa type of sea bream
chorizo spicy sausage made of pork, garlic, and paprika
chuletas chops
chupe de mariscos scallops served with creamy sauce and gratinéed with cheese
churro sugared tubular fritter
cigalas sea crayfish
cincho (queso de ...) hard sheep-milk cheese
ciruelas plums; **~ pasas** prunes
clavo clove
cochifrito de cordero highly seasoned stew of lamb or kid
cochinillo asado crispy roasted Castilian suckling pig
cocido boiled; beef stew with ham, fowl, chickpeas, and potatoes

cocido al vapor steamed
coco coconut
codorniz quail
cohombrillos pickles
cola de mono blend of coffee, milk, rum, and pisco
coles de bruselas Brussels sprouts
coliflor cauliflower
comida meal
comino caraway
compota stewed fruit
con hielo on the rocks
con leche with milk
con limón with lemon
condimentos herbs
coñac brandy
conejo rabbit; **~ al ajillo** rabbit with garlic; **~ de monte** wild rabbit
confitura jam
congrio conger eel
consomé al jerez chicken broth with sherry
copa nuria egg yolk and egg white, whipped and served with jam
corazonada heart stewed in sauce
corazón heart
cordero lamb
Cordoníu brand of Catalonian sparkling wine
cortadillo small pancake with lemon
corto strong coffee
corzo deer
costilla chop
crema cream; **~ batida** whipped cream; **~ catalana** caramel pudding; **~ española** dessert of milk, eggs, and fruit jelly; **~ nieve** with beaten egg yolk, sugar, rum

cremoso cream
criadillas sweetbreads
(a la) criolla with green peppers, spices, and tomatoes
croqueta fish or meat cake
crudo raw
Cuarenta y Tres egg liqueur
Cuba libre rum coke
cubierto cover charge
cuenta check
curanto dish of seafood, vegetables, and suckling pig

D

damasco variety of apricot
dátiles dates
de cordero lamb's
de cuerpo full-bodied
de lechuga green
de ternera calf's
del tiempo in season
desayuno breakfast
descafeinado decaffeinated
doble double (a double shot)
dulce dessert wine; sweet
dulce de naranja marmalade
durazno peach
duro hard (egg)

E

edulcorante sweetener
embuchado stuffed with meat
embutido spicy sausage
empanada pie or tart with meat or fish filling; ~ **de horno** filled with ground meat; ~ **gallega** tenderloin of pork, onions, and chili peppers in a pie

empanadillas small savory pastries stuffed with meat or fish
emperador swordfish
en dulce boiled
en escabeche marinated
en salazón cured
en salsa braised in casserole
en su jugo pot roasted
enchilada stuffed tortilla served with vegetable garnish and sauce
encurtido pickled
endibia endive
eneldo dill
ensalada salad; ~ **rusa** diced cold vegetables with mayonnaise
entremeses (variados) (assorted) appetizers
escabeche de gallina chicken marinated in vinegar and bay leaves
escarola escarole
espaguetis spaghetti
espalda shoulder
(a la) española with tomatoes
especialidades de la casa specialties of the house
especialidades locales local specialties
especias spices
espinacas spinach
espumoso sparkling
(puntas de) espárragos asparagus (tips)
esqueixado mixed fish salad *(Cat.)*
(al) estilo de in the style of
estofado braised; stewed
estragón tarragon

F

fabada (asturiana) stew of pork, beans, bacon, and sausage
faisán pheasant
fiambres cold cuts
fideo thin noodle
filete steak; **~ de lenguado empanado** breaded filet of sole; **~ de lomo** filet steak (tenderloin); **~ de res** beef steak
fino pale, dry sherry
(a la) flamenca with onions, peas, green peppers, tomatoes, and spiced sausage
flan caramel pudding
frambuesas raspberries
(a la) francesa sautéed in butter
fresas strawberries
fresco fresh, chilled
fresón large strawberry
fricandó thin slice of meat rolled in bacon and braised
frijoles beans; **~ refritos** fried mashed beans
frito de patata deep-fried potato croquette
fritos fritters
fritura mixta meat, fish, or vegetables deep-fried in batter
fruta fruit; **~ escarchada** candied fruit
frío cold
fuerte strong
Fundador wine-distilled brandy

G

galletas cookies; **~ de nata** cream cookies; **~ saladas** crackers

gallina hen
gallo cockerel
gambas (grandes) shrimp; **~ a la plancha** grilled; **~ al ajillo** with garlic
ganso goose
garbanzos chickpeas
garrafa carafe
gaseosa carbonated
gazpacho cold tomato soup
ginebra gin; **~ con limón** gin-fizz; **~ con tónica** gin and tonic
(a la) gitanilla with garlic
gordo fatty, rich
granadas pomegranates
granadina pomegranate syrup mixed with wine or brandy
granizados iced drinks
gratinado gratinéed
grelos turnip greens
grosellas espinosas gooseberries
grosellas negras black currants
grosellas rojas red currants
guacamole spicy avocado salad
guarnición garnish, trimming
guayaba guava
guinda sour cherry
guindilla chili pepper
guisantes peas

H

habas broad beans
habichuela verde green beans
hamburguesa hamburger
hayaca central cornmeal pancake, usually with ground meat filling
helado ice cream
hielo ice

hierbas herbs; ~ **finas** mixture of herbs

higaditos de pollo chicken livers

hígado liver

higos figs

hinojo fennel

hoja de laurel bay leaf

hongos fungi

horchata de almendra/chufa ground almond drink

(al) horno baked

hueso bone

huevos eggs; ~ **a la española** stuffed with tomatoes and served with cheese sauce; ~ **a la flamenca** baked with tomato, onion, and diced ham; ~ **al nido** "eggs in the nest"; ~ **al trote** with tuna; ~ **cocidos** boiled; ~ **duros** hard-boiled eggs; ~ **escalfados a la española** poached egg on onions, tomatoes, peppers, and zucchini; ~ **fritos** fried eggs; ~ **revueltos** scrambled eggs

humita boiled corn with tomatoes, green peppers, onions, and cheese

J

jabalí wild boar

jalea jelly

jamón ham; ~ **en dulce** boiled and served cold; ~ **y huevos** ham and eggs

(a la) jardinera with carrots, peas, and other vegetables

jengibre ginger

jerez sherry

judías blancas white beans

judías verdes green beans

jugo fresh juice; gravy, meat juice; ~ **de fruta** fruit juice

jurel kind of mackerel (fish)

L

lacón shoulder of pork

lampreas lampreys

langosta lobster; ~ **con pollo** with chicken

langostinos shrimp

lavanco wild duck

leche milk

lechón suckling pig

lechuga lettuce

legumbres legumes

lengua tongue

lenguado sole; ~ **a la vasca** baked with potatoes and vegetables

lentejas lentils

licor liqueur

liebre hare; ~ **estofada** jugged

lima lime

limonada lemonade

limón lemon

lista de platos menu

lista de vinos wine list

litro a liter

liviano light

lobarro type of bass

lombarda red cabbage

lomo loin; ~ **de cerdo al jerez** pork loin

loncha slice of meat

longaniza long, highly seasoned sausage

lubina bass

M

macedonia de frutas mixed fruit salad
(a la) madrileña with chorizo sausage, tomatoes, and paprika
magras al estilo de Aragón cured ham in tomato sauce
Mahón (queso de ...) type of goat cheese
(a la) mallorquina highly seasoned (fish and shellfish)
maíz sweet corn
manchego (queso de ...) ewe's milk cheese
mandarina tangerine
mantecado rich almond ice cream
mantequilla butter
manzana apple
manzanilla dry, pale sherry
maní peanut
marinera fish and seafood only
(a la) marinera with mussels, onions, tomatoes, herbs, and wine
mariscos seafood
matambre rolled beef stuffed with vegetables
mazapán marzipan
media botella half bottle
medio pollo asado half a roasted chicken
mejillones mussels
melaza molasses
melocotón peach; **~ en almíbar** in syrup
melón melon
membrillo quince paste

menestra green vegetable soup; **~ de pollo** casserole of chicken and vegetables
menta mint
menudillos giblets
merengue meringue
merienda afternoon snack
merluza hake
mermelada jam; **~ amarga de naranjas** marmalade
mero sea bass
miel honey
(a la) milanese with cheese, generally baked
minuta menu
mojo picón piquant red sauce *(Can.)*
mojo verde green herb sauce served with fish *(Cat.)*
mole poblano chicken served with sauce of chili peppers, spices, and chocolate
mollejas sweetbreads
moras mulberries
morcilla blood sausage
morilla morel mushroom
moros y cristianos rice and black beans with diced ham, garlic, green peppers, and herbs
mostaza mustard
mújol mullet
muslo de pollo chicken leg
muy seco very dry

N

nabo turnip
naranja orange
naranjada orangeade

nata cream; **~ batida** whipped
natillas custard
níspola medlar (fruit)
nopalito young cactus leaf served with salad dressing
nueces walnuts
nueces variadas assorted nuts
nuez moscada nutmeg

O

olla stew; **~ gitana** vegetable stew; **~ podrida** stew made of vegetables, meat, fowl, and ham
oloroso dark sherry
oporto port
ostras oysters
oveja ewe

P

pa amb tomàquet bread with tomato and salt (*Cat.*)
pabellón criollo beef in tomato sauce, garnished with beans, rice, and bananas
paella paella
paletilla shank
palitos skewered appetizer **~ de queso** cheese sticks
palmito palm heart
palta avocado
pan bread; **~ de pueblo** plain white bread
panecillos rolls
papas potatoes; **~ a la huancaína** with cheese and green peppers; **~ arrugadas** new potatoes baked and rolled in rock salt (*Can.*)
parrillada grill; **~ mixta** mixed

pasado done, cooked; **~ por agua** soft (egg)
pasas raisins
pastas pastry; pasta
pastel cake; **~ de choclo** corn with ground beef, chicken, raisins, and olives; **~ de queso** cheesecake
pasteles cakes; pastries
patatas potatoes; **~ (a la) leonesa** potatoes with onions; **~ fritas** french fries; **~ nuevas** new potatoes
pato duck/duckling
paté pâté
pavo turkey
pechuga de pollo breast of chicken
pepinillos pickles
pepino cucumber
(en) pepitoria stewed with onions, green peppers, and tomatoes
pera pear
perca perch
percebes goose barnacles (seafood)
perdiz partridge; **~ en escabeche** cooked in oil with vinegar, onions, parsley, carrots, and green pepper; served cold; **~ estofada** served in a white-wine sauce
perejil parsley
perifollo chervil
perilla (queso de …) firm cheese
pescadilla whiting
pescado fish **~ frito** fried fish
pez espada swordfish
picadillo ground meat, hash
picado ground
picante sharp, spicy, highly seasoned
picatoste deep-fried slice of bread

pichón pigeon
pierna leg
pimentón paprika
pimienta pepper
pimientos a la riojana sweet peppers stuffed with ground meat
pimientos morrones sweet red peppers
piña pineapple
pincho moruno grilled meat on a skewer
pintada guinea fowl
pisco grape brandy
pisto green pepper stew
(a la) plancha grilled on a griddle
plato plate, dish, portion; **~ del día** dish of the day
platos fríos cold dishes
platos típicos specialties
plátano banana
pollito spring chicken
pollo chicken; **~ a la brasa** grilled; **~ asado** roast; **~ pibil** simmered in fruit juice and spices
polvorón almond cookie
pomelo grapefruit
ponche crema eggnog liquor
porción small helping of tapas
postre dessert
potaje vegetable soup
puchero stew
puerros leeks
pulpitos baby octopus
pulpo octopus
punto de nieve dessert of whipped cream with beaten egg whites
puré purée; **~ de patatas** mashed potatoes

Q
queso cheese
quisquillas common shrimp

R
rábano radish; **~ picante** horseradish
rabo de buey oxtail
ración large helping
raja slice, portion
rallado grated
rape monkfish
raya ray, skate
rebanada slice
rebozado breaded, fried in batter
recomendamos … we recommend …
refrescos cold drinks
regular medium
rehogada sautéed
remolacha beet
repollo cabbage
requesón (queso de …) cottage cheese
riñones kidneys; **~ al jerez** braised in sherry
róbalo haddock
rodaballo turbot
(a la) romana dipped in batter and fried
romero rosemary
romesco sauce of nuts, chili, tomatoes, garlic, and breadcrumbs *(Cat.)*
ron rum
roncal (queso de …) sharp ewe's milk cheese
ropa vieja cooked, leftover meat and vegetables, covered with tomatoes and green peppers
rosado rosé

rosbif roast beef
rosquilla donut
rubio red mullet
ruibarbo rhubarb

S

sal salt
salado salted, salty
salchichas sausages
salchichón salami
salmonetes red mullet
salmón salmon; **~ ahumado** smoked salmon
salsa sauce
salsa a la catalana sauce of tomato and green peppers
salsa a la vasca parsley, peas, garlic; a delicate green dressing for fish in the Basque country
salsa alioli garlic sauce
salsa de tomate ketchup
salsa en escabeche sweet and sour sauce
salsa española brown sauce with herbs, spices, and wine
salsa mayordoma butter and parsley sauce
salsa picante hot pepper sauce
salsa romana bacon/ham and egg cream sauce
salsa romesco green peppers, pimentos, garlic; popular chilled dressing for fish on the east coast around Tarragona
salsa verde parsley sauce
salteado sautéed
salvia sage
sandía watermelon

sangrita tequila with tomato, orange, and lime juices
sangría wine punch
sardinas sardines
seco dry
sencillo plain
sepia cuttlefish
serrano cured
sesos brains
setas mushrooms
sidra cider
sobrasada salami
soda soda water
sol y sombra blend of wine-distilled brandy and aniseed liqueur
solo black (coffee); straight/neat
solomillo de cerdo tenderloin of pork
sopa soup; **~ de buey** oxtail; **~ de ajo** garlic; **~ de arroz** rice; **~ de camarones** shrimp; **~ de cangrejo** crab; **~ de castellana** baked garlic; **~ de cebolla** onion; **~ de cocido** kind of broth; **~ de espárragos** asparagus; **~ de fideos** noodle; **~ de mariscos** seafood; **~ de patatas** potato; **~ de pescado** fish; **~ de tomate** tomato; **~ de verduras** vegetable; **~ juliana** bouillon of finely shredded vegetables; **~ sevillana** highly spiced fish soup
sorbete (iced) fruit drink
suave mild
suizo bun
suplemento sobre ... ...extra
surtido assorted

T

taco wheat or cornflour pancake, usually with meat filling, garnished with spicy sauce

tajada slice

tallarín noodle

tamal pastry dough of coarsely ground cornmeal with meat or fruit filling, steamed in corn-husks

tapas snacks

tarta de almendras almond tart

tarta de manzana apple tart

tarta de moka mocha cake

tarta helada ice-cream cake

tartaletas small open tarts filled with fish, meat, vegetables, or cheese

taza de café cup of coffee

té tea

ternera veal

tinto red

Tío Pepe brand of sherry

tipo roquefort blue cheese

tocino salted fresh lard, **~ de panceta** bacon, **~ entreverado** streaky bacon

tocino/tocinillo de cielo dessert of whipped egg yolks and sugar

tojunto rabbit stew

tomates tomatoes

tomillo thyme

tónica tonic water

toronja type of grapefruit

tortilla omelet; **~ al ron** rum; **~ de alcachofa** artichoke; **~ de cebolla** onion; **~ de espárragos** asparagus;

~ de jamón ham; **~ de patatas** potato; **~ de queso** cheese; **~ de setas** mushroom; **~ gallega** potato omelet with ham, chili; **~ paisana** with potatoes, peas, shrimp, or ham

tortitas pancakes/waffles

tostadas toast

tripas tripe

Triple Seco orange liqueur

trucha trout; **~ a la navarra** stuffed with ham; **~ frita a la asturiana** floured and fried in butter, garnished with lemon

trufas truffles

tumbet ratatouille and potato-type casserole with meat or fish *(Maj.)*

turrón nougat

U

ulloa (queso de ...) soft cheese from Galicia

uvas grapes; **~ blancas** green; **~ negras** black

uvas pasas raisins

V

vaca salada corned beef

vainilla vanilla

valenciana a type of paella, the classic version

variado varied, assorted

varios sundries

vaso glass

venado venison

veneras scallops

verduras vegetables

vermut vermouth

vieira scallop
villalón (queso de ...) mild cheese
vinagreta piquant vinegar dressing
vino wine; **~ de mesa** table wine;
~ del país local wine
(a la) vizcaína with green peppers,
tomatoes, garlic, and paprika

W

whisky whisky; **~ americano**
bourbon; **~ con soda** whisky and
soda; **~ escocés** Scotch

X

xampaña Catalonian sparkling
wine
xató olive and endive salad *(Cat.)*

Y

yema egg yolk
yemas dessert of whipped egg
yolks and sugar
yogur yogurt

Z

zamorana ham, pork loin, pig's
feet, chili pepper
zanahorias carrots
zarzamoras blackberries
zarzuela savory stew of assorted
fish and shellfish *(Cat.)*;
~ de pescado selection of fish
with highly seasoned sauce
zumo fresh juice; **~ de fruta**
fruit juice

SWEDISH

ESSENTIALS

Hello.	**Hej.** *hay*
Good evening.	**God afton.** *goo afton*
A table for ..., please.	**Kan jag få ett bord för ..., tack.** *kun yaag faw et boord fur ... tuck*
1/2/3/4 (people)	**en/två/tre/fyra** *en/tvaw/treh/fewra*
Thank you.	**Tack.** *tuck*
The check, please.	**Kan jag få räkningen, tack.** *kun yaag faw rairkningen tuck*
Good-bye.	**Adjö.** *ayur*

PLACES TO EAT

Cocktail bar *kocktailbaar*
These "bars" serve canapés and other small snacks

Dansrestaurang *dansresteurang*
Restaurants offering dining and dancing, found in large towns and cities

Fiskrestaurang *feeskresteurang*
Fish and seafood restaurants

Gatukök *gaateuchurk*
"Kitchen on the street," serving quick snacks such as sausages, hamburgers, mashed potatoes, French fries

Grillbar *grilbar*
Self-service restaurants offering hamburgers, steaks, French fries, beer, and soft drinks

Gästgivargård _yestyeevargord_
Old country inns, with rustic décor and excellent cuisine; good choice for a **smörgåsbord**

Kafé _kaffeh_
Coffee shops serving hot drinks, soft drinks, and snacks

Konditori _kondeetoree_
Coffee shops serving hot drinks, soft drinks, and a mouthwatering selection of pastries and cakes; also serve sandwiches and snacks

Korvstånd _koorvstond_
Hot-dog stands

Kvarterskrog/Lunchrestaurang _kvaartehrskroog/leunschresteurang_
Small neighborhood restaurants with good, inexpensive food, and beer and wine

Restaurang/Restaurant _resteurang_
Not officially rated; in Stockholm, don't miss a memorable meal on a boat taking you out into the archipelago

Stekhus _stehkheus_
Steak houses

Värdshus _vairdsheus_
Old inns in smaller towns, often offering local specialties such as reindeer, moose, and poultry

MEAL TIMES
Frukost _freukost_
Breakfast: 7–10 a.m.

Lunch _leunsch_
Lunch: served from as early as 11 a.m.; the best time to try the **dagens rätt** (specialty of the day)

Middag *middah*

Dinner: eaten early, around 6 or 7 p.m.

SWEDISH CUISINE

Most visitors and tourists equate Swedish food with the **smörgåsbord**. Whereas the **smörgåsbord** does indeed represent a great many delicacies from Swedish cuisine, there are many other excellent Swedish dishes that visitors should sample. Swedes are fish lovers and some of their favorite seafood dishes include **sill** (marinated herrings), shrimp in their shells, **gravlax** (marinated salmon), and **kräftor** (crayfish, available in August)—all eaten with new potatoes, boiled with dill. Don't miss the opportunity to sample venison, moose, or reindeer, served with rowanberry or wild cranberry jam. In the countryside, you will find desserts made with fresh **smultron** (wild strawberries) and **blåbär** (blueberries, bilberries).

FINDING A PLACE TO EAT

Can you recommend a good restaurant?	**Kan ni rekommendera en bra restaurang?** *kun nee rekomendehra en braa resteurang*
Is there a(n) … near here?	**Finns det någon … i närheten?** *fins det nawgon … ee nairhehten*
inexpensive restaurant	**billigare restaurant** *billigareh resteurang*
traditional local restaurant	**värdshus** *vairds-heus*
vegetarian restaurant	**vegetariansk restaurant** *vegetaree-ansk resteurang*
Where can I find a(n) …?	**Var finns …** *vaar fins*
café	**ett kafé** *et kafeh*
fast-food restaurant	**en grillbar** *en gril-baar*
ice-cream parlor	**ett glasstånd** *et glas-stond*

pizzeria	**en pizzeria** *en pitsereea*
steak house	**ett stekhus** *et stehk-heus*
coffee/pastry shop	**konditori** *kondee-toree*

RESERVATIONS

I'd like to reserve a table …	**Jag skulle vilja reservera ett bord …** *yaag skeulleh vilya reservehra et boord*
for two.	**för två.** *fur tvaw*
for this evening/ tomorrow at …	**till ikväll/imorgon klockan …** *til eekvel/eemorron klockan*
We'll come at 8:00.	**Vi kommer klockan åtta.** *vee kommer klockan otta*
A table for two, please.	**Ett bord for två, tack.** *et boord fur tvaw tuck*
We have a reservation.	**Vi har reserverat ett bord.** *vee haar reservehrat et boord*

YOU MAY HEAR

| **Till vilken tid?** | For what time? |
| **Tyvärr, det är fullbokat.** | I'm sorry. We're very busy/full. |

Could we sit …?	**Kan vi sitta …?** *kun vee sitta*
over there	**där borta** *dair borta*
outside	**ute** *euteh*
in a non-smoking area	**vid bord för icke-rökare** *veed boord fur ickeh-rurkareh*
by the window	**vid fönstret** *veed furnstret*
Smoking or non-smoking?	**Rökare eller icke-rökare?** *rurkareh eller ickeh-rurkareh*

ORDERING

Waiter!/Waitress!   **Ursäkta.** *eurshekta*

May I see the wine list, please?   **Kan jag få se vinlistan?** *kun yaag faw seh veen-listan*

YOU MAY HEAR

Vill ni beställa?	Are you ready to order?
Vad vill ni beställa?	What would you like?
Jag kan rekommendera …	I recommend …
Smaklig måltid.	Enjoy your meal.

Do you have a set menu?   **Har ni en meny?** *haar nee en menew*

Can you recommend some typical local dishes?   **Kan ni rekommendera några typiska rätter från den här regionen?** *kun nee rekomendehra nawgra tewpiska retter frawn den hair regeeoonen*

Could you tell me what … is?   **Kan ni tala om vad … är?** *kun nee taala om vaad … air*

What's in it?   **Vad är det i den?** *vaad air det ee den*

I'll have …   **Jag tar …** *yaag taar*

a bottle/glass/carafe of …   **en flaska/ett glas/en karaff …** *en flaska/et glaas/en karaff*

SPECIAL REQUESTS

Could I have a salad instead of vegetables, please?   **Kan jag få sallad istället för grönsaker?** *kun yaag faw salad ee stellet fur grurn-saaker*

Does the meal come with vegetables/potatoes?	**Inkluderar varmrätten grönsaker/ potatis?** *inkleudehrar varm-retten grurn-saaker/pootaatis*
May I have some …?	**Kan jag få lite …?** *kun yaag faw leeteh*
bread	**bröd** *brurd*
butter	**smör** *smur*
lemon	**citron** *seetroon*
mustard	**senap** *sehnap*
pepper	**peppar** *peppar*
salt	**salt** *salt*
oil and vinegar	**olja och vinäger** *olya ock vinairger*
sugar	**socker** *socker*
artificial sweetener	**sötningsmedel** *surtnings-mehdel*
vinaigrette	**vinaigrettesås** *vinnegret-saws*
Could you bring a child's seat, please?	**Kan jag få en barnstol, tack?** *kun yaag faw en baarn-stool tuck*
Where can I change the baby?	**Var kan jag byta på babyn?** *vaar kun yaag bewta paw baybin*

GENERAL QUESTIONS

Could I/we have a(n) …, please?	**Kan jag/vi få …, tack?** *kun yaag/vee faw … tuck*
ashtray	**en askkopp** *en ask-kop*
cup/glass	**en kopp/ett glas** *en kop/et glaas*
fork/knife	**en gaffel/en kniv** *en gaffel/en kneev*
plate/spoon	**en tallrik/en sked** *en tallrik/en shehd*

napkin	**en servett** *en servett*
I'd like (a) …	**Jag skulle vilja ha …** *yaag skeulleh vilya haa*
tea/coffee	**thé/kaffe** *teh/kaffeh*
black/with milk	**utan/med mjölk** *eutan/mehd myulk*
(hot) chocolate	**(varm) choklad** *(varm) shooklaad*
cola/lemonade	**cola/sockerdricka** *kawla/socker-dricka*
fruit juice	**fruktjuice** *freukt-yoos*
orange/pineapple/tomato juice	**apelsin-/ananas-/tomat-juice** *apelseen-/ananas-/toomaat-yoos*
That's all, thanks.	**Det var allt, tack.** *det vaar alt tuck*
Where are the restrooms?	**Var är toaletten?** *vaar air tooaletten*

SPECIAL REQUIREMENTS

I can't eat food containing …	**Jag kan inte äta mat som innehåller …** *yaag kun inteh airta maat som inneholler*
salt/sugar	**salt/socker** *salt/socker*
Do you have any dishes/drinks for diabetics?	**Har ni några rätter/drinkar för diabetiker?** *haar nee nawgra retter/drinkar fur deeaabehtiker*
Do you have vegetarian dishes?	**Har ni vegetarianska rätter?** *haar nee vegetaree-anska retter*

COMPLAINTS

| That's not what I ordered. | **Det här har jag inte beställt.** *det hair haar yaag inteh bestelt* |
| I asked for … | **Jag beställde …** *yaag besteldeh* |

I can't eat this.	**Jag kan inte äta det här.** *yaag kun inteh airta det hair*
The meat is …	**Köttet är …** *churtet air*
overdone	**för mycket stekt** *fur mewcket stehkt*
underdone	**inte genomstekt** *inteh yehnom-stehkt*
too tough	**för segt** *fur sehgt*
The food is cold.	**Maten är kall.** *maaten air kal*
This isn't fresh.	**Det här är inte färskt.** *det hair air inteh fairskt*
How much longer will our food be?	**Hur länge till behöver vi vänta?** *heur lengeh til behurver vee venta*
We can't wait any longer. We're leaving.	**Vi kan inte vänta längre. Vi går nu.** *vee kun inteh venta lengreh. vee gawr neu*

PAYING

Tipping: See page 332.

The check, please.	**Kan jag få notan, tack.** *kun yaag faw nootan tuck*
We'd like to pay separately.	**Vi vill betala var för sig.** *vee vil betaala vaar fur say*
It's all together.	**Allt tillsammans.** *alt til-sammans*
I think there's a mistake in this check.	**Jag tror det måste vara fel på notan.** *yaag troor det mosteh vaara fehl paw nootan*
What's this amount for?	**Vad står den här summan för?** *vaad stawr den hair seumman fur*
I didn't have that. I had …	**Jag åt inte det. Jag åt …** *yaag awt inteh det. yaag awt*

Can I pay with this credit card?	**Kan jag betala med det här kreditkortet?** _kun yaag betaala mehd det hair kredeet-koortet_
Could I have a receipt, please?	**Kan jag få ett kvitto, tack?** _kun yaag faw et kvittoo tuck_
That was a very good meal.	**Det var en mycket god måltid.** _det vaar en mewcket good mawl-teed_

COURSE BY COURSE

Breakfast Frukost

Most hotels and guest houses offer a buffet breakfast, including the items listed below and also cold meats, cereals, and cheeses. Breakfast is usually a cup of coffee with an open-faced sandwich or a bowl of porridge (**gröt**) or cereal. For a special treat, try Swedish yogurt, **filmjölk**, with your cereal.

I'd like …	**Jag skulle vilja ha …** _yaag skeulleh vilya haa_
eggs	**ägg** _egg_
boiled/fried/scrambled	**kokt/stekt/äggröra** _kookt/stehkt/egg-rurra_
fruit juice	**fruktjuice** _freukt-yoos_
grapefruit/orange	**grapefrukt/apelsin** _grape-freukt/apelseen_
honey	**honung** _hawneung_
jam/marmalade	**sylt/marmelad** _sewlt/marmelaad_
milk	**mjölk** _myulk_
rolls/toast	**småbröd/rostat bröd** _smaw-brurd/rostat brurd_

Appetizers Förrätter

rökt lax	*rurkt lax*	smoked salmon
gravlax	*graavlax*	marinated salmon
sillbricka	*sil-bricka*	variety of marinated herrings
viltpaté	*vilt-pateh*	game paté

Färska räkor *fairska rairkor*
Unshelled shrimp—shell the shrimp and eat with toast, butter, and mayonnaise

S.O.S. (smör, ost och sill) *es oo es (smur oost ock sil)*
A small plate of marinated herring, bread and butter, and cheese

Toast skagen *toast skaagen*
Toast with chopped shrimp in mayonnaise, topped with bleak* roe

Löjrom *lur'-rom*
Bleak* roe, served with onions and sour cream on toast

* Bleak is a small silvery fish belonging to the carp family.

Soups Soppor

Soups are eaten in fall and winter, and many are a meal in their own right. **Spenatsoppa** (spinach) and **ärtsoppa** (pea) are specialties.

buljong	*beull-yong*	broth/consommé
fisksoppa	*fisk-soppa*	fish soup
grönsakssoppa	*grurnsaaks-soppa*	vegetable soup
kycklingsoppa	*chewkling-soppa*	chicken soup
löksoppa	*lurk-soppa*	onion soup
oxsvanssoppa	*ooxsvans-soppa*	oxtail soup
potatissoppa	*pootaatis-soppa*	potato soup
sparrissoppa	*sparris-soppa*	asparagus soup

Ärtsoppa *airt-soppa*
Pea soup, made from dried yellow peas and served with lightly salted pork or pork knuckle; traditionally followed by pancakes

Köttsoppa *churt-soppa*
A soup of boiled pieces of beef, vegetables, and dumplings

Spenatsoppa *speh<u>nat</u>-soppa*
A rich soup made from fresh spinach, potatoes, milk, and cream

Egg dishes Äggrätter

äggröra	*<u>egg</u>-rurra*	scrambled eggs
stekta ägg	*stehkta egg*	baked eggs

Omelet *ome<u>let</u>*
Omelets, filled with pieces of ham, mushrooms, or spinach

Pannkaka/Fläskpannkaka *<u>pan</u>kaaka/<u>flesk</u>-pankaaka*
Pancakes, eaten with raspberry or blueberry jam; **fläskpannkaka** is a thick pancake filled with bacon and baked in the oven

Fish and seafood Fisk och skaldjur

If you visit Sweden in August, enjoy a **kräftkalas** (crayfish party)—when helped down with a few glasses of **akvavit** (aquavit) and some salad and cheese, it makes for an unforgettable evening.

forell	*foo<u>rel</u>*	trout
hummer	*heummer*	lobster
kolja	*kolya*	haddock
lax	*lax*	salmon
makrill	*makril*	mackerel
musslor	*<u>meuss</u>loor*	mussels
ostron	*oostron*	oysters
räkor	*rairkoor*	shrimp
röding	*<u>rur</u>ding*	char

rödspätta	_rurd-spetta_	plaice
sjötunga	_sjur-teunga_	sole
skarpsill	_skarp-sil_	herring
tonfisk	_toonfisk_	tuna
torsk	_torshk_	cod

Strömming _strurming_

Sprats (Baltic herring) fileted and sandwiched with dill and butter
in the middle; fried and eaten hot with mashed potatoes or just cold

Böckling _burkling_

Buckling—(or bloaters) smoked Baltic herring

Rimmad lax med stuvad potatis
reemahd lahks mehd stewahd potahtihs
Lightly salted salmon with creamed potatoes and dill

Halstrad forell med färskpotatis
hahlstrahd forel mehdfairskpotahtihs
Grilled trout with new potatoes

Stuvad abborre _stewahd abborreh_

Perch poached with onion, parsley, and lemon served with potatoes

Smörgåsbord

If you have never heard of typical Swedish food, you may at least
have heard of the famous **smörgåsbord**. It is a buffet meal on a
grand scale, laid out on a large, beautifully decorated table.

You start at one end of the table, usually the one with the cold
seafood dishes, marinated herrings, **Janssons frestelse**, and salads.
Then you work your way through the cold meat, **köttbullar**,
sausage, omelets, and vegetables, and end up at the cheeseboard
and desserts. Then you start all over again. The price is set, and
you can eat as much as you like.

At Christmastime, the **smörgåsbord** becomes a **julbord**, served in
homes and restaurants alike. Swedes tend to drink **akvavit** (aquavit)
or beer with this.

Meat and poultry Kött och fågel

anka	*anka*	duck
bacon	*baykon*	bacon
biffkött	*bif-churt*	beef
biffstek	*bif-stehk*	steak
fasan	*fasaan*	pheasant
fläskkött	*flesk-churt*	pork
hare	*hareh*	rabbit
kalkon	*kalkoon*	turkey
kalvkött	*kalv-churt*	veal
korv	*korv*	sausages
köttbullar	*churt-beullar*	meatballs
kyckling	*chewkling*	chicken
lamm	*lumb*	lamb
skinka	*shinkaa*	ham

Älgstek (Renstek) med svampsås
ail-stehk (rehnstehk) mehd svampsos
Roast moose (reindeer) with mushroom sauce; served with baked potatoes

Kåldomar med gräddsås och lingon
koldolmahr mehd graidsos ok leengon
Ground meat and rice stuffed in cabbage leaves; served with a cream-based gravy and wild cranberries

Sjömansbiff *shurmahnsbif*
Casserole of fried beef, onions, and potatoes; braised in beer

Vegetables Grönsaker

blomkål	*bloom-kawl*	cauliflower
champinjoner	*shampin-yooner*	mushrooms
grönsallad	*grurn-salad*	lettuce

gurka	geurka	cucumber
haricots verts	arikaw vair	green beans
(röd) kål	(rurd) kawl	(red) cabbage
kålrot	kawlroot	rutabaga
lök	lurk	onions
morötter	moorurter	carrots
paprika	paaprika	peppers (red, green)
potatis	pootaatis	potatoes
rovor	roovor	turnips
schalottenlök	shalotten-lurk	shallots
tomater	toomaater	tomatoes
vitlök	veet-lurk	garlic
äggplanta	egg-planta	eggplant
ärtor	airtoor	peas
ättiksgurka	ettiks-geurka	pickled gherkins

Salad Sallader

blandsallad	blandsalad	mixed salad
grönsallad	grurn-salad	green salad
potatissallad	pootaatis-salad	potato salad
skaldjurssallad	skaal-yeurs-salad	seafood salad
tomater och lök	toomaater ock lurk	tomato and onion salad

Sillsallad sil-salad
Beet and herring salad with apples, pickles, potatoes, onions, cream

Västkustsallad vestkeust-salad
Shrimp and mussel salad with mushrooms, tomatoes, lettuce, cucumber, asparagus, dill

Cheese Ost

Herrgårdsost *hairrgawrds-oost*
A semi-hard cheese with a nutty flavor

Svecia *svehsia*
One of the most popular semi-hard cheeses; varies in strength

Grevé *greveh*
A semi-hard cheese with a taste between Gouda and Emmentaler

Mesost *mehs-oost*
A soft, sweet, yellowish whey cheese

Ädelost *airdel-oost*
A blue cheese with a sharp taste, similar to French Roquefort

Kryddost *krewdd-oost*
A sharp, strong cheese with caraway seeds

Västerbotten *vester-botten*
A sharp, tangy, hard and strong cheese from the north of Sweden

Dessert Efterrätter

äppelpaj/äppelkaka	*eppel-pie/ eppel-kaaka*	apple pie/apple tart
fruktsallad	*freukt-salad*	fruit salad
glass	*glas*	ice cream
jordgubbar med grädde	*yoord-geubbar mehd greddeh*	strawberries and cream

Friterad camembert med hjortronsylt
fritehrad camembert mehd yoortron-sewlt
Deep-fried camembert with cloudberry jam

Ostkaka *oost-kaaka*
A traditional curd cake dessert from southern Sweden; sometimes made with almonds and served with jam

Våfflor *voffloor*
Waffles served with jam and whipped cream

Marängsviss *mareng-svis*
Meringues served with whipped cream and chocolate sauce

Fruit Frukt

apelsiner	*apelseener*	oranges
bananer	*banaaner*	bananas
blåbär	*blaw-bair*	blueberries
citron	*seetroon*	lemon
grapefrukt	*grape-freukt*	grapefruit
hallon	*hallon*	raspberries
jordgubbar	*yoord-geubbar*	strawberries
körsbär	*churs-bair*	cherries
persikor	*pairshikoor*	peaches
plommon	*ploommon*	plums
smultron	*smeultron*	wild strawberries
(vatten)melon	*(vatten)meloon*	(water)melon
vindruvor	*veen-dreuvor*	grapes
äpplen	*epplen*	apples

DRINKS

Apart from wine, alcoholic drinks in Sweden are probably the most expensive in Europe, due to high taxes. Alcohol (with the exception of class I and II beers, see below) is sold in state-run shops (**systembolaget**). **Systembolaget** and restaurants carry all types of drink; make sure you know the price of a drink before you order.

Aperitifs Aperitif

Pre-dinner drinks; as anywhere, with sherry, Martini, and whisky topping the list, followed by gin and tonic and vodka.

Beer Öl

Beer is probably the most popular drink in Sweden. Beer with an
alcohol content above 3% (**starköl**—class III) can only be bought in
systembolaget; classes I (**lättöl**) and II (below 3% alcohol content)
can be bought in ordinary stores.

Do you have (any) …?	**Har ni …?** *haar nee*
bottled beer/canned beer	**öl på flaska/burköl** *url paw flaska/beurk-url*
draft/low-alcohol	**fatöl/lättöl** *faat-eurl/let-url*

Wine Viner

Wine prices are very competitive in the state-run stores as well as in
restaurants, since the government imports wine in bulk. You can
find good, reasonably priced table wine as well as Champagne.

Can you recommend a … wine?	**Kan ni föreslå ett … vin?** *kun nee furreh-slaw et … veen*
red/white/blush [rosé]	**rött/vitt/rosé** *rurt/vit/ro<u>seh</u>*
dry/sweet/sparkling	**torrt/sött/mousserande** *tort/surt/moo<u>seh</u>rande*
I'd like the house wine, please.	**Jag skulle vilja ha husets vin, tack.** *yaag skeulleh vilya haa heusets veen tuck*
I'd like a corkscrew.	**Jag skulle vilja ha en korkskruv.** *yaag skeulleh vilya haa en <u>kork</u>-skreuv*

Aquavit Aqvavit

Aqvavit, a grain- or potato-based spirit, is something of a national
drink, served in very small, ice-cold glasses. It goes excellently
with marinated herring dishes, crayfish, and **smörgåsbord**.

Renat (Brännvin) *rehnat (bren-veen)*
Colorless type of **aqvavit**, without flavor

Skåne *skawneh*
Flavored with aniseed and caraway seeds

Herrgårdsakvavit *hairrgawrds-akvaveet*
Flavored with caraway seeds and whisky

Spirits and liqueurs Sprit och likör

Glögg *glurg*
Similar to a mulled wine, **glögg** also contains sugar, port, lemon rind, and various spices—and is very much a part of Christmas celebrations

Punsch *peunsh*
An after-dinner, sweet liqueur, made from arrack, sugar, and pure alcohol; often served warm with pea soup (**ärtsoppa**)

brandy/gin/whisky	**cognac/gin/whisky** *konyak/jin/whisky*
rum/vodka/port	**rom/vodka/portvin** *rom/vodka/port-veen*
liqueur	**likör** *likurr*
straight/neat	**ren/"som den är"** *rehn/som den air*
on the rocks [with ice]	**med is** *mehd ees*
with water/tonic water	**med vatten/med tonic** *mehd vatten/mehd tonik*
I'd like a single/double …	**Jag skulle vilja ha en liten/ dubbel(stor) …** *yaag skeulleh vilya haa en leeten/deubbel (stoor)*
Cheers!	**Skål!** *skol*

Non-alcoholic drinks

For afternoon tea or coffee, try typical Swedish **konditori** (patisserie/coffee shop). You can help yourself to as many cups as you like while indulging in a slice of **prinsesstårta** (sponge cake with cream and custard, covered with green marzipan), **mazarin** (almond tart, topped with icing), or a **wienerbröd** (Danish pastry). Try the **saffransbulle** (saffron bun) and **pepparkaka** (ginger cookies) at Christmas. Tea is commonly drunk with lemon, no milk.

Kaffe *kaffeh*

Coffee—a national drink, and always freshly brewed; commonly drunk black, but you can ask for **mjölk** (milk) or **grädde** (cream)

I'd like (a/an)…	**Jag skulle vilja ha …** *yaag skeulleh vilya haa …*
tea/with milk/with lemon	**thé/med mjölk/med citron** *teh/mehd myulk/mehd ceetroon*
(hot) chocolate	**(varm) choklad** *(varm) shooklaad*
cola/lemonade	**coca-cola/sockerdricka** *kawka-kawla/socker-dricka*
fruit juice	**fruktjuice** *freukt-yoos*
orange/pineapple/tomato	**apelsin/ananas/tomat** *apelseen/ananas/toomaat*
milk shake	**milkshake** *milk-shake*
mineral water	**mineralvatten** *mineraal-vatten*
carbonated/non-carbonated	**med kolsyra/utan kolsyra** *mehd kawl-sewra/eutan kawl-sewra*

MENU READER

bakad	_baakad_	baked
blodig	_bloodig_	rare/underdone
brynt	_brewnt_	sautéed
bräserad	_brehsehrahd_	braised
friterad	_freetenrahd_	deep-fried
fylld	_fewld_	stuffed
förlorat	_furlooraht_	poached (eggs)
genomstekt	_yehnomstehkt_	well-done
grillad	_grillahd_	grilled
i bitar	ee _beetahr_	diced
i gryta	ee _grewtah_	stewed
inlagd	_inlagd_	marinated
kluven	_klueven_	diced
kokt	_kookt_	boiled
kryddad/kryddstark	_krewdahd/ krewd-stahrk_	spicy
marinerad	_mahreenehrahd_	marinated
medium	_mehdeeyewm_	medium
panerad	_pahnenrahd_	breaded
pocherad	_poshehrahd_	poached
riktigt blodig	_reekteegt bloodig_	very rare
rökt	_rurkt_	smoked
stekt	_stehkt_	fried/sautéed
stuvad	_stewad_	stewed
ugnsbrynt	_ewngns-brewnt_	oven-browned
ugnstekt	_ewngnstehkt_	roasted
ångkokt	_ongkookt_	steamed

A

abborre perch
alkoholisk dryck alcoholic drink
alkoholfria drycker non-alcoholic drinks
ananas pineapple
anka duck; duckling
ansjovis anchovies; marinated anchovies
apelsin orange
apelsinjos/apelsinjuice orange juice
aprikoser apricots
avokado avocado
älgstek (renstek) med svampsås roast moose (reindeer) with mushroom sauce

B

bakverk pastries
bakelse piece of cake
banan banana
barnmatsedel children's menu
basilika basil
bål punch
ben leg/on the bone
biff steak
bigarråer sweet morello cherries
bit slice
björnbär blackberries
björnstek roast bear
blandade assorted
blandade grönsaker mixed vegetables
blandade kryddor mixed herbs
blandade nötter assorted nuts
blandsallad mixed salad
blomkål cauliflower
blåa vindruvor black grapes
blåbär blueberries
blåbärssylt blueberry jam

blåmusslor mussels
bog shoulder (cut of meat)
bondbönor broad beans
bordsvin table wine
bouquet garni mixed herbs
braxen bream; sea bream
broiler spring chicken
brylépudding crème caramel
brysselkål Brussel sprouts
brytbönor kidney beans
brännvin aquavit (grain- or potato-based spirit)
bröd bread
brödsmulor bread crumbs
bröst breast
buljong consommé
bulle bun
böckling smoked herring
bönor beans
bönskott bean sprouts

C

champinjoner mushrooms
chilipeppar chili pepper
chips potato chips
chocklad chocolate
citron lemon
citronjuice lemon juice
cognac brandy

D

dadlar dates
dagens meny menu of the day
dagens rätt dish/speciality of the day
dessertvin dessert wine
dillsås dill sauce
dragon tarragon

E

efterrätt dessert
enbär juniper berries

endiv endive
en dubbel double (a double shot)
en halv flaska half bottle
enkel plain
entrecote sirloin steak

F

falukorv lightly spiced sausage for frying
fasan pheasant
fatöl draft beer
fet fatty, rich (sauce)
fikon figs
filé filet mignon
filmjölk drinking yogurt
fisk fish
fläsk pork
fläskben pork on the bone/leg of pork
fläskfilé filet of pork
fläskkarré loin of pork
fläskkorv spicy, boiled pork sausage
fläsklägg knuckle of pork
fläskpannkaka thick pancake filled with bacon
forell trout
franskbröd white bread (French recipe)
friterad camembert med hjortronsylt deep-fried Camembert with cloudberry jam
friterade fritters
frukost breakfast
frukostflingor cereal
frukt fruit
fruktjuice fruit juice
från grillen grilled
fullkornsmjöl whole wheat flour
fylld (med) stuffed (with)
fyllda oliver stuffed olives

fylligt full-bodied (wine)
fågel poultry
får mutton
fårost ewe's milk cheese
fänkål fennel
färsk (frukt) fresh (fruit)
färska fikon fresh figs
färska räkor unshelled shrimp
färskpotatis new potatoes
förlorat ägg poached egg
förrätter first course

G

garnering garnish/trimming
gelé jelly
get kid (goat)
getost goat's milk cheese
gin och tonic gin and tonic
glass ice cream
glutenfritt gluten free
glögg mulled wine with port and spices, served hot
grapefrukt grapefruit
gratinerad au gratin
gratäng gratin
gravlax marinated salmon
greve semi-hard cheese
grillad kyckling grilled chicken
grillspett skewered
gryta pot roast, stew or casserole
gurka cucumber
gås goose
gädda sea perch
grädde cream
gräddfil sour cream
gräslök chives
grön paprika green peppers
gröna bönor green beans
grönsaker vegetables
grönsakssoppa vegetable soup
grönsallad green salad

gröna vindruvor white grapes
gröt porridge

H
hallon raspberries
halstrad fisk grilled fish
halstrad forell med färskpotatis grilled trout with new potatoes
hamburgare hamburger
haricots verts string beans
hasselbackspotatis oven-baked potatoes, coated in bread crumbs
hasselnötter hazelnuts
havre corn
havsabborre sea bass
havskräfta large shrimp (sea crayfish)
hemlagad homemade
herrgårdsakvavit aquavit flavored with caraway seeds and whisky
herrgårdsost semi-hard cheese with a nutty flavor
het hot (temperature)
hjort deer
hjortron cloudberries
hjortronsylt cloudberry jam
honung honey
hovmästarsås dill sauce (for marinated salmon)
hummer lobster
husets specialitet specialties of the house
huvudrätter main course
hårdkokt hard-boiled (egg)
hårt bröd crispbread
hälleflundra halibut

I
i olja in oil
ingefära ginger

inlagd i ättika (vinäger) marinated in vinegar
inlagd sill marinated (pickled) herring
is ice
isterband sausage of pork, barley, and beef, for frying

J
jordgubbar strawberries
jordnötter peanuts
jos/juice juice
julbord buffet of hot and cold Swedish specialties served at Christmas time
järpe hazel hen

K
kaffe coffee
kaka cake
kalkon turkey
kall soppa cold soup
kallskuret cold dish
kalops beef stew
kalvbräss sweetbreads
kalvkött veal
kalvsylta pickled pig's feet
kammussla scallops
kanderad frukt candied fruit
kanel cinnamon
kantareller chanterelle mushrooms
kapris caper
karaff carafe
karameller candy
karré tenderloin (smoked)
katrinplommon prunes
kex cookies
kikärtor chickpeas
kiwifrukt kiwi fruit
klimp dumpling

kokosnöt coconut
kokt stewed
kokta katrinplommon stewed prunes
kokt potatis boiled potatoes
kokt skinka boiled ham
kokt ägg boiled egg
kolgrillad charcoal-grilled
kolja haddock
kolsyrad/t carbonated (drinks)
kompott stewed fruit
konserverad frukt canned fruit
korv sausage
korvar sausages
kotlett cutlet
kotletter chops
köttsoppa substantial beef and vegetable soup with dumplings
krabba crab
krasse watercress
kronärtskockor artichokes
kroppkakor potato dumplings, filled with bacon and onions
krusbär gooseberry
kryddad pepparsås hot pepper sauce
kryddost sharp, strong cheese with caraway seeds
kryddor seasoning/spices
kryddstarkt spicy
kräfta crayfish
kummel hake
kummin caraway
kvark fresh curd cheese
kyckling chicken
kycklingbröst breast of chicken
kycklinglever chicken liver
kycklingsoppa chicken broth
kylda drycker cold drinks
kylt chilled (wine, etc.)

kål cabbage
kåldolmar cabbage leaves stuffed with ground meat and rice
kålrot turnip
källkrasse watercress
körsbär cherries
körvel chervil
kött meat
köttbullar meat balls
köttfärs ground beef
kött och grönsakssoppa meat and vegetable broth
köttsås bolognese sauce

L
lagerblad bay leaf
lageröl lager
lamm lamb
lammgryta lamb stew
landgång long open-faced sandwich
lax salmon
lever liver
leverpastej pâté
lingonsylt lingonberry jam
linser lentils
liten förrätt appetizers
lägg shank (top of leg)
läsk soft drink
löjrom bleak roe with chopped, raw onions and sour cream, eaten on toast
lök onions
löskokt soft boiled (eggs)
lövbiff thinly sliced fried beef with onions

M
mackrill mackerel
majonnäs mayonnaise
majs sweet corn

mald ground
mandarin tangerine
mandel almond/sugared almond
mandeltårta almond tart
marmelad marmalade
marsipan marzipan
marulk monkfish
maräng meringue
marängsviss meringues served
with cream and chocolate sauce
matjesill marinated herring
matsedel menu
medaljong small filets of cut meat
med benet kvar on the bone
med citron with lemon
med florsocker icing
med grädde with cream (coffee)
med is on the rocks/iced (drinks)
med kolsyra carbonated (drinks)
med mjölk with milk (coffee)
med socker with sugar
med vitlök in garlic
mellanmål snacks
meny set menu
mesost soft, sweet, whey cheese
middag dinner (evening mealtime)
mineralvatten mineral water
mjukost soft cheese
mjuk pepparkaka ginger cake
mjöl flour
mjölk milk
mogen ripe
morkulla woodcock
morötter carrots
mot extra kostnad extra charge
mousserande sparkling
mousserande vin sparkling wine
mullbär mulberry
multe mullet
munk donut
muskot nutmeg

musslor clams
mustigt full-bodied (wine)
mycket kryddad highly seasoned
mycket torrt very dry (wine, etc.)
mynta mint (herb)
mäktig rich (sauce)
mördegstårta tart (sweet or
savory)
mört roach (type of fish)

N
nejlikor cloves
nejonögon lamprey
nektarin nectarine
njure kidney
nudlar noodles
nyponsoppa rose-hip compote
served with whipped cream and
almond flakes

O
odlade champinjoner cultivated
mushrooms
ojäst bröd unleavened bread
oliver olives
omelett omelet
ost hard cheese
ostkaka curd cake served with
jam
ostkex crackers
ostron oysters
oxkött beef/ox
oxrullader braised rolls of beef
oxsvans oxtail

P
paj pie
palsternacka parsnips
pannbiff hamburger (when listed
as main meal)
pannkakor pancakes
pasta/pastarätter pasta

pastej pâté
peppar pepper (condiment)
pepparkakor ginger cookies
pepparrotssås horseradish sauce
persika peach
persilja parsley
piggvar turbot
pittabröd pita bread
plommon plums
plättar baby pancakes served with jam and whipped cream
pomegranat äpple pomegranates
pommes frites french fries
portion portion
portvin port
potatis potato
potatismos mashed potato
prinsesstårta sponge cake with vanilla custard, whipped cream, and jam, covered in light green marzipan
prinskorv small pork sausage, similar to frankfurters
pumpa pumpkin
punsch sweet liqueur, made from arrack, sugar, and pure alcohol
purjolök leeks
pytt i panna chunks of fried meat, onion, potatoes, often served with a fried egg
på beställning made on request
pärlande sparkling
pärlhöns guinea fowl
päron pear

R
rabarber rhubarb
ragu beef stew
rapphöna partridge
ren neat (straight)
ren reindeer
renat flavorless, clear spirit (aquavit)

renskav ground leg of reindeer
renstek roast reindeer
revbensspjäll spareribs
rimmad cured
rimmad lax lightly salted salmon
ris rice
riven grated
rocka ray, skate
rom rum
rosé blush (wine)
rosmarin rosemary
rostat bröd toast (bread)
rostbiff roast beef
rova turnip
rumpstek rump steak
russin raisins
rå raw
rådjur venison
rådjursstek roast of venison
rågbröd rye bread
rädisa radish
räkor shrimp
rätt dish
röda vinbär red currants
rödbeta beet
rödkål red cabbage
röd paprika sweet red peppers
rökt smoked
rökt ål smoked eel
rökt fisk smoked fish
rökt lax smoked salmon
rökt renstek smoked reindeer
rökt skinka smoked ham
rönnbärsgelé rowanberry jelly
rörd soppa cream soup
rött red (wine)

S
sadel saddle
saffran saffron
saffransbulle saffron buns (served at Christmas)

saft squash (fruit cordial)
salamikorv salami
sallad salad
salladshuvud lettuce
saltad salted
saltade jordnötter salted peanuts
saltgurka salted, pickled gherkins
salvia sage
sardiner sardines
schalottenlök shallots
schnitzel escallope
selleri celery root/celery
senap mustard
sherry sherry
sill herring
sillsallad beet and herring salad
sirap syrup
sjömansbiff casserole of fried beef, onions, and potatoes, braised in beer
sjötunga sole
skaldjur seafood
skaldjurssallad seafood salad
skinka ham
skogssvamp all field fungi
sky gravy
skåne type of aquavit flavored with aniseed and caraway
smultron wild strawberries
småbröd rolls
småkakor cookies
smårätter snacks
småsill whitebait
smör butter
smördeg pastry
smörgås sandwich/Swedish open-faced sandwich
smörgåsbord buffet of hot and cold Swedish specialties
sniglar snails
socker sugar

sockerdricka lemonade
sockerkaka sponge cake
sockerärtor sugar snap peas
sodavatten soda water
soppa soup
S.O.S. (smör, ost och sill) small plate of marinated herring, bread and butter, and cheese
sparris asparagus
specialitet för landsdelen local specialty
spenat spinach
spenatsoppa spinach soup
sprit spirits
spädgris sucking pig
squash squash (vegetable)
stark sharp/strong (flavor)
starkt kryddad hot (spicy)
stek roast
stekt fisk fried fish
stekt kyckling fried chicken
stekt potatis sautéed potatoes
stekt ägg fried egg
strömming sprats (Baltic herrings)
strömmingsflundror Baltic herrings, fileted and sandwiched in pairs, fried, with dill and butter filling
stuvad abborre perch poached with onion, parsley, and lemon
sufflé soufflé
sultana sultana/raisin
sur sour (taste)
svamp mushroom
svart black (coffee)
svarta vinbär black currants
svecia semi-hard cheese
svensk punsch Swedish punch (sweet liqueur)
sylt jam

sås sauce/gravy
söt sweet
sötningsmedel sweetener
sötpotatis sweet potato
sötsur sås sweet-and-sour sauce

T

T-benstek T-bone steak
thé tea
tillägg supplement
timjan thyme
tomater tomatoes
tomatsås tomato sauce
tonfisk tuna
tonic tonic water
torkade dadlar dried dates
torkade fikon dried figs
torr dry
torsk cod
toast skagen toast with chopped shrimp in mayonnaise, topped with bleak roe
tunga tongue
tunnbröd Swedish flat bread (similar to pita bread)
tunn sås light (sauce, etc.)
två personer for two
tårta sponge-based fruit or cream cake

U

ugnsbakad fisk baked fish
ungsstekt kyckling roast chicken
ugnsstekt potatis roast potatoes
utan kaffein decaffeinated

V

vaktel quail
valfria tillbehör choice of side dishes
valnötter walnuts
vanilj vanilla

vaniljsås custard
varm chocklad hot chocolate
varm korv hot dog
varmrätter main course
varmt hot
vatten water
vattenmelon watermelon
vaxbönor butter beans
vegetarisk meny vegetarian menu
vermouth vermouth
vetemjöl plain flour
vilda champinjoner field/button mushrooms
vildand wild duck
vilt game
vin wine
vinaigrettesås vinaigrette
vinbär currants
vindruvor grapes
vinlistan wine list
vispgrädde whipped cream
vit sås white sauce
vitkål white cabbage
vitkålssallad coleslaw
vitling whiting
vitlök garlic
vitlöksmajonnäs garlic mayonnaise
vitlökssås garlic sauce
vitt bröd white bread
vol au vent vol-au-vent (pastry filled with meat or fish)
våfflor (med sylt och grädde) waffles (with jam and whipped cream)
vårlök spring onions
västerbotten strong, tangy, hard cheese
västkustsallad seafood in mixed green salad, asparagus, and dill

WXYZ

wienerbröd Danish pastry
wienerschnitzel breaded veal cutlet
yoghurt yogurt
zucchino zucchini

Å

ål eel
ångkokt fisk steamed fish

Ä

ädelost blue cheese
ägg eggs
äggplanta eggplant
äggröra scrambled eggs
äggula egg yolk
äggvita egg white
älg elk
älgfilé filet of elk
älgstek roast of elk
äppelpaj apple pie/tart
äppelringar apple fritters
äpple apple
ärtor peas
ärtsoppa yellow pea soup
ättiksgurka sweet, pickled
gherkins

Ö

öl beer

WEIGHTS & MEASURES

Conversion Charts

1 gram (gr)	= 1000 milligrams	= 0.035 oz.
1 kilogram (kg)	= 1000 grams	= 2.2 lb
1 liter (l)	= 1000 milliliters	= 1.06 quarts
		= 2.11 pints
		= 34 fluid oz.
1 centimeter (cm)	= 10 millimeter	= 0.39 inch
1 meter (m)	= 100 centimeters	= 39 in./3.28 ft.
1 kilometer (km)	= 1000 meters	= 0.62 mile

Oven Temperatures

100° C – 212° F   177° C – 350° F

121° C – 250° F   204° C – 400° F

154° C – 300° F   260° C – 500° F

When you know	Multiply by	To find
ounces	28.3	grams
pounds	0.45	kilograms
inches	2.54	centimeters
feet	0.3	meters
miles	1.61	kilometers
gallons (US)	3.8	liters
Fahrenheit	5/9, after subtract 32	Centigrade
Centigrade	9/5, then add 32	Fahrenheit

TIPPING GUIDE

The figures below are shown as a percentage of the bill or in local currency. They indicate a suggested tip for the service described. Even where service is included, additional gratuities are expected by some. It's also customary to round off a bill and leave the small change.

Tipping is an individual matter and the correct amount to leave varies enormously with category of restaurant, size of the city, and so on. The figures suggested below represent normal tips for average middle-grade establishments in big cities.

Austria
Service charge	10–15% included
Waiter	10–15%

Belgium
Service charge	15% included
Waiter	optional

Czech Republic
Service charge	generally included
Waiter	round up the sum

France
Service charge	12–15% generally included
Waiter	round up the sum or leave an extra euro (optional)

Germany
Service charge	15% generally included
Waiter	round up the sum (optional)

Greece
Service charge	15% included
Waiter	round up the sum (optional)

Netherlands
Service charge	included
Waiter	10% optional

Italy
Service charge	12–15% included
Waiter	10%

Poland
Service charge	10% generally included
Waiter	round up the sum

Portugal
Service charge	15% included
Waiter	10%

Russia
Service charge	10–15% included
Waiter	10%

Spain
Service charge	15% generally included
Waiter	10%

Sweden
Service charge	included
Waiter	round up the sum (optional)

Switzerland
Service charge	15% included
Waiter	1–3 (Swiss) francs, depending on the amount of the bill (optional)